In Pieces

a memoir

Sally Field

**SIMON &
SCHUSTER**

London · New York · Sydney · Toronto · New Delhi

A CBS COMPANY

First published in the United States by Grand Central Publishing, an imprint of
Hachette Book Group, Inc., 2018
First published in Great Britain by Simon & Schuster UK Ltd, 2018
This paperback edition published by Simon & Schuster UK Ltd, 2019
A CBS COMPANY

13 5 7 9 10 8 6 4 2

Simon & Schuster UK Ltd
1st Floor
222 Gray's Inn Road
London WC1X 8HB

www.simonandschuster.co.uk
www.simonandschuster.com.au
www.simonandschuster.co.in

Simon & Schuster Australia, Sydney
Simon & Schuster India, New Delhi

Additional copyright information is on page 403.

A CIP catalogue record for this book is available from the British Library.

Paperback ISBN: 978-1-4711-7578-7
eBook ISBN: 978-1-4711-7577-0

Interior design by Marie Mundaca
Printed and bound by CPI Group (UK) Ltd, Croydon, CR0 4YY

Sally Field is a two-... ...and three-time
Emmy Award-winning actor who has portrayed dozens of iconic roles
on both the large and small screens. In 2012, she was inducted into the
American Academy of Arts and Sciences, and, in 2015, she was honoured
by Presi... ... ... A... ... ...
the board ...irectors of Vital Voices since 2002, and also served on the
board of the Sundance Institute from 1994 to 2010. She has three sons
and five grandchildren.

Praise for *In Pieces*

'Impressive, candid and vivid.' ***The Times***

'One of the most revelatory memoirs of the year.' ***Sunday Times***

'Beautifully written...vividly captures the people who have meant most in
her life...All come to life as if they are walking into the room where you are
reading.' ***Daily Telegraph***

'*In Pieces* is a book that feels wrenched from its author's soul.' ***Mail on Sunday***

'The revelations come thick and fast...Field is a real writer, her prose
uncluttered and direct...beautiful in its descriptive simplicity.' ***Daily Express***

'Hardly a traditional showbiz autobiography...tells a story illuminated by its
author's abundant grace and dignity, and her authentic desire to plumb the
depths of her feelings.' ***Independent***

'Blisteringly honest.' ***Sunday Express***

'A painfully honest attempt to confront and understand all the personal
heartbreak...an unusually intimate, heartfelt voyage of self-discovery.'
The Herald

'Written by the actor over seven years, without the aid of a ghostwriter (a crutch
often used by celebrity authors), this somber, intimate and at times wrenching
self-portrait feels like an act of personal investigation – the private act of a
woman, now 71, seeking to understand how she became herself, and striving to
cement together the shards of her psyche that have been chipped and shattered
over the course of her life.' ***New York Times Book Review***

'Beyond the headlines...there's a smart woman's reckoning with her complicated past.' *People*

'Unflinchingly honest.' *Choice Magazine*

'A complex cri de coeur [and] shockingly frank...A rarity in the world of celebrity memoirs.' *USA Today*

'As soulful, wryly witty and lyrical as it is candid and courageous...Eye-opening and deeply affecting...Arresting in its dark disclosures, vitality, humour, and grace, Field's deeply felt and beautifully written memoir illuminates the experiences and emotions on which she draws as an exceptionally charismatic, empathic, and powerful artist.' *Booklist*

'Such affecting literary depth...Field fuels this aching, lyrical memoir with frankness about her emotional childhood, her conflicted relationship with the late Burt Reynolds, and how acting helped her interpret life in all its pain and beauty.' *Entertainment Weekly*

'Award-winning actress Sally Field could have written a typically dishy Hollywood memoir. But *In Pieces* is an intensely personal, vulnerable accounting of her life and career. Field's meditations on memory, fear and love will leave you shattered. Her lyrical prose and sly humour will glue you back together again.' *NPR*

'Field's "pieces" are raw, heartbreaking, sometimes maddening but each builds insight to who she is – and that's the point. This work, as she thinks of it, is meant to reveal her, not to name-drop or tell unimportant tales about movies made long ago.' *AARP*

'Engrossing...Field holds nothing back...This powerful, timely narrative resonates with pain and triumph.' *Library Journal*

For Peter, Eli, and Sam

And all of theirs

Contents

Part Three

In Pieces

My mother and me.

Prologue

THERE WAS NO proscenium arch, no curtains or lights to create an illusion, no proper stage at all. It was just a classroom with all the chairs and their seventh-grade occupants pushed aside in disorganized clumps.

It wasn't even a real classroom. The entire school had originally been part of an army hospital built at the end of World War II, specializing in central nervous system injuries, syphilis, and psychiatry. It had once even included a small compound for prisoners of war—a building now stuffed with classrooms and students held captive until the sound of the bell. This particular room was long and narrow, each side lined with windows, which made it look exactly like a hospital ward and nothing like a junior high school drama class. But on that day, through my twelve-year-old eyes, I saw only the faint interior of a swank apartment.

I remember watching my feet as they stomped across the worn wooden floor, and for one instant the feet weren't mine anymore. Then I was back in the classroom again, wondering what to do with my hands, my armpits sweating so much I dripped. I stopped at the door (a wobbly contraption hinged to a freestanding frame made by the boys in wood shop), took hold of the handle, then turned back toward the thirteen-year-old playing my uncouth gangster boyfriend. With one clammy hand gripping the knob, and my whole body twisted around to face the actor—my arm awkwardly wrapped in front of me—I stood listening to the boy deliver his dialogue. When he had finished spraying words through his braces, I paused a beat, then yelled, "Drop dead, Harry," and exited in an indignant huff, slamming the door behind me. That was it, my first moments as an actor, a scene from *Born Yesterday* and my pubescent version of the brassy Brooklyn bombshell Billie Dawn.

I wasn't good. I knew I wasn't. It was like Heidi, the little goat girl, had taken a stab at Hedda Gabler. But it didn't matter. A new sensation had brushed past me and for one moment, I felt free. My body moved—maybe not gracefully but all on its own—without me telling it where to go, tiny flashes when it didn't belong to me at all, and I was watching from far away with no anxious sense of time. In those cracks of light, the pressure of what people thought of me or didn't think of me, who they wanted me to be or didn't want me to be, completely stopped. A bell had rung, everything focused and sharpened. I could hear myself. Then it was gone again.

In the eighth grade—a year later—I had my first performance night in the school auditorium. For the first time I walked on a stage in front of an audience of parents and friends, there to watch, among other things, my Juliet—not the whole play, just two scenes: the potion scene and the death scene. My mother drove me home afterward, and I clearly remember sitting in that dark car beside her. I desperately wanted to know what she thought but was afraid to ask, so I just watched her drive. Sometimes the headlights of an oncoming car would light up the whole interior, making it seem even darker after it passed. But when her face was bright with light she looked at me, and as if we were hiding from someone, she whispered, "You were magical."

I whispered back, "I was?" Then everything was dark again and I could barely see her at all.

"What does that mean?" I asked.

"Just that." Another flash of headlights lit up the front seat and I could see her mouth edging toward a smile, the light bleaching her beautiful face white, then slowly fading to black.

PART ONE

There is a pain—so utter—
It swallows substance up—
Then covers the Abyss with Trance—
So Memory can step
Around—across—upon it—
As one within a Swoon—
Goes safely—where an open eye—
Would drop Him—Bone by Bone.

—Emily Dickinson

Little Ricky and Sally in 1948.

My beautiful mother with all three of her children.

1

My Grandmother's Daughter

I WAIT FOR my mother to haunt me as she promised she would; long to wake in the night with the familiar sight of her sitting at the end of my bed, to talk to her one more time, to feel that all the pieces have been put into place, the puzzle is solved, and I can rest.

Sometimes I think I've seen something out of the corner of my eye and I stop still in the middle of my Pacific Palisades kitchen, looking for the flutter of a sign; or I'm walking in the West Village, headed to my New York apartment, loaded down with groceries, when I hear her laugh ring out. I turn in circles, looking for her. Where are you, Mom? Why won't you come?

This isn't new, this longing I have for her. It's the same ache I had when I was five, sitting on the bench outside the nurse's office at school, feeling embarrassed and ashamed because I had once again panicked for no apparent reason. I waited and waited, counted to ten hundreds of times, knowing that if I could see her eyes I'd be safe. Then suddenly, as if I'd conjured her out of wanting, there she was. My throat would lock as I watched her coming toward me, hugging her purse to her stomach like a hot-water bottle, and when she got close enough, I'd jump to my feet, hiding my face in her legs.

I still don't know why grammar school was so agonizing for me. Still can't figure out whether the agony was waiting for me in the school or I brought it in with me. Either way, it didn't matter because nothing and no one could distract or engage me enough to lessen the dread I felt. I don't remember having any friends or playdates—basically, in those days no one had playdates, or they weren't called playdates. But whatever they were called, I didn't have any. Maybe that's one of the reasons why I hated all the games at recess. "Red Rover, Red Rover," for instance, which was not only terrifying but, let's face it, a truly mean, totally stupid game. A group of kids would lock their arms together, then call the other students, one at a time, to run full blast into their wall of arms. If the runner was successful, the wall opened, and that runner was allowed to join the barricade. I hated this no-win situation of a game. I was the smallest one, and even if they did call my name, I couldn't break through, only bounced off and had to return to the land of the losers. But there was always the chance that they wouldn't call my name, and I'd have to stand there as everyone else broke through, joining the line one at a time, until they were all holding hands and looking at me, alone.

I guess you'd have to say that in my early school days—at five and six—I was a problem. A little stress case with a brand-new family and a constant stomachache that no one could explain. I remember my mother's concern, but I certainly couldn't tell her how to help me because I didn't have a clue why I felt so anxious, why I wanted to hide from everyone and couldn't act like the rest of the kids. Maybe I needed a good hard push toward socialization, and maybe my loving mother was too consumed with her own evolving life to realize that. But I'll tell you right now, if she had tried to organize a little "get-together" for me with one of those five-year-old strangers, I would have had a conniption fit, and my mother was not a battler. So as I watched everyone picking their friends, forming clusters of companions, I felt the hill to friendship getting steeper.

Then again, maybe it wasn't about that at all. Maybe I just needed my mother.

I have a memory of clinging to her, a vision so dimly lit that it slips from my grasp like a dream after waking. Barely out of toddlerhood, I have blond-brown bangs hanging in my eyes and one very chapped thumb tucked into my mouth. With the other hand, I'm gripping her robe at the neck, snugly hooked onto her hip as she stands, slowly stirring a pot on the old gas range. Behind us, my brother, Ricky—who is two and a half years older—sits on the hollow wooden box of a bench, rhythmically banging his feet while holding a tiny metal cowboy in one hand and a matching Indian in the other, hopping them around the oilcloth-covered table. My mother's eyes are focused on a book lying open atop the crowded butcher-block counter, and after a moment, she turns her head as if to look out the window, then speaks in a deep, loud, slightly false voice. Ricky looks up at her, then out the window to see who's there, while I watch for my brother's reaction. But when she stops abruptly, shakes her head, and looks back down at the book, we relax again into her cocoon.

I still have that book. All those books of hers I now own, hardcover Modern Library editions of Ibsen, Odets, and Chekhov, her barely faded notes jotted on the pages...the same copy she was using to memorize Chekhov's *The Cherry Orchard* in that envelope of a kitchen.

Margaret Morlan had eyes the color of dark chocolate, laced with feathery black lashes, and was clearly drop-your-jaw beautiful. She resembled Jennifer Jones, except she had a cleft in her chin and a kind of lit-up giggle in her face that left Ms. Jones standing in the shadows, as far as I was concerned. When she looked at me, it was never through me, but into me, lifting me off the ground in an invisible embrace. I wonder if

Margaret in 1945.

everyone felt that way. If they did, I don't think she was aware of it, of her power. I never felt that she leaned on her looks in any way, though maybe she did before I knew her, before she was my mother. I wish I'd known her then, wish I had known what hopes and dreams she might have had.

I do know that in 1942 she was a twenty-year-old sophomore at Pasadena City College, where she'd been studying literature. Then when she met a soldier and married him three months later, her education came to a screeching halt. And maybe that's what she'd been hoping for, to marry someone and to travel with him, to immediately move to Camp Barkeley in Texas. And when he was shipped overseas a year later, promising to write as often as he could, she waited for his return back in her California home, lovesick and pregnant. Maybe that's exactly what she wanted to be: a wife and mother. But one fortuitous night, when her husband was far away in the war and my brother was barely a year old, when the world was caught in a tremendous struggle, something reached out of nowhere and changed my mother's life.

It happened when a man named Milton Lewis approached her while she was sitting in the audience of the Pasadena Playhouse, waiting for the curtain to go up. "Excuse me," he said. "I love how you look. Would you like to come to Paramount Pictures tomorrow for a meeting?"—or something to that effect. He then handed her his card, verifying that he was indeed a talent scout for Paramount. The next day, she traveled to Hollywood, where she met with Lord knows who and said God knows what (and as I picture her in my mind, with her soft shy demeanor, only now does it dawn on me how much gumption that must have taken on her part). She was immediately put under a three-year contract. Suddenly, without looking for it, my twenty-three-year-old mother had a career.

No one in her family had ever had a career. The men worked to earn money as best as they could: Her father had been a piano salesman, her brother a bank manager, and the whole time my mother was married to my father, he was in the army. They had jobs, but nothing anyone would call a career. Certainly, none of the women had ever dreamed of such a thing. But now, my not-yet-mother had one. Leaving her baby son in the arms of her own mother, my grandmother, she would take a bus from Pasadena to Hollywood, then transfer to a streetcar that took her within walking distance of Paramount Studios, where she was given movement classes and elocution lessons, all in an effort to help her walk and talk like Jean Arthur or her look-alike, Jennifer Jones.

Most important, my mother was also given the chance to study acting with the brilliant Charles Laughton, eventually becoming a member of his acting company, the Charles Laughton Players, performing Chekhov and Shakespeare in a small theater on Beverly Boulevard, on the outskirts of Hollywood. Not only did she find herself onstage with Mr. Laughton, but she had the amazing good fortune to be directed by him as well. These moments stayed alive in her always.

Much of this change and challenge happened before the war was over, before my father had returned, and before I was born. My memories begin here, with the book, memorizing words, and the comforting smell of noodle soup...all connected to this world where my mother grew up, this world of women, and to the house where my grandmother lived as long as I knew her.

Located in Altadena, nestled in the foothills above Pasadena, her cottage was a uniquely Californian two-bedroom wooden bungalow, trimmed in gray river rock. It had a back porch converted into a third bedroom and a front porch elevated by five big wooden stairs, where a green canvas glider always stood, waiting for us kids to give it some action. It wasn't a big place, I know that, but to a child it seemed huge, a trusted member of the family that crackled and groaned when you walked from room to room, a comforting murmur that added to the soft chatter of female voices or the occasional pop of freshly washed clothes right off the line, snapped in the air before being folded into a pile.

My mother had spent her late adolescence and early adulthood in this house, living with her parents and older brother. It was where she had stayed when she was the lonely wife of a soldier expecting their first child, and where her beloved father had suffered a fatal heart attack—a loss that jolted her into early labor, delivering my brother six weeks premature. Then in 1949, when my mother decided to pack up her two small children and leave her marriage not quite four years after her husband's return, this is where we came to live: my grandmother's house.

When I look for that house in my mind, I have a blurry vision of my great-aunt Gladys standing in the dining room cutting flat rubber padding into tiny circles to paste onto her sore feet. Behind her I can see my grandmother sitting at the sewing machine by the big window, guiding a swatch of fabric under the foot, pumping the wide flat pedal back and forth. There's a rocking chair beside the mesh-curtained fireplace where my seventy-six-year-old great-grandmother sits under a halo of white hair, her hands dancing around two thin knitting needles with a steady stream of twine-like yarn flowing from the paisley bag resting on the floor. I remember that chair, how it chirped like a cricket when my great-grandmother would rock me, quietly patting my back the whole time.

These are the women who raised my mother, whose influence had been ingrained in her. My grandmother and her sister Gladys, and their mother, Mimmie or Mama, as they called her. The two sisters lived in the house together since both of their husbands had passed away several years before, one right after the other. My great-grandmother didn't have a permanent home of her own but moved around from daughter to daughter, sometimes making her way to South Carolina to visit Mae, the only one of her four daughters who'd stayed in the Deep South. The youngest sister, Perle, lived in nearby Glendale but was in and out of the house constantly. She was the only one whose husband was still alive, yet I don't remember seeing Uncle Chet very often, and never for any other reason than to pop in and fix something. My mother's brother would drop by, but I can't remember him pausing to sit down, and even though my father must have entered the house at some point, I have no memory of it. It was a kind of no-man's-land. A world filled with women who would straighten up if a man walked in, who would set aside the triviality of their own work and quickly move everything out of the way. But the men, whoever they were, never stayed long, and when the door slammed behind them, the house seemed to breathe a sigh of relief.

Gladys was the most imposing of the sisters and the only one who made me nervous. She'd sit at the end of the dining room table, always in the same chair, playing solitaire or one-handed canasta while she soaked her feet in a pan of hot water and Epsom salts after working all day at Bullock's department store in Pasadena. I wanted her to like me the best, but no matter how hard I tried, Ricky was always Aunt Gladys's favorite. Instead I had to content myself with being my grandmother's favored child, and when I was little I always felt as though I'd been stuck with the shorter end of the stick. It has taken me a long time to see that it was my grandmother's sturdy presence in my life—never full of tender touches or hugs and kisses, just a quiet, fierce devotion—that created a rock inside me, a safe spot I've always relied on but never knew I had. When I hear a house creaking under my feet, I'm instantly back there, in the safety of my grandmother's world.

Her name was Joy and that's what I called her. Never Grandma or Grammy or Newnee, just Joy. Which is ironic, actually, because I don't think I ever saw an ounce of it in her. Well, maybe tiny glimpses of glee, never joy. Like years later, when we'd come to visit and she'd be waiting on the sofa, watching out the window. Then she'd quickly move to the backyard as our car came up the driveway, ready for us to scramble out. When I'd say a simple "Hi, Joy," she'd fling her hand over her face as if to hide the smidgen of delight seeping out. The only reason I knew she was smiling was because her big puffy cheeks elevated her glasses, the cheeks that got handed down to me, along with a smaller version of her cow eyes with long lashes—spider-leg lashes, I called them.

Other than that, it was hard to read what was going on

inside my grandmother. One time she caught Ricky and me playing in her "nasty, bug-infested" garage after she told us not to, and I don't know if she was mad that we had disobeyed or scared that we'd get hurt, but for whatever reason, she chased us around the lemon tree with a switch, a switch she must have had waiting somewhere, 'cause there she was, instantly armed, red in the face and at a gallop. It was the only time in my life I saw tears rolling down my grandmother's face, which was the most upsetting part of that whole event—those tears. Emotions, in general, were not encouraged, and if I got angry as a child, Joy would pucker her face and say, "Don't be ugly." So when she came at us in a blaze of fury and flowing tears, Ricky and I were totally befuddled, not knowing whether she was mad or sad, or what the hell was going on. Needless to say, we spent the rest of the day trying to make her laugh.

All of the women in Joy's house, even Perle (whom I knew the least), were linked together like they were playing a life-long game of "Red Rover," except they never called anyone else to come over. They'd cluster in the backyard, just the sisters and their mama, sharing the task of turning the crank on the wooden ice-cream maker filled with cream and peaches from Joy's tree, while we all waited for my mother to come home from her day at the studio. I would lie on the quilt one of them had spread out over the grass and dreamily listen to that bubbling chatter, punctuated by the occasional slam of the screen door as Joy moved in and out of the kitchen. Taking turns, one would talk and then another as they pleasantly gabbed on about what needed to be fixed, or what to cook for Thanksgiving, or whether the cream had set, but never about themselves, never about their past, or even their present. I never learned anything about them from eavesdropping or any other way, and for some reason I never asked. It seemed as if there was nothing I needed to know. And clearly my mother had never asked, because these women had been the backbone of her life, and yet she didn't know any more about them than I did. And I knew nothing.

Many years later, long after Mimmie had passed away, just as all the sisters were heading toward the end of their lives, Joy slowly began to talk, revealing the memories that had been hidden for so long. It is Joy's history, handed to her by Mimmie, her mother, but somehow a thread of that history got woven into my mother's history and then into mine. I have always felt that, always thought that Joy's story is somehow an important piece of this puzzle, the puzzle of me and my mother. Even though I've never really known why.

Born in Alabama in the late 1800s, Joy came from a long line of farming folk on both her mother's and father's sides. They were not the landowners, but worked on the land and were, for the most part, uneducated. When Joy's father, Grover Bickley, suddenly died of malaria, her mother, Mimmie, was left penniless, with no means of support and four little girls to care for, my eight-year-old grandmother being the oldest. Immediately, Joy's sisters Mae, age three, and Perle, not quite two, were sent to live in South Carolina on a farm with one of their father's brothers, while Joy and five-year-old Gladys were sent to live nearby in the Epworth Children's Home, where they stayed for almost ten years.

What shadowy information Joy gave us about the children's home was all very Dickensian: It was cold, many little children died, the education was all hellfire and damnation, men are the devil and sex is evil. She told us about picking bugs—weevils, I presume, and God knows what else—out of the oatmeal, and that Gladys was sickly, refusing to eat. Joy had to force food into her. Maybe she dramatized some of the details but, bless her heart, she lived there for a good chunk of her childhood, years that no doubt shaped who she was. So if there was some creative accounting on her part, that's fine with me.

Long after my grandmother had passed away, I began to research her life, eventually stumbling upon the 1910 U.S. Federal Census report for Columbia, South Carolina. I just sat there, staring at my computer. There they were, Joy and Gladys Bickley recorded as "inmates," along with a list of other children. That same day, hours later, I found Mimmie, whose legal name was Redonia Ethel, living alone in a hotel located in another town. Her occupation was listed as "housekeeper," which fits the story that Joy had told us: Her mother had worked cleaning houses during the day and as a seamstress at night, saving everything she could in an effort to reunite with her daughters.

Nine and a half years after the sisters had entered Epworth, Mimmie somehow arranged to have fourteen-year-old Gladys, who had become deathly ill, moved to the farm where her two younger sisters had been living. But while Gladys was being welcomed by Mae and Perle, seventeen-year-old Joy was being sent to Texas to live with another one of her father's brothers, where it seems she immediately lost her voice. She simply lost the ability to speak. And who could blame her? She was now separated not only from her mother but from her sister as well.

One afternoon, while sitting on the front porch with a young man who'd come to call—conversation being pretty sparse, since she was still without her voice—a letter arrived with a check to cover the cost of a train trip to Chicago, requesting she arrive as soon as possible. It was signed, *James L. Bynum, Your Father.*

This is where the story goes from one of plain ol' hardship to something else altogether. Joy had always thought her father was Grover Bickley, the same as her sisters'. But he was not. When Mimmie was nineteen, she'd run off with the local schoolteacher. After she returned home, claiming she'd been married by a justice of the peace, it was then discovered that whatever had happened, legal hadn't been a part of it. It was also discovered that several other young women in town had fallen under the spell of the dark-eyed devil, and as the story goes, the scallywag was then run out of town with a pack of yapping dogs on his heels. Who knows what truly happened, but what can't be denied is the fact that my teenage great-grandmother was now pregnant and had no husband to show for it. As a result, Mimmie's mother—who had by then given birth to eleven children—kicked her oldest daughter out of the house. And though Grover, a young farmhand who had always fancied Mimmie, swiftly married her, it wasn't enough to erase the taint that now enveloped the jilted young woman. Mimmie never set eyes on her mother again.

Before receiving Bynum's letter, Joy had never wondered about her mama's family or why she'd never met them, and maybe she never thought to ask. I can't imagine the impact it must have had on her when she finally put the pieces together. Not only had she grown up in an orphanage and felt the humiliation of that, but she was now shamed with the sudden knowledge that she was illegitimate. Be that as it may, she was still curious enough to take that train trip to Chicago (presumably with her voice) and meet the rascal of a man she would forever after refer to as her father. Joy would cover her face and actually giggle when she talked about him, always making sure I heard the fact that, though he had a mistress, her successful father—who had by then become an educated lawyer—never married.

During that trip, Bynum invited his daughter to live with him. Joy declined the offer, choosing to travel back to Texas—a decision she would chew on for the rest of her life. But she never lost contact with him, visiting several more times. She did accept Bynum's offer to pay for her tuition to secretarial school, and soon my grandmother was making enough money to bring Mimmie to Texas to live with her, along with her sisters Perle and, most especially, Gladys. It was there that Joy met and married my grandfather, Wallace Miller Morlan, and on May 10, 1922, it was there—in Houston, to be exact—that Margaret Joy Morlan entered the world with a full head of black hair and huge dark eyes that matched both her mother's and her grandfather's, the dark-eyed devil she would never meet.

At the bottom of an old mildewed storage box—one of the various containers that were left with me—I found a crumbling leather diary of my mother's, written in 1935, when she was only thirteen. By this time, she and her family, which included Mimmie, had been living in California for about six years. I know she wouldn't have wanted me to read it, but I did (sorry, Mom).

Besides a lot of little-girl chitchat, she writes about her

daddy losing his job, writes about money worries again and again, always ending with the fear that they will have to move out of their home. The diary stops there, but I know that not long after the entry was written, everything changed when Joy was awarded a small inheritance from the last will and testament of James Bynum, her father. And that small allotment allowed my grandmother to purchase the cottage that still lives in my heart, Joy's house.

The day my grandmother passed away I was cowering in the corner of the hospital room where she had been taken three days before. I kept my eyes on the hypnotic bouncing line of the heart monitor, afraid to look death in the face as Joy hovered, not in this world and not eternally in the other. Now in her early nineties, she'd been hospitalized only once before, had stayed a week to regulate her heart rate and was released to my mother by the medical staff, who said that they wouldn't keep my grandmother any longer, complaining that she spat on the floor and refused to be touched by any of the male nurses.

A few months after her first episode, she was back in the ICU, disoriented and declining. It was late evening on that third day of waiting, of my mother and I whispering and pacing, frequently laughing at nothing, always trying to be respectful while Joy lay suspended, the beeping of the monitor getting slower and slower. Suddenly, without warning, my gentle mother moved close to Joy, leaned down to her face while boldly grabbing her arm. "Where are you, Joy?" she demanded in her ear. "Tell me where you are." I couldn't understand what my mother was doing, much less why. But when Joy's eyes immediately fluttered, and she calmly replied,

"I'm with Bynum," we looked at each other, chilled. That night my grandmother stayed with her father, forever.

I have never stopped thinking about that moment. At the time, I know we were both charmed by Joy's response, felt that it was romantic to think that in death Joy had looked for her father to come and take her away. But right now, as I try to understand how all of this fits, I am struck... finally seeing the truth. This man, the "scallywag" who took what he wanted without any consequences and left my great-grandmother's life irrevocably changed, had forever remained a dashing figure, a hero in his daughter's eyes. Yet it was that woman, Joy's mother, who had struggled her entire life to be beside her child. Who is the dashing figure in this scenario?

I went back into my mother's things, and in another box I found a short typewritten account of a conversation she'd had with Joy at some point. In it my grandmother tells how angry she stayed toward Mimmie. How as time went on, Mimmie had slowed her visits to the orphanage, eventually coming only once a year, saying it was too hard for her to witness the conditions in which her daughters were forced to live. And though, as a child, I never picked up on any of that, never perceived my grandmother's complex feelings toward her mother, I can see in my memory how Mimmie was always hovering around the edges of her daughters' lives, not completely ignored but never invited into their center. As I put it all together, I wonder if Mimmie spent her life seeking their forgiveness for the things they never talked about. And Mimmie must have felt no small amount of fury toward her own mother as well, the mother who abandoned her, who shut the door in her pregnant daughter's face. All of them with wounds that wouldn't heal because no one acknowledged they were bleeding, and yet each of them needing the other to be near. And that—I realize—is how this story fits into my life. These generations of women, weaving a pattern into a lifelong garment, unconsciously handed down from mother to daughter to granddaughter to me.

The women: Gladys, Joy and Mimmie are
standing behind my mother as she proudly
holds baby Ricky.

2

Dick

MY FATHER LIVED down the hill from Joy's cottage in a beige stucco house identical to all the other beige stucco houses lining Foothill Boulevard, homes that sprang up quickly after the war to accommodate the returning servicemen and their families. If I close my eyes and dig down, I can conjure up his house again, can put my little-girl self in that living room and feel how still it is. My father's house isn't breathing, not like Joy's. It isn't alive. All I can hear is the muffled voice of Vin Scully saying, "Easy, to the inside. That's strike two," and from the mantel, above the unused fireplace, comes the crisp ticking of a travel clock, louder than you'd think possible for such a small device.

This is where I was born—well, not literally in the house. I was born at Huntington Memorial Hospital, not far away. But when my mother carried me home to meet my toddler brother, she brought me to this house, where we lived with my father until I was about three. I remember it as being sparsely furnished, with a feeling of randomness, as if it held nothing cherished, a place to stop but not to live. Maybe it wasn't always that way, but by the time my brain could hold any images of the place, my mother had already left, taking me and Ricky and every bit of life out of it.

My father grew up in Warren, Pennsylvania, with his very Catholic family and didn't migrate to California until right before the U.S. entered World War II. He was drafted into the army in November of 1941, receiving notice to report to the Pennsylvania Railroad Station in Warren at 8:30 a.m. on December 1—six days before the bombing of Pearl Harbor. And yet it's recorded that he enlisted in Riverside, California, on January 16, 1942, when he was twenty-eight years old— over a month later. I'm guessing that by the time he received his draft notice, he was already living in California, where he was working as a pharmaceutical salesman. His paternal grandmother had been living in Pasadena for many years, so perhaps my father went to California to be near her, or even to live with her. None of his three older siblings had left home yet, so maybe he was a young man with a bit of adventure in him.

My mother and father met during that same year, 1942, when my grandfather invited several young men in uniform to dinner at Joy's house, saying he knew what it was like to be away from home and preparing to go to war. Three months later, Margaret Morlan and Private Richard Field married and immediately moved to Texas, where he had been accepted into Officer Candidate School at Camp Barkeley. Upon graduating in December, he became Captain Richard Field. Exactly one year later, my father kissed his newly pregnant

My mother and father before I was born.

wife goodbye and was shipped off to Europe, serving for three years as a medical registrar for First General Hospital in London and then outside Paris.

Perhaps my father changed during his time away or perhaps when he returned he was expecting things to be as they had been before he'd left. I don't know. But when he got back, early in 1946, he found that the young housewife he'd left behind was now an independent working actress, plus the mother of a rambunctious baby boy. And, as the story goes, the army captain took one look at his new son, Richard Field Jr., and flat-out didn't like him. Then when I was born, in November of that year, he completely adored me but still didn't care for little Ricky. Or that's what the women who lived in Joy's house always told us.

I never felt any of it, how he delighted in me and rejected my brother. But it was the story that Ricky and I grew up hearing. Even after we stopped believing that we'd dry up and blow away if we didn't eat enough, or that swallowed watermelon seeds would sprout in our stomachs, we continued to accept the tale of our father's preferences. And the idea that I was his chosen one was like being accused of a crime I didn't commit. I worried that I'd somehow wronged everyone, was a traitor to the female tribe up the hill. No matter if it was accurate or not, the story hurt my big brother and it was my fault.

I never knew if it was true. I never knew anything about my father, never asked him a single question about who he was, or what he was feeling, never relaxed around him long enough to be curious. Even at four, maybe before, I felt guarded, afraid to allow him into my heart for fear that his need to be comforted or to feel important or successful or even loved would suffocate me. One of my first memories—one that stays on the tip of my mind—is of my father sitting on the edge of his big bed (the bed that would never hold my mother again) with his head in his hands. My eyes can barely see over the mattress as I stand beside him, my face so close to his weeping bent body I can smell the heavy odor of his Brylcreemed hair. "Have I lost my little girl?" he sobs through his fingers. "Will I never see my little girl again?" I'm not sure if I'm the little girl he's weeping about or if it's my absent mother, but his anguish is terrifying. I want to run or cry myself, but instead I put my arm around his neck as best I can, and pat him the way Mimmie pats me when we're in Joy's chair. "It's okay, I won't leave, don't worry. I'm here, Dick."

*　　*　　*

I called my mother Baa most of my life—probably because Ricky did—always called my grandmother Joy, and my father I called Dick, short for Richard. And short he was, barely five feet seven inches, looking a bit like Alan Ladd—in a slightly less handsome way. Audie Murphy reminded me of him too, as did Donald O'Connor, except Audie seemed more menacing and Donald more adorable. Actually, Dick was all of those things: slightly handsome, somewhat menacing, and fleetingly adorable. Which happened to be his father's name: Fleet.

Fleet Folsom Field was another man in my family whom I never knew, since he died when I was two. I do have one tissue-paper memory of my father's mother, whom I called Jen—even though her name was Jane. She and I are sitting together on Dick's sepia-toned sofa and she's reading the Little Golden Book of Disney's *Cinderella* to me, carefully enunciating each word. I sit enthralled at her side, the skirt of my dress fanning out over the cushion as I noiselessly suck my thumb and gaze at the only bit of color in the room: the pages of Cinderella's world. Every time Jen reaches the end, she gently asks if I'd like to hear it again and I nod my head, while trying not to lean on her unfamiliar shoulder. I remember I liked her and didn't want her to stop, but though she lived until 1961, I don't recall ever seeing her again. I never had a conversation with her, never learned anything about her, and it's only now that I wish I had. Dick's older sister, Betty, wrote to me through the years, letters that I kept but never read because I wasn't interested, until this very moment. In one she writes that her mother desperately wanted to be a concert pianist and that Jen's father, Betty's grandfather, refused to allow it, claiming that displaying herself onstage was inappropriate behavior for a woman. I don't know what kind of image I had of my grandmother Jen, but that was not it. Not of a young woman who had dedicated herself to a skill, who had become an accomplished pianist and was forbidden the opportunity to perform. Where did she put that longing? Where does anyone? Carl Jung wrote, "Nothing has a stronger influence psychologically on their environment and especially on their children than the unlived life of the parent."

Next to the container of Aunt Betty's letters I have a tattered suitcase of Dick's that found its way to me after my father passed away in 1992. The small cardboard valise is old and almost as fragile as the memorabilia stuffed inside, a mishmash of things I'm examining for the first time. In it is a yearbook from the University of Pennsylvania, where he received a business degree, and inside the big padded book are pictures of him as a member of the baseball team, where his nickname was "the runt." There are also some newspaper clippings reporting that he was a prominent member of the "Mask and Wig Club," which put on an annual musical performed by men dressed as women. The crumbling articles and faded photos lead me to think that maybe you had to be there to get the whole—less than dazzling—concept. But I remember how Dick would boast about his time onstage, seeming to get a big kick out of it, then he'd pause and shrug, as if discarding the unimportant thought.

His sister Betty never shrugged away that thought. She was the only family member to remain on the East Coast, where she struggled to become a dancer, and when that didn't happen, she taught dancing. The rest of the family treated her ambition as though it were a frivolous fancy, calling her passions "idiosyncrasies." Eventually, Betty became an usher at the Lunt-Fontanne Theatre on Forty-Sixth Street in New York, where she spent most of her life. In her letters, which I'm only now appreciating, she sends me clippings and reviews, plus pages and pages describing the magic in her world of the theater, while she proudly led patrons to their seats with a flashlight in her hand.

My mother told me that Betty had been kind to her during my parents' divorce when the rest of the Field family gave depositions or testimony—or whatever was required back then—all in an attempt to have my mother declared unfit, hoping to take her children away from her. That was all my mother ever told me about the divorce and I never asked for more or asked anyone else—meaning Dick. The court must have declared that the custody of the children should be shared in some capacity but how that sharing schedule was worked out and by whom, I really don't know.

Dick always seemed nervous when Ricky and I first walked into his house for our required time, which initially was every weekend—though at four, I'm not sure I knew what a weekend was. The car ride was fine, but once we were settled inside the house it seemed as though my father didn't know what to do with us, as though we were not young humans but another species; puppies or kittens that needed a little feeding, then could be left on their own. It's not that my father didn't try. I remember him doing a silly tap dance for us in the kitchen as he flipped our grilled cheese sandwiches in the skillet or telling us the same jokes over and over on the long car rides to and from his house after we moved from Joy's. "Who flung gum in Grandpa's whiskers?" he'd ask and pause, expecting us to laugh. I did, of course—even though how that was a joke, I'll never know. Half the time Ricky didn't seem to be listening, but I was and made sure to laugh in all the appropriate places. I always tried to deliver whatever unspoken need he had of me—his chosen one.

But once the little pets were fed and amused for a moment, my father would wander back into his life, totally ignoring our existence. And that was okay when Ricky and I were there together, but as we got older, Ricky would often be excused from his obligation, mainly because the women—our mother, grandmother, and especially Aunt Gladys—sympathized with him, muttering how difficult it must be for him to spend time with a father who didn't care for him. Although I swear I never saw any evidence of my brother's mistreatment by my father, and to this day, Rick doesn't remember any. Believe me, Dick ignored us both equally.

I felt like the sacrificial lamb. I had to go no matter what—with my brother or without—and I hated it. I fought and whined or faked illness: anything to try to get out of the visit. Sometimes, but not often, my mother would cave to my desperation, reluctantly calling Dick to explain that I was sick and couldn't come, but then the crushing weight of guilt made my freedom hardly worth it. So, I gritted my teeth and endured countless weekends with my father, totally forgotten and ignored. If I wanted to spend some "quality time" with him, I could sit on the sofa listening to Vin Scully announce the ball game on the radio. That would have been just fine with Dick, but I would've preferred to eat dirt. I'd sit in the room with him, not to be completely alone, and play with all the things he'd give me from his desk, organizing and reorganizing the pencils, paper clips, and sheets of stationery with his employer's name, National Drug Co., printed on top. And that was great for a while, but I've got to tell you, if you're four or five or even six, this solitary game of office runs thin. I felt so deeply lonely I was afraid.

When I got older, and I knew I was in for a quiet, mind-numbing few days, I'd bring Nancy Drew books and *Little Lulu* comics with me. Hell, I'd have brought *War and Peace* if I'd been a better reader. Once, when my father waited for me in his car, I asked my mother to hold a small red book titled *One Hundred and One Famous Poems* close to her heart for a few moments so that when I felt panicked with loneliness during the long days of being held prisoner, I could hug the book like a doll, and feel her essence—though trust me, hugging that book didn't cut it either. I really didn't understand why I was there. Dick never took me to the movies or the park, never played games. He hardly even talked to me. Not really. Except once I remember he walked in when I was sitting on the toilet and carefully instructed me that I must always wipe from the front to the back. I was mortified, but I did remember his words and oddly think about them, often.

One day, about a year or so after my mother had vacated the premises, I was sitting on the floor of my father's house, in front of the big living room window, carefully cutting out the paper dolls I'd brought to help me endure my weekend. Ricky, who had once again been excused from duty, was waiting for me up the hill at Joy's house. And as I sat there focused on my scissors—scraps of paper scattered on the faded rug—the boxwood shrubs in front of the house began to move, scratching against the glass panes. Suddenly, out popped my brother's little round face, which he then smooshed against the window. I nearly jumped out of my skin. But when he signaled for me to come outside, I was up and out the door.

Huddled down in the cool damp dirt—a world of spiders and sow bugs—Ricky took my hand and whispered, "I've come to rescue you. Don't make a sound." Without giving it another thought, we crawled from our hideout under the bushes and ran hand in hand, dashing tree-to-tree. We were absolutely certain that our stealthy getaway had been masterfully executed, but most likely we were two kids, one five and the other seven, in plain sight the entire time had anyone bothered to look.

In 1951, many of the streets in Pasadena had deep, stone-lined gullies on either side, with short bridges connecting the street to the driveway of each house. Most of these gullies and bridges have disappeared over time, but fortunately, on the day of the great escape, North Marengo's gullies were still intact, and that's where we walked, hidden from the world all the way up to East Las Flores. It was probably only a mile—maybe not even that—but to me it seemed like a massive undertaking, like Lawrence of Arabia crossing the desert to the port of Aqaba.

The entire trek up the hill, my brother excitedly chattered about the huge fort he'd built for me in Joy's backyard, how he'd planned a dinner for us and convinced our grandmother to build a fire in the outdoor grill that stood deep in the yard, adjacent to the big stone incinerator (where she burned her rubbish every Thursday). It was the most exciting thing that had ever happened to me. We never worried that Dick might panic when he discovered I was gone or that we might be punished for our dangerous adventure, and if either of those things happened, I don't remember.

What I do remember is finally dashing up the driveway to Joy's backyard and standing there, horrified. It looked like the aftermath of a battle. Nothing was left of the fort but a tangle of robes still attached to the trees, blankets and quilts strewn

The two escapees. Pretty sure that's not what I was wearing.

across the grass, and clothespins scattered everywhere like shell casings. When Ricky saw his work of art, now torn to shreds, he sat down and started to cry. I was heartbroken, not for my lost gift but for my brother. Then from behind a row of hydrangea bushes came the triumphant giggles of the culprit, the little boy next door, taunting us as he witnessed our reaction. Like an attack dog, I dashed at him, flinging my whole body against the chain-link fence that stood between us as the boy backed up, stunned by my behavior. Ricky didn't say a thing—also stunned by my behavior—and quietly walked into the house, refusing to speak, much less play with me, the rest of the day. I was his little sister, and he should have been the one to go after the creep for wrecking the fort, not me. But Rick never would have. Somewhere inside, I knew he couldn't and I could.

When I said my father never took me anywhere, that wasn't completely true. He took me to church on Sundays, and on Saturdays to the racetrack. I felt equally stupefied at both locations. At Sunday's Catholic church service, I'd sit with my rosary in hand, feet dangling, unable to touch the ground, as I tried to entertain myself by wrapping the beads around my fingers. Dick sat with a solemn face, meeting my eyes only when he'd shoot me a mean look if I squirmed around trying to pull my dress down so my legs didn't stick to the seat. I knew all the prayers and recited each one loudly at the proper time. Dick had taught them to me, but he never told me why I was saying them, never explained why I had to kneel until my knees were dented and bloodless, or why I had to hit myself in the heart asking for God's forgiveness. What had I done? Except want out of this boring church, except wiggle around too much, except leave with my mother when she broke his heart.

When I was about eight, Dick moved from his house in Pasadena to one in nearby Arcadia, two blocks from the beautiful Santa Anita Park racetrack. On Saturdays, he'd take me with him to bet on the horses, which you'd think would have been great, except Dick never got anything but general admission tickets. If there was a seat somewhere, I never sat in it. We'd always stand in a herd of people near the rail, though I'm only guessing that we were near the rail because I never saw that either. Matter of fact, I never saw anything but a bunch of butts. I do remember my father trying to hold me up every now and then, but I'd feel his arms begin to tremble and very soon he'd put me down again. Plus, he didn't seem to want to hold me, or to hug me, as if it made him uncomfortable to be close to my face. I'd spend most of the time standing at his side examining people's back pockets or their shoes, but honestly, after fifteen or twenty minutes, tops, I was about ready to eat dirt again. So, I developed a game. Trying not to be stepped on, I'd scoot around and gather up the tickets that had accumulated on the ground, stuffing them into grocery bags I'd brought with me. When I got back to Dick's house, I'd sit at the dining room table with the racing form and check, ticket by dirty ticket, to find hidden treasure, convinced that someone had accidentally discarded a winner. Needless to say, I never found one.

It was two weeks after my thirty-eighth birthday in November of 1984. I had long since quit trying to please my father—mostly because I avoided him—and had successfully tucked the thought of him into an unused corner of my brain. Occasionally he'd call to ask how I was doing and whenever I heard his voice on the other end of the phone, I'd grit my teeth, bracing myself as if preparing to give blood. He'd immediately segue into asking who I was dating and did we want to meet at his club for a round of golf, finally offering to teach me to play. The only time I'd try to conjure up his image was when a writer from *Ladies' Home Journal* or some such magazine would ask about my parents in an attempt to create a profile on me. Most of their inquiries about my childhood I'd dance around, telling only an edge of the truth, but when they asked about Dick, my answer was always the same: I didn't really know my father. On that November day, now with two children of my own and about to enter into my second marriage, I received a manila envelope addressed to me in my father's instantly recognizable handwriting. I didn't read what it contained. I couldn't face it. I put it away, but I didn't throw it away.

The thought of that small manila envelope, stacked in a plastic shoe box with notes and letters I've kept over the years, has floated to the top of my memory—belly up—many times. But only now, as I dig to uncover all the pieces of some life-long puzzle, do I feel brave enough to read his words.

Inside the envelope are two folded documents and a note from my father, written on two small sheets of lined notebook paper dated November 12, 1984. I read that first. It's curt and angry.

Unfortunately I picked up this month's McCall's Magazine and read about your happy life and successful career. As usual I was depicted as the man who divorced your mother when you were three years old. This time, however, I was categorized along with some of your past boyfriends as missing something you desired in a man. For your reference, I am sending copies of a letter to you and Rick written in 1951 after your mother had left.

Even now I feel a stab of—what? Guilt? Sadness? Fear? I can feel my father's anger, the jolt that I've disappointed him. I set the small note aside without finishing it and pick up another of the envelope's contents. It's a copy of the legal document stating that on January 23, 1953, the Superior Court of the State of California for the County of Los Angeles, after the required one-year waiting period had elapsed, decreed that the divorce was finalized. Margaret Field and Richard Field were no longer married.

Then I look at the last of the documents: a mimeographed copy of a letter my father wrote to Ricky and me on October 23, 1951, a month before the divorce papers were originally filed. It's a three-and-a-half-page handwritten letter on the National Drug Co. stationery, never finished and never mailed, but clearly never thrown away either. This letter has had a long history: First it was never sent; then it was sent, but never seen. Now, sixty-six years later, I hold that letter, or rather its mimeographed copy.

They are the words of a man who feels wronged, who wants his children to know why they are not going to be with their father, who thinks his children are entitled to know him. If he had been forced to live separately from his dad, he writes, he would have wanted to know why, so that his "judgment of him could have been fairly appraised." He in turn wants us, his children, to consider him fairly and for us to know he "craves" the love and respect of his little boy and his little girl too, and that on this day, he has signed the divorce papers, to give our mother her freedom. "Without going into it," he writes, "the divorce is being settled out of court because of what any published proceedings may someday be to you" (meaning if the press got hold of the story). He goes on to say that in no way would such proceedings reflect on his character, adding that he'd been told that, had he chosen to contest the divorce, he would've had a good chance of keeping his children (meaning sole custody). Instead, he will lose his two children, whom he wants—giving us up, without a fight, to protect us from gossip. He tells us that he has loved our mother, perhaps too much, "for if I hadn't, I might have been able to keep her from wading in until she got over her head." He writes that there has never been anyone else but her and there isn't now. The letter stops, almost midsentence.

With reluctance, I pick up the smaller letter and continue reading.

> I've included the final divorce papers of your parents. As you might notice, it doesn't take a mathematician to see why it was necessary for your mother to divorce me. For twenty years, I have been hurt and belittled by the media concerning you and now with the days dwindling down to probably a precious few, I had to speak my piece and remind you a little of the past... Happy Birthday. Your Dad.

From wading in until she got over her head.

3

Jocko

BAA NEVER IGNORED us, not like Dick. But during all the many months we were living at Joy's house, my mother was moving from one job to the next, so even when she was with my brother and me, I'm sure that part of her was somewhere else, thinking about other things. She wasn't being cast in leading roles, and many times she's listed as "uncredited"— meaning she had no lines at all. But she was working steadily and gaining ground, appearing in a few major films as a minor character, co-starring in a couple of B movies and beginning to work in the expanding world of television, even starring in the science fiction classic *The Man from Planet X*. But whether she was preoccupied or not, I always felt thrilled to be in the same room with her, intoxicated by her childlike glee, which was just the same as mine. She was my mother and I know that in a lot of ways the connection between us was hardwired, but that doesn't completely explain how I felt. I was enchanted by her.

One morning, she packed up Aunt Gladys's car and drove us kids into the San Gabriel Mountains above Altadena where we found the perfect spot near a stream that we would forever call "our little place." I can't remember why that one day, that obscure spot, stayed in our minds, and my brother can't figure it out either. But if I let my subconscious mind walk back there, I hear my mother laughing while we lie flat on our backs, looking up at the sky. She's describing a magical, anything's-possible world, seeing things in the masses of condensed water vapor that I couldn't imagine. A world where everything has a hidden treasure in it, including Ricky and me. If we ever went back there again I don't recall, but my brother and I never forgot "our little place."

And when Baa would occasionally leave for an evening with this man or that, my grandmother would stand with her hand on the knob, preparing to close the front door behind them, sending off a less than friendly air as she loudly sucked her teeth. It was usually too late to build a fort, so when they were gone, Ricky would try to fill the void by listening to the radio—we didn't have a television yet. We'd lie on the pallet Joy had made for us on the living room floor, a quilt and two pillows spread out in front of the big wooden box, waiting for the creepy voice announcing, "With the speed of light, a cloud of dust and a hearty 'Hi-yo Silver.'" My brother stayed wide awake and fascinated while I, curled up next to him, fell asleep listening for the sound of my mother's footsteps on the front porch. Always needing her.

Then Jocko appeared. I was only four and some-odd months at that point, so this shadowy memory may not be a true recollection, but the essence of it is: I see him entering Joy's house for the first time, making the living room seem suddenly small as he ducks his head to pass through the front door. I hear my mother introduce him to my no-frills grandmother, and watch Joy as she stands in the corner, draping her hankie across her hiccupping giggle, peeking at him over the top like a harem dancer. When I look for my brother in my memory, I find him standing stiff and awkward, keeping his eyes on his feet, stuffing his hands deep in his pockets. And my mother is looking around at all of us, with her focus only on Jocko. Abruptly, giving a loud "ten-hut" laugh, he swoops down and gracefully snatches me off the floor, enfolding my body to his chest in one quick grab.

And shadowy or not, I know this part of the memory is true: When Jocko and I met it was face-to-face, nose-to-nose, high above everyone else in the room. I was looking down at my mother now, watching her, wanting her to take me away from him, to safely plant me on her hip. But I heard her wordless plea—even in my child's mind—as clearly as if she'd spoken it out loud: *Don't disgrace me by pushing this man away, don't be frightened.*

I wanted to please her, above all else, so I remained tearlessly in his grasp, though clearly terrified. And slowly, I realized that everyone in the room was looking at me—or at least in my direction—making me feel I'd done something wonderful. Maybe to be comforted and admired, I had to be terrified as well, maybe that's what I was supposed to learn. I watched my mother and this man beaming at each other, while I was caught in the middle. She wanted to show Jocko something appealing about herself, and I, her little girl, was it. Jocko wanted to show her something grand and manly about himself, and I, her little girl who appeared comfortable in his arms, was it. Tag—you're it.

Early in 1952, my mother and Jocko were married in Mexico, and we became a family. My little sister was born six months later and only now have I done the math.

His name was Jacques O'Mahoney but everyone called him Jocko, and that's what he was: a jock. Though he was born in 1919 in Chicago, Illinois—the only child of Ruth and Charles O'Mahoney—he actually grew up in Davenport, Iowa, and attended the University of Iowa, where he excelled at swimming and diving. It claims in one of his bios that he had hopes of becoming a doctor, but I never heard him talk about his lost dreams in the medical profession or saw any sign of a diploma, pre-med or pre-anything. I do know that in 1943, when he was twenty-four years old, he enlisted in the Marines, where he learned to fly the airplanes used on aircraft carriers and

Baa and Jocko on The Range Rider *set. Don't know why he's dressed like that.*

later became an instructor. But by the time he entered my life, he was no longer teaching men how to get planes off the deck of a carrier and back down again. His troops now consisted of two kids, Ricky and me—and later our little sister, who was born when I was five and a half. "I always wanted my own little princess," I heard Jocko say after seeing his infant daughter for the first time. So that's what he named her: Princess.

Jocko looked to me like a cross between Errol Flynn and Randolph Scott, two of the actors he "doubled" during his career as a stuntman through the 1940s and into the '50s. At that time, stunt work was very different than it is in today's world of digital possibilities. Stunt people just did the "gags" without the aid of special effects cables or hidden padding, and with little or no safety net. And what "gear" they did use was rudimentary, like falling into a bunch of cardboard boxes instead of the modern, specially designed airbags. In those days, they simply fought the choreographed sword fight, ending with a bouncing roll down twenty-five brutally hard stone steps. Or they leaped—without cables or airbags—from balcony to balcony, thirty feet in the air, or jumped from the buckboard of a runaway stagecoach onto the nearest galloping horse of the rig, then vaulted to a lead horse, grabbing the reins and saving the day.

Jocko preferred quarter horses, never Thoroughbreds. They were big working horses, with long necks held high over sleek muscular bodies, which pretty much describes Jocko. At six feet, four and a half inches, he moved like a horse, his long legs loping forward while his upper body stayed straight, the movement registering in the swing of his hips. He never strolled, but walked with a sense of purpose as if he were needed somewhere, which made people look at him if for no other reason than to see where he was going with such deliberateness. He demanded to be noticed. With a strong sculptured face and classic Roman nose, Jocko's looks were striking. Everywhere he went he left behind the impression of a very handsome man, whether anyone in the room thought he was or not.

My mother met him in the early months of 1951 while doing a guest spot on his television series *The Range Rider,* a half-hour show with very little story and a whole lot of horse stunts performed by Jocko and his co-star, Dickie Jones. He and Dickie had a stunt show they performed all over the country, and according to Jocko, he'd broken every bone in his body at least once. One of the legendary tales about him was of the night when he shattered his collarbone halfway through the Madison Square Garden performance and just kept on going. Jocko was a stuntman turned actor who was only an average actor but a great stuntman. He was good with the sword, could throw a punch with the best of them, and his horsemanship was nothing short of astonishing.

I found four black-and-white snapshots taken in 1951, photographs that are like pieces of a map, leading to places where memories are buried. One of the pictures is a three-shot taken from behind as the group leans toward the edge of a cliff, looking down to the rushing, boulder-filled river below. The young boy is wearing a camp T-shirt neatly tucked into the elastic band of his shorts and his hands are hanging meekly at his side. Standing next to the boy is a towering shirtless man in white shorts and work boots with a little girl held securely to his bare torso. One of her hands is resting on the big man's back; the other is out of sight. I suspect the thumb of that hand is in her mouth. He held

Our first family trip to Yosemite.

me a lot. I don't recall that trip to Yosemite we took as a newly formed family, but when I look at the photo of him holding me, I have to stop. I remember the feeling of that. I remember...

I'm looking down at my feet, tiny in his huge hands, the grip so tight it feels like they will fold in half. If I look past my toes, I can see him lying with his back pressed into the patchy grass, his knees bent toward the sky as he holds me high above him. Sometimes Baa will poke her head out of the back door, or glance at us through the window above the sink as she continues doing whatever she's doing. Always, I wait for her to caution him, to tell him to be careful or say that it's time to come in, that it's getting dark or cold or dinner is ready—anything that will bring a halt to these acrobatics. To come and get me. Or at least watch me and be pleased—*just watch me, Baa*. But she rarely does.

"Eyes straight," he coaches. "Arms at your side...tight. Don't look down. I've got you. You won't fall." He moves his hands together, tightens his grasp, and carefully transfers one of my feet to join the other, until I stand—eyes straight, arms plastered to my side—with both feet in one of his hands. I want to do "good," to please him, but in equal amounts I also want him to stop. I can't speak for fear of revealing what a sniveling coward I really am, unworthy of his attention, or anyone's. I'm in a pickle—a baseball term I've heard Dick use—but at least I'm not being ignored. The same choices in this emotional relish dish: to be safe and ignored or to be terrified and seen. So I stay. I look down at my feet and see his sculpted arm holding me securely where I don't want to be.

My feet. I see them, so small as they cautiously walk on his sore back, his skin warm against my bare soles. At first it took many steps to cover the distance from the top of his shoulders to the curve of his waist, where I'd carefully turn to point my toes toward his shoulders again, never allowing a toe to slip under the sheet that draped over the bottom half of his body. I wanted to look up to the windows of his bedroom, out into the morning beyond, but I also wanted to do a good job. Caught in that pickle again. I longed to focus on the leaves of the big tree outside, to watch their rustling movement, but I kept my eyes down, wordlessly performing my task. When I was seven and eight my feet could almost dance across his back, if I'd wanted—but I didn't. Later, as my feet got bigger, there was no room to dance and no dancing in my heart.

*　　*　　*

The first house where we lived as the O'Mahoney family, located on Califa Street in the San Fernando Valley, was small, dark, and rented. That's all I can remember about it. I could find only two small scalloped-edged photos of that time, not much of a map. One picture is too blurry to uncover anything of interest but in the other I can see a six-year-old Sally, with a pillow and a blanket, nestled on the new sofa in front of the living room window—cheeks flushed with fever and the chicken pox—which leads me to the memory of the delicate pink blossoms on the big oleander bush in the backyard of that house, a wall of leaves that twinkled in the wind and poisoned Dr. Quack, my first pet—obviously, a duck. I remember thinking, *Yikes, so this is death. You get totally stiff and smell funny, then you're stuffed into an old shoe box and buried in the backyard next to the very thing that killed you.* Which takes me to the memory of my brother and me hanging over the toilet as Baa tried to make us puke up the rancid ground beef that the babysitter had mistakenly fed us, meat my mother had intended to throw away. Everyone seemed to panic, and though we stuffed our fingers down our throats as best we could, no half-digested ptomaine-laced meat appeared. I never felt sick from whatever it was I'd eaten, but that night I was worried I'd end up in the backyard buried next to Dr. Quack in my own Keds coffin. This is probably around the time I started having meltdowns at school so maybe it's all beginning to make sense. Part of it at least.

I have a 1953 issue of a fan magazine entitled *TV Show*. Inside these deteriorating pages is a story called "The Range Rider and His Queen," which includes thirteen awkwardly posed pictures of us all, photos meant to show a family caught in the midst of real life like only a fan magazine can do. There's the one showing the three kids sitting directly in front of a television, staring with intense fascination at a round, *blank* screen, and one of eight-month-old Princess sitting in her high chair, mouth wide open like a baby bird as she waits to get the bottle that is being suspended in front of her by Jocko, looking like a resident of the Ponderosa. Baa—dressed to match— stands on the other side, holding a bowl of something Gerber,

If my mother was the Range Rider's queen,
then we must have been his court.

both parents beaming with exaggerated adoration toward the camera. Then there's the picture of my brother and me sitting on the counter next to the kitchen sink, my mother standing slightly in front of Ricky as we watch a now shirtless Jocko scrubbing the bottom of a skillet with an S.O.S pad. Ricky and my mother look intently at Jocko's helpful hands but I, pressed against the dish rack, have my eyes focused on his face as if awaiting further instructions.

My favorite photo is an eight-by-ten print of a picture that was obviously taken at another shoot, because my hair is longer, while Baa's is shorter, and if it was ever in a publication, I don't have the magazine. In this shot, I'm in the foreground, spinning, arms out straight with the gathered skirt of my dress in midair, and everyone, except Princess—who must have been taking her nap—is in the background watching me twirl. My mother and I are dressed in Navajo-style attire, me with my rickrack-trimmed dress and Baa wearing an enormous turquoise necklace. Jocko looks like the grand marshal of the Tournament of Roses Parade in his fringed leather jacket and huge white cowboy hat, with an "I've got the answer, if you've got the question" smirk on his face. Poor Ricky sits next to Baa on the new redwood patio bench, drowning in cowboy clothes that are clearly the wrong size and looking as though he's lost the will to live. What I love about the photo—other than the look on my brother's face—is the fact that I can see our new backyard, fenceless and carpeted in deep St. Augustine grass, plus I can see all the fenceless yards down to the end of the block. Every one exactly the same.

Twirling in Van Nuys.

This was the place on Hayvenhurst Avenue in Van Nuys, where we lived next. It was a little California ranch–style house in a new development of similar ranch-style houses, the first home we had purchased and the house where Ricky turned nine. I remember my mother filling out the party invitations for my brother's one and only birthday party, putting them in a bag for Rick to distribute to each of his fourth-grade classmates. Unfortunately, only four of the invited guests showed up and all of them were girls who stood around the paper-covered picnic table looking lost. To this day, my brother insists that the party was a tremendous success, but

I'm telling you, it was a life-altering experience. Ricky's hair was so slicked down he looked like he belonged in a barbershop quartet, and the only entertainment was watching him wandering around the yard blindfolded, determined to pin that damn tail on the donkey's ass. I vowed, then and there, never to have a party of my own. And since my mother was good at a whole lot of celebratory things but throwing a successful birthday party was not one of them, the vow was easy to keep. My mother was simply not a people person.

Ricky and I weren't exactly surefooted in the people department either, so our house was never filled with kids from the neighborhood or classmates from school all laughingly full of mischief, and none of this seemed to concern anyone except the woman who lived next door. Shortly after we moved in, she began to gently but regularly invite me to her quiet, neatly kept home, and though it was extremely unusual for me, I slowly began to go. If she was married—and I think she was—her husband was never around, and clearly she had no children. I wish I could remember her name, this nice woman. She wasn't as pretty as my mother, but she had a careful, eager way. She showed me how to dunk a cube of sugar in my cup of tea— which she served in a flowered cup with matching saucer—then pull the cube out before it melted and suck on it really quick. A sweet treat as we sat at her kitchen table, talking about the day. I started making drawings and little art projects at home, gifts I'd then give to her, my secret friend. I never told anyone about her, especially not Baa. I felt that I was doing something wrong, that there were things about me I should hide. Maybe I worried that it would hurt her feelings knowing that my best friend, my only friend, was a woman her age. I don't know.

But at that time, both my mother and Jocko were seated in the front car of a huge roller coaster: their lives. Everything was moving at such a dazzling speed—their love affair, the birth of their child, the liftoff of their careers—they must have found it hard to do anything but hang on. Not only was Jocko filming *The Range Rider* (which ended after seventy-eight episodes) but he was also the lead actor in two B movies and a short film with the Three Stooges. Baa was now working in a constant stream of episodic television, which included performing regularly in the new live television shows, *Playhouse 90, Lux Video Theatre, Chevron Theatre,* and four episodes of *Schlitz Playhouse of Stars*. But even if you're working regularly, being a professional actor doesn't offer a lot of security. It's not a nine-to-five job and no two days are the same, no two jobs are the same. When you finish one, you have no idea when, or even if, the next will appear. At that time, however, the work kept coming, and Jocko kept spending the money that rolled in. He also spent the money that hadn't rolled in.

We lived in the Hayvenhurst house only long enough to harvest a few baskets of walnuts from our front yard tree and for Jocko to teach me to ride a bike. I won't say he was appalled that I hadn't learned to ride one by the age of seven, but close enough. In my defense, I'd never had a bike or a safe place to ride it, much less anyone who could or would teach me. But if my stepfather was critical about my lack of cycling skills, he was apoplectic about Rick's. Grandiose to a fault, one day Jocko brought home a tricycle for his eighteen-month-old daughter and two shiny Schwinn bicycles, big red boys' bikes with crossbars…both. Neither of them the step-through girl's type. These were bikes meant for older guys of eleven or twelve, not a small boy of nine and a tiny girl of seven. And if training wheels existed at the time, I never saw any.

As I remember, Ricky sailed right into it, literally took off, and I was too confounded with the big red thing to even be jealous. Day after day, Jocko would run alongside my bike holding the back of the seat as I tried to pedal this huge vehicle. Then after the four-hundredth shove, with knees skinned and virginity compromised after slamming down on that damned "boy's bar" again and again, I finally wobbled my way into the cycling world. I was actually doing it, truly under way and thrilled to feel Jocko's pride in me. Although pedaling backward was not easy, so working the brakes was always a problem. I had to slow enough to put one foot down—the crossbar making it impossible for both feet—then hop along, tiptoeing to a stop. Eventually, with my heart slamming against my ribs as though it wanted out of my body, I could ride and I could stop…ish.

Shortly after completing the training sessions, after maneuvering through all obstacle courses, when Ricky and I had proven we could fly the craft off the ship, then land again safely, Jocko allowed us—even me—to ride our bikes to school, which was a few blocks away. Never in my life had I experienced a feeling like that, the freedom of sailing along under a canopy of eucalyptus trees while keeping the safety of my brother and his red bike from getting too far ahead. I felt so much love for my stepfather, the man who had cared enough to give me the gift of gliding, untethered.

*   *   *

And then on Sunday mornings, or any morning during the long months of summer, Jocko started calling me to his bedroom, the room he shared with my mother, who was downstairs cooking breakfast. We had moved again, leaving the tract homes of Van Nuys behind to enter the lush world of Encino and the house on Libbit Avenue. Definitely coming up in the world, the Libbit house had a pool, a paddle tennis court, and even a corral for horses, which Jocko promptly populated with a pinto and a huge roan—horses only he was allowed to go near. There was also an enormous garage, home to Baa's old silver Ford and the white Cadillac convertible with red leather seats that had suddenly appeared in our lives.

Shortly after we expanded ourselves to fit into this grand space, my stepfather started sending for me, using my mother as the messenger. Princess in her shorty PJs and I in my ankle-length nightgown would be quietly playing in our room, frolicking in the delicious "let the day present itself" feeling of childhood, when Baa would poke her head in the door. "Sal?" she'd say, her face puffy with sleep. "Jocko needs you to walk on his back." It never felt like a request, more like a summons and a great honor. I'd been singled out, the chosen one again.

I'd climb up the stairs, barely aware of the carpet under my feet or the flannel clinging to my legs, glance out the big window halfway up, then stop for a beat at the top of the landing—for what reason I didn't know—and step into his room, their room. The bright day was visible through the windows and the glass-topped Dutch door, which opened out onto a balcony overlooking the backyard. But even though the bedroom was large, it always smelled musty—thick with sleep and privacy. Keeping my eyes down, I walked to the big bed where my mother's husband lay facedown, naked and tangled in the sheets.

"Go, baby," he'd crackle as he sensed me moving in. It was what we did. It was what I was good at—walking on his back—and surely it was what every little girl did, so the distinct "fingernails down the blackboard" feeling I had was to be ignored. It was what I did for him and I was good at it.

I walked on his back until he rolled over, commanding me to keep going. One foot in front of the other, up his chest I tiptoed, my nightgown hanging loose as his hands slid over my legs, then moved up. I'd turn my feet around, walking toward his stomach to be out of reach, and he'd whisper instructions, "Lower, lower." My steps got tinier as he muttered, "Lower." I walked on this much loved non-father of mine, carefully trying to avoid where he was aiming my feet, and looked up at the world outside, inhaled the comforting smell of bacon frying downstairs, and part of me wasn't in the room anymore.

4

Libbit

NESTLED IN THE heart of Encino, surrounded by eucalyptus and sycamore trees, stood the rambling two-story Libbit house. Lime-green lawns stretched out on either side of the circular driveway, and running next to the horse corral, on the south side of the estate, was another driveway—a kind of service entrance off Noeline Avenue. I don't need photos to uncover buried bits, not of the house or the grounds. I remember it all like an endless loop of film in my brain.

The minute we moved in, the enormous backyard was almost instantly transformed into Jocko's playground and everywhere you looked was some kind of apparatus he'd either made or quickly acquired, equipment that eventually we were all expected to perform on. Standing next to the swimming pool was a crude split-level pinewood diving platform, about ten feet high on the upper level, maybe seven or eight on the lower. Several two-by-fours were nailed to the back of the wood framing, which were used as a ladder to climb to the shorter platform, where more two-by-fours would take you to the top.

Underneath the platform, of course, was a whole lot of water, and needless to say, I didn't know how to swim. If I hadn't had access to a bicycle before I met Jocko, I sure as hell hadn't had access to a swimming pool, unless you count the one at Joy's house—which was plastic, barely inflated, and had a foot of bug-infested water. I did know how to float, however; I was really good at floating. While hopping around the shallow end of our new pool, I found that when Ricky pushed my head underwater—which he did again and again—if I went totally limp, playing dead, I would miraculously float to the top.

But knowing how to float and jumping from the high dive were two different things, and by the time I could safely dog-paddle myself around, that's what my stepfather wanted me to do. Climb up and jump off; ready, set, GO. I stood there, rocking back and forth, my toes gripping the edge of the plat-form while I repeated Jocko's instructions in my head over and over: legs together, toes pointed, hands at my sides, until finally I'd push off, pointing everything I could point, and jump in. But that wasn't the end of it. After I could climb up and jump in without too much hesitation, pushing off with enough force to distance myself from the platform, out came the pool pole—a long aluminum stick with a net fastened to one end used to scoop leaves out of the water—now being used as a piece of training equipment. Jocko would hold the pole out in front of me while issuing new commands: Arms over your head, tight to your ears, legs straight, toes pointed. Push off hard and dive over the pole. "Go!"

But I couldn't move. Not just because I was afraid of the smack in my face or the breath-grabbing sting on my stom-ach, even though that played a big part in it. It was that

A weekend in Palm Springs. Legs together, toes pointed, hands at my side.

Jocko's tone had changed. Nowhere in sight was the loving patience he had shown during our bicycle training days. Now he sounded mocking and condescending, as if my inability was purposely done to challenge him. Was he teaching me to dive or trying to make me cry? And if I fell on my face would he applaud my attempt or enjoy my pain?

Directly across from the pool, on a lawn to the side of the house, Jocko had erected a square made of iron pipes, standing about eight or nine feet above the ground—a minimalist version of monkey bars. In those days, women with muscles were not considered attractive, so I was rarely expected to perform on this bastardized version of gymnastic equipment. No, the bars belonged to Ricky, and when Jocko started demanding feats of strength that the chubby eleven-year-old wasn't capable of achieving, no matter how hard he tried, it was not an ownership my brother wanted. With each clumsy attempt, it seemed that Jocko's need to disgrace my brother, to reveal him as unmanly and incapable, increased. And to top it off, at the end of every demoralizing session, Jocko would push Ricky to the side, then hop up himself, looping around and around on the bar like a toy you get at the five and dime, ending each performance with a dozen effortless chin-ups. Even though he avoided my eyes, I knew my big brother felt just as he was being taught to feel: ashamed.

In the center of the yard was an unfenced, unused paddle tennis court with its shaggy net lying in a neglected heap to one side. A big trampoline now stood between the two metal poles where the net would have been strung. The trampoline—ah, yes. I could bounce—we could all bounce—and I could definitely point my toes. I could land on my knees and then bounce back up. I could land on my butt and bounce back up. I could even land on my butt, bounce, change direction in midair, then land on my butt again, facing the opposite way. But I could not, under any circumstances, do what Jocko demanded: flip. I couldn't do a flip of any kind, no matter how much he pushed. I wouldn't even try. So out came the pool pole again, as if this aluminum stick were somehow the answer, the surefire way to address my incompetence. If I could dive over the pole, curling into a somersault before I landed, I could eventually translate that well-executed move into the same kind of smooth aerial display that Jocko so gracefully demonstrated.

But I never could because some part of me wondered if his reasons for pushing us were not about our successes, but about our failures. A tiny cell in my head began to distrust.

On the right side of the yard lived the tree: a sycamore so huge that when I put one hand on its mottled torso, balanced on the low brick wall that encased the roots, and slowly walked around the massive trunk, I counted out thirty little-girl steps. If you stood back and looked at it through squinted eyes, the tree became a monstrous giant with two large branches dipped down, one slightly lower than the other, as if they were arms waiting to catch something in flight.

And that's exactly what we were expected to do: fly. Jocko had somehow attached a long thick rope to each of the sycamore's arms. Ropes so thick they were impossible to grip and so coarse they tore up your hands, ropes you'd imagine being used to tie the *Queen Mary* to its moorings. A flier might take off using one of two methods: As you held one of the ropes, Jocko would grab you around the waist, then walk backward until he stood in the camellia bushes, under the kitchen window, as far as he could go. He'd then launch you into the wild blue with an enormous push and if the initial heave didn't knock you off, the momentum at the top most likely would. Therefore, the method of launch I preferred was the entanglement approach. I'd stand on the low picket fence that edged the pink flagstone walkway surrounding the tree, lace my hands around the rope hanging from the lower branch, then jump backward into the air. While using the rope connected to the taller branch (which was therefore longer) and standing on a much higher launching point (sometimes from the balcony above), the opposing flier, who was often Jocko, would time it just right and take off, gathering more speed than me with my tiny jump back. The performer on the longer rope would then swing out and around my shorter one and when the ropes engaged, it would whip me with a snap of centrifugal force that was both thrilling and horrifying. We'd twirl round and round each other, caught in "the dance of the ropes," ending when the two partners finally collided. I learned to loop the rope around one foot when I was dizzy and slipping, then I could use my legs plus my not-quite-big-enough hands and have a prayer of staying on. If not, I'd be flung to the walkway below.

The yard echoed with screams and shrieks, the kind of laughter that comes from riding the Intimidator or from being tickled to the point of peeing in your pants. I desperately hated the diving platforms, felt a failure on the trampoline, but the ropes I could do. I could cling to that knot of hemp and live.

The inside of the house kept changing too, as Jocko began accumulating bigger and better things. Furniture, television consoles, and in the living room, a new stereo was set up, allowing the music of Dean Martin and Peggy Lee and Martin Denny to rumble through the house constantly. I remember watching them dance: two people, four feet, my mother on tiptoe while Jocko's big hand lightly gripped her waist, guiding her to move with him, pushing her back, drawing her in. I watched, fixated, as they danced the cha-cha, that one, two, one-two-three pulse vibrating the floor where I sat with the roaring fireplace hot on my back. When the music stopped, they continued to embrace, Jocko running his hand down her back, cupping her butt, then pulling her toward him. I watched as my mother pushed him away, then headed toward the den to refill their drinks, making a distinct "tsk-tsk" sound with her tongue, the same sound my grandmother would make—a "naughty" reprimand. Was that because of me? Because she suddenly saw me sitting there with my chin resting on top of my bent knees?

Jocko always described Baa as a prude, overly uptight about most things, especially sex. If a crude or suggestive word was uttered in her presence, she'd blush, putting her hand to her face—just as Joy would—and I could feel her embarrassment radiate across the dinner table. It was no secret that Jocko thought my mother was loving but limited and while she could kiss our boo-boos, it was his job to bring us fully alive, to unleash in us all the important primary colors of being human; colors my mother felt uncomfortable or incapable of revealing and he did not. We were her children, for goodness sake, so perhaps she felt it was inappropriate to behave in an openly sensual way in our presence. That's true, I'm sure, but it was more than that. Joy had raised her, and my grandmother's troubled childhood, complete with daily lectures on the sin of sex, clung to Baa. It was like a cloud that floated through my mother's life, dimming her brightness, sometimes making it difficult to see her clearly.

When my mother had left the room, her "tsk-tsk," floating away, Jocko turned to me. "Come on, Doodle, let's dance." I jumped to my feet, having recently attended the Tap, Ballet, and Acrobat class at the dance studio down the street, which oddly enough had included the cha-cha. But Jocko didn't put one hand on my waist and hold the other out straight, like he had with my mother. He put both his big familiar hands on my hips while he stepped with me—one, two, an' cha-cha-cha—all the time instructing, "Move your hips. Move your hips," pushing them this way and that. "That's my girl."

They both looked impossibly perfect: he in his dark suit with just a hint of cowboy, she with the black lace bodice of her dress cinched at the waist above layers and layers of a black tulle skirt that whispered when she walked. After a fleeting good-night kiss, followed by the tip-tap of her heels and the thud of his boots, they floated off together on a cloud of glamour, the white Cadillac carrying them away for the evening. As soon as the door was closed, Mrs. Roberts, the new live-in housekeeper, went to her room above the garage—assured that the kids were safely tucked in front of the television—and I drifted up to my mother's big walk-in closet.

Hiding behind the forest of Baa's clothes—hers on one side, his on the other—I sat against the wall looking up at the hanging garments, hypnotized by the lingering smell of my mother's Femme perfume, then chose one beautiful dress, stepped out of my nightgown and into the silk and satin. When it wouldn't stay on my body, I got a handful of big safety pins from the sewing basket on a shelf in the back, pinned the dress everywhere in a suggestion of a fit, and moved out into their bedroom. Lost in a world of pretend, I danced around the room, remembering Jocko's hands directing me to move this way and that, the whole time trying to keep the gown from falling off my child's body. When I finally tripped on the hem—breaking the illusion—I took Baa's sewing scissors and cut the bottom of the beautiful dress . . . off. Maybe I just needed to make it work. Or maybe destroying the dress was a message, trimmed in lace.

The Libbit house, the new white Cadillac, and the perfect couple.

When she finally found her once-beautiful dress, now wadded into a ball and hidden in the back of her closet, she sat with her head down, confused and disappointed. She didn't ask me why I had done such a thing, or demand to know what on earth I was thinking—which were two questions I couldn't have answered anyway. She never yelled or even raised her voice in anger. Not ever. She expressed hurt. And that was much worse. Somewhere in me I had the feeling that I needed to protect her from hurt and as I got older, that meant protecting her from me. There were times when I longed to have her explode in a fury, times when I knew she was silently disturbed by my stepfather's rough treatment of Ricky—ridiculing him for no other reason than to make him

65

cry—times when I wanted her to rescue me, and on the rare occasions when she did try to dry our tears or soothe our fears, Jocko would call her a worrywart, discrediting her, claiming she would surely ruin us as she had been ruined herself.

One summer afternoon when I was about eleven, my mother and Jocko were sitting on the patio with a group of their friends. It was a hot day and I kept asking if I could go into the pool, since by that time, I'd become a fairly strong swimmer. The answer was always a distracted "in a while," and when I asked one too many times, Jocko, in a quick flash, picked me up and threw me, fully clothed, across the patio into the pool—a distance of perhaps thirty feet. The water slapping me in the face didn't hurt nearly as much as the sound of laughter spewing from Jocko and his friends. It's the only time I remember Baa actually reprimanding him (even though it was done lightly) and, against his orders, coming to my aid, folding her arm around me when I pulled myself from the pool, then walking me to my room as I hid my tears in her chest. But if she ever told Jocko definitively to stop or expressed her dissatisfaction with his form of parenting, I was never aware of it.

Yet, outside of Jocko's sphere, if I was troubled about something or needed to talk, to work something out, she was endlessly patient and supportive. When I was in the eighth grade I was abruptly kicked out of the circle of girls with whom I had tried to be friends. As soon as I got home from school that day, I went directly to my closet, shut the door, and lay on the floor crying, saying I could never go back to school again. Baa sat on the carpet, talking to me through the crack under the door for hours. She was always like that. Whenever I felt I'd hit a hopeless dead end, she had a way of making me think of alternate routes by suggesting a long list of choices I hadn't seen. And even though most of them were maddeningly unacceptable, her ability to look for that little bit of sunshine in a situation that seemed pitch black always gave me the sense that if everything went out, I had a backup generator: my mother.

It would have been so much easier if I'd only felt one thing, if Jocko had been nothing but cruel and frightening. But he wasn't. He could be magical, the Pied Piper with our family as his entranced followers. He had a rule that on Christmas morning we weren't allowed to get out of our beds until the sky was fully light, so every Christmas Eve I'd just lie there, watching the night creep by. On one particular wide-eyed eve, a big storm had rolled in with a hammering rain that lashed my bedroom window and as I listened to the relentless splashing, I started to hear something else behind it, a very faint pounding that didn't seem to be connected to the downpour on the roof or the branches tapping against the glass panes. If I stopped breathing and tried to open my ears, I could hear it: a faint slam, a rhythmic popping, and then I guess sleep had its way with me because when I opened my eyes again, the rain had stopped and the color of the night had shifted. Not that it was light, but it wasn't totally dark either. Five-year-old Princess, whose twin bed stood an arm's distance from mine, didn't seem to have any trouble sleeping, and even after I poked her in the side several times she stayed blissfully zonked. But when I saw the dim outline of something sitting at the foot of my bed I let out a small squeal, and that got her up. It was a big stuffed monkey with arms and legs long enough to tie around me in a constant hug, and Princess had one sitting at the end of her bed too. Wrapped in our monkeys, off we went to wake the rest of the family, stopping for a moment in the living room to behold the magic stacked high under the huge illuminated tree.

After much haggling over what color the sky truly was, and what constitutes "light," dawn was reluctantly declared and the festivities could finally begin. There were presents everywhere: under the tree and hidden out of sight in the branches, turning into a game of "hot and cold" conducted by the grown-ups. When, at last, the cacophony of ripping paper, excited screams, and fleeting words of gratitude had faded away, Jocko said, "Put your shoes on, Doodle," then took my hand and led me through the den into the backyard, with everyone following. There, a few feet from the big sycamore, was a structure made of pale pinewood—a two-story square with a pitched roof, a front porch, and windows on either side of the doorway. It was big enough for me to walk around in and had an attic-like top floor where I couldn't quite stand, but almost. Yes, two-by-fours had been nailed to the wall to be used to climb up to the second floor and Jocko had made it, all of it. He had worked all night in the rain. My brother, whose face was now glowing with pride, had spent the night at Jocko's side, helping him accomplish this feat. A little house and they had both made it . . . just for me.

I stood there, in that damp yard filled with Jocko's contraptions, staring at my gift—dumbfounded. Why had Jocko done that? Why was I given a whole house when Princess and

Ricky didn't get anything like it, not in any way? Where was the extravagance usually heaped on my mother? There was only a little house for me.

A part of me still lives in that little raw house. I would lie in the upstairs loft looking out the thick mesh-covered window, besotted by the hot dusty summer air, alone.

All my life I've tried to figure out why I didn't have a constant stream of friends. We lived in a neighborhood filled with children. I'd see them every morning as we stood on the corner, waiting for the school bus. Pam, a girl in my class, lived down the street but I only remember going to her house once, feeling anxious and awkward the whole time.

When I was in the sixth grade, I asked a classmate over to play. I don't remember her name, only that I was nervous. It was somehow decided that she would come on Saturday at noon, but when that Saturday came around Jocko was home, working in the yard, intent on keeping me near. I felt intoxicated with his attention and forgot all about my new friend. And as we worked side by side—Jocko issuing orders that I dutifully followed—he took his shirt off, then casually suggested I take mine off too. I was wearing shorts and a T-shirt with my two-piece bathing suit underneath and though the sun was hot, the air was cold. Leaving my shirt on seemed like a better idea in every way, but I didn't decline his suggestion. I took my shirt off as if I were happy to do so. When he told me to take the top of my bathing suit off as well, that I didn't need it, declaring I'd feel better if I were free, I felt the familiar fingernails on the blackboard of my insides. Lord knows I

Little Doodle, age eleven, in the Libbit backyard.

didn't need it, but at twelve I didn't want to be free, I wanted to be covered. But as he moved behind me, untying the strings to my top, whipping it off, then stuffing the little wad of pink fabric in his back pocket, I just stood there, wordlessly.

We planted marigolds and raked leaves, Jocko beaming at me as if he needed my help. And I felt important, forgetting that there was anyone else in the world other than him. When the doorbell rang, I dashed inside to answer it without thinking and found myself standing in near nakedness before my would-be friend and her father. She awkwardly stammered something about bringing her new set of jacks and I, without a moment's hesitation, told her to leave. When they stepped away bewildered, I closed the door, then leaned my forehead on it, listening to the sound of their car driving away, feeling profoundly alone and numbed with shame.

And always, always I was called.

I watch my feet as they travel the length of his back. Little steps, baby steps, toe to heel. I want to look up...look up to the window where I can see the tree. The tree I love to touch. I can see my hand against the tree, gliding across its ragged bark skin. But I must watch my feet. I don't want to slide off his back. I want to do a good job. I'm glad he's on his stomach. Maybe that will be all. I wonder if he's asleep and I'm alone here. I'd rather be alone. But no, he moves, begins to turn over, careful to hold the sheet, the sheet that once covered my mother too. He lays it loosely across his waist with a sigh. "Keep going, Doodle."

I watch my feet, careful little feet, my feet, not his, mine! I stay high on his chest but he puts his face under my nightgown. I don't pull it back. I can't. He watches his own hands as they slide up my legs and my bare body, gliding across everything that is girl of me, not invading, savoring, and I want away. I want away. He murmurs directions. "Down." I'm stepping on his stomach. "Down." I'm on the edge of the sheet. "Down." I see what he wants me to walk on. I don't want to. I look up through the window to the moving leaves outside. "Down," he crackles. I walk carefully, keeping the man of him between my little-girl feet.

I didn't want to be there. I wanted to be alone. But I was there. Constantly, endlessly, there. And as I grew, the game grew too. He started calling me when my mother wasn't at home, often in the middle of the day, no longer looking for my feet to soothe his morning-stiff back.

When I was twelve or so I would lie awake in my bed, not because Christmas was near or the following day offered something special, but because I was terrified. My sleeping sister was so close, but I couldn't reach for her, or call her name. I'd lie in the dark with my heart pounding, listening to the oleanders smack against the windows, waiting for the sound of a window sliding open. I waited and when the wind's tapping never altered, I was sure that whatever was lurking out there was already inside—and was waiting too. Waiting for the right moment. I pulled the blankets to my chin, feeling something getting closer, ducking under the covers before the icy hand could grip my neck. I was sure if I jumped from the bed in a mad dash to get my mother, the thing would grab my ankle and drag me under—under the bed, I guess, or just under altogether. I wanted to call Baa but couldn't make my mouth move. *Call her, call her now, call her*, a voice inside my head kept demanding. Sometimes I actually did manage to call softly, "Baa. Baa…Please hear me." *Too soft. Call her again.* "Baa!"

Every once in a while, she came. Not often. Usually Jocko's voice bellowed from somewhere—under the bed, I presume— "Go to sleep. Your mother's busy." Mostly I lay with the blankets under my nose, stiff with fear, listening and waiting for something I was afraid of. The thing that I was sure would get me.

And then I am not as young as I had been. I am twelve and then thirteen, almost fourteen—and I knew. I knew. I felt both a child, helpless, and not a child. Powerful. This was power. And I owned it. But I wanted to be a child—and yet.

I'm naked. How did I get naked? Did I do that? Did he? He pulled the plastic bags off the dry cleaning that hung in the closet with the sliding doors, the sliding doors with big mirrors on them. He wraps the plastic bags around me—just so. Through my legs, around my chest. He lays me down on the white shag carpeting in the big bathroom and gets into the adjacent shower.

"Okay, Doodle, let me see. Move."

The merengue. I am learning to do the merengue. The dance he showed me one night in the den with everyone watching as he instructed. I practiced in the den and now I'm practicing here.

"Come on, let me see."

I push my face down into the carpet that smells of dust, trying hard to thrust my butt high in the air and down and side to side. I want to be good, but more than anything I want it to be over. And some part of me feels I'm in danger. I hold my face deep in the shag. Hide in the carpet. Not to be at all anymore—and yet. And yet...

This man's focus is totally on me; at this moment, I've won him. I am flypaper, the sweet sticky temptation, and he's caught. A tiny sliver inside me starts to stir, feels powerful. I am powerful. No...no. I want to be a child.

And then he slides from the shower, wet and erect and I don't know how he ever gets that thing in his pants, since I never see it in any other condition. He gently picks me up and sets me on the bathroom counter. I sit on the cold tile surrounded by mirrors, me in my Saran-wrap dress. He kisses me, not any different than other times. And yet it's different, it's different. Many times, he would playfully try to push his tongue into my mouth. I would always clamp my teeth closed. I'd never been kissed by anyone and didn't know what would happen if my teeth weren't clamped shut.

"Open your mouth," he breathes.

I don't.

He sets his penis, as muscular as the rest of him, between my legs and pulls my littleness toward him . . . and it.

He loved me enough not to invade me. He never invaded me. In all the many times. Not really. It would have been one thing if he had held me down and raped me, hurt me. Made me bleed. But he didn't. Was that love? Was that because he loved me?

5

What Goes Up

In 1954, when we moved into the Libbit house, Jocko's career was on a solid climb upward: from B movies to co-starring in A movies with important actors like Rock Hudson and Jeff Chandler and then eventually becoming the lead actor in A-ish movies. The ride went up and up, until 1958, when he was cast to star in a half-hour series on CBS. As popular as *The Range Rider* had been, it was only regionally televised, so *Yancy Derringer* was a much bigger deal. I can't say that the series thrust him into the same arena as James Garner of *Maverick* or Clint Eastwood of *Rawhide*, who were starring in more prestigious, hour-long shows, but it came very close. The whole house seemed to vibrate with the swagger of achievement. Jocko walked taller, his voice got deeper, and I swear the fringe on his jacket grew longer. He was a peacock with his tail fully spread and fluttering.

But when *Yancy Derringer* was suddenly canceled after one thirty-two-episode season, down went the ride. Even as a twelve-year-old, I remember feeling a sense of hush in the house as though there'd been a death in the family. Ricky and I didn't talk about it and Princess was too young to understand, but we all felt it. Outraged conversations were taking place in the den behind closed doors, and loud debates with someone on the phone upstairs could be heard all over the house. Muffled tidbits of the tragedy floated through the air: The new management at the network, Jim Aubrey—who was now executive vice president—had been systematically canceling all the shows he hadn't participated in from the beginning, or Aubrey had some kind of problem with Jocko, or this or that. But the truth is, "That's show biz, folks." And after all the indignant smoke had cleared, we discovered that the financial bubble we'd been living in had popped. We were standing in mid-air without a parachute or any rainy-day savings account... flat broke. Jocko needed a job, but as the weeks and months went by, the more he needed one, the less likely it seemed he might get one. And the less likely it seemed, the more he would inflate himself, going from a peacock to a puffer fish as he tried to pretend to be bigger than he actually was.

I'm sure this first real slam in his career was devastating, but I never saw Jocko take the punch like the brilliant stuntman he'd always been, never saw him register the blow or pause to reassess who he was, as an actor or a human. Righteously fuming, he would blame it on everyone else's spiteful incompetence, saying that it was the network who had lost, not him. But when the ride seems to be headed nowhere but down, how can you change your course if you won't recognize where you're headed? How can you change who you are and learn what it takes to get up, over and over, if you can't allow yourself to feel how much it hurts to be knocked down?

My mother continued to work, but erratically and without

*We didn't go out much. I think this was
opening night of the circus.*

the same energy, as if inch by inch, day by day, she was losing her confidence. The proud twinkle in her eyes was starting to fade along with her flawless face, now beginning to puff
from vodka's nightly numbing. And as the tension in the house
increased, so did the size of those evening cocktails. Though it
never happened in our presence, I had the sense that she and
Jocko were fighting and I felt frightened for my mother. Once,
Jocko told us that we had to stay completely quiet all day, that
Baa was in bed, that she'd taken a hard fall and hit her head.
We couldn't go upstairs to see her, or talk to her in any way. All
we could do was keep quiet. We whispered, tiptoeing around,
afraid to move, as if we were hiding from the Nazis.

*   *   *

Over the years, I slowly created a place where I could toss all the feelings I didn't understand, or the ones I didn't want to understand, was afraid of. Emotions that many times came to me as physical sensations without words, like the uncomfortable fingernails on the blackboard inside me. Instead of trying to verbalize what I was feeling, even to myself, I'd shove them away. I would pack them up and send those parts of me out the window to stay safe with the tree, while only one piece remained, muted and dulled, though dutifully performing the required tasks. But as adolescence approached, my emotions began to overload. The man I had lived with most of my life, the father figure whom I had looked to for love and affection, now seemed only dangerous, and I couldn't expect protection to come from my mother, who had lost sight of everyone, including herself. So, I unconsciously created an internal sycamore tree, a safe place. What I didn't want to see or feel, I would send off into a cloud of fog, hidden in a mental whiteout.

I began to live in that foggy world to such a degree I couldn't focus on my schoolwork, could barely read a book much less write a report on it. Subjects I might have loved and excelled in, like language or history, would go in one ear and out the other so fast, I couldn't remember any of it. Mathematics was simply out of the question. I started thinking of myself as being stupid because I couldn't hold anything in my head. What I could do was memorize a poem, or focus completely on anything relating to the drama department, which luckily, I discovered at this exact moment. Other than that, it was all a muted fog, and floating through the fog was the familiar feeling of fear. Always, I felt afraid.

*   *   *

Then, when I was newly fourteen, I just stopped talking to him. One day I was his little Doodle and the next, I refused to look him in the face or acknowledge he even existed, answering his questions with as few words as possible. Without touching him or knowing why, I pushed him away. And he felt it as surely as if I had hit him with a club. I shut down, tucked everything so completely inside my fog that, at the time, I couldn't clearly see what had happened, what had finally tripped the wire. I used the only words I could, which were no words at all, and my about-face infuriated, confounded, and hurt him. After that, Jocko and I entered a war together,

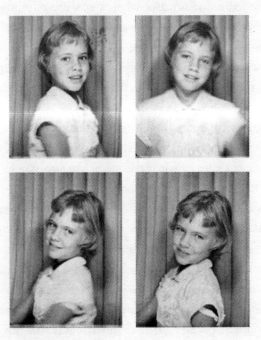

Turning fourteen.

mortal enemies, communicating with the only language our intense relationship could speak: anger on his part and silence on mine.

With each day, a new theater of war opened up. He began spying on me, listening on the other phone if anyone called, accusing me of behaving in ways I couldn't even fathom, things he saw only through his eyes. I was a teenager who desperately needed her peers, trying hard to be friends with a group of girls, to be invited to their slumber parties, to be included. Once, he lay spread-eagle on the big front lawn, flat as a pancake and undetected by the light of the moon or passing cars as he waited for me to return from an eighth-grade party I'd been allowed to attend. But when I was securely dropped off by the parent of another girl at exactly eleven o'clock—my curfew—his hopes of trapping me in some kind of deception were thwarted. God knows how long he'd been planted out there on the damp grass—which definitely needed mowing.

Then there was the time a boy I knew from school impulsively walked me home from the Little League field, less than a mile away. I remember feeling flustered, but, thinking Jocko wouldn't be home until late, I invited the young man to stay for dinner. Ricky and Princess joined us, thank God, because they did most of the talking, making the conversation seem friendly and fun. As we all sat around the kitchen banquette, eating Baa's dinner of pan-fried pork chops and canned corn, I was so caught up with the novelty of having this impromptu guest that I didn't notice Jocko's unexpected entrance through the back door.

Suddenly he stood looming over our giggling group. And as I introduced my stepfather to the first and only boy I'd ever invited into the house, Jocko turned to me with a sly look and the interrogation began. "What the hell have you got on your face, smart-ass?"

I was not allowed to wear lipstick, ever. I knew that, but since all the other girls wore it, when I was with them, I sometimes did too. Usually I was careful to wash it off, terrified to be caught behind enemy lines with Revlon on my face, but this time I'd forgotten and I got caught. I sat stunned on the sticky Naugahyde cushion, my mind began searching for possible excuses: I was in dress rehearsals for a play, I was testing it for a friend, my lips were really chapped so I grabbed the only thing I could find. Yet only a weak "I don't have anything on my face" dribbled out of my bright pink mouth. I could usually lie like a pro, not because I ever had anything to hide—well, except lipstick—but because I liked lying to him. If he wanted the truth from me, he wasn't gonna get it. He could ask if I'd had orange juice that morning and even if I had, I'd tell him it was apple. This time, however, I had actually broken a rule and needed a good lie. But I just sat there, so flooded with embarrassment that everything went white in my mind and I couldn't think.

Desperate to show everyone—most especially this poor bewildered boy—what a lying sniveler I was, Jocko went to the sink, wet a dishrag, loaded it with soap, and as my mother stood silently at the stove with her hand over her mouth, proceeded to wash my face in front of all those who could bear to watch. He needed to beat me in whatever game this was.

Mom, where are you? Even now I want to call out to you. I want to look up and see you coming to help me. Gathering up these memories, forcing myself to look at ones that have been lying out in the open the whole time, I don't know what to think. I've adored you all my life. But I've camouflaged the truth, fiercely believing my own fairy tale about you. I dressed you in clothes borrowed from the emperor, ones that didn't actually exist, and during those important years you abandoned me. I don't understand. I don't want to discover that the piece I've been looking for is something I don't want to see, I've never wanted to see... my anger toward you. I still need to hold on to you. Please help me to see something else.

I have a stack of letters Jocko wrote to my mother at different times during their marriage. Letters I'm sure she never wanted me to read, yet she didn't rip them to shreds and flush them down the toilet, so she must have known that they'd eventually land in my box of puzzle pieces, helping me to see her and put it all together. I look at them now with my eyes squinted, my grasp light, ready to drop the onionskin airmail pages if I feel I need to take a break—maybe a quiet jog to the nearest fog bank. I'm surprised to read Jocko's words, constantly pleading for her love, frantic for her approval, while she keeps him waiting for her answers. And though I have none of the letters she finally did write in return, I have a few pages of her journal writings, sometimes typed on an electric typewriter, sometimes written by hand in a spiral notepad. But there are so few entries—dashed off in a disorganized, misspelled way—it leads me to think that she put her feelings on paper only when she was at an overload point and blurry with booze; other than that, she kept her real anguish locked away.

On her private pages she nonchalantly writes that because we now had no money, she was faced with the overwhelming task of selling the Libbit house and finding us somewhere else to live as quickly as possible, while Jocko vanished. Hired to play the villain in the film *Tarzan the Magnificent*—which starred Gordon Scott and was being shot in Africa—Jocko had decided to leave weeks earlier than the production needed him. Baa writes that he had to leave, that he couldn't watch, that he found it too painful to witness everything, all his cherished possessions, dissolve. And so, during the next few months we packed up our belongings and moved from our sprawling house in Encino to a small home in, yes, it's true... Tarzana. Everything seemed to disappear at once: the house, the Cadillac, and for a while, Jocko.

Unlike the law stating that I couldn't wear lipstick until I was five feet tall (which didn't happen until 1963), one of my step-father's ironclad rules doesn't seem completely unreasonable in retrospect. This edict—which Jocko had repeated regularly and emphatically for years—pertained to dating: I was not allowed to do anything that resembled a date, could not go anywhere with a boy alone, until I turned fifteen years old. But I was not quite fifteen when I started the tenth grade and met a boy. And even though I was terrified of Jocko's scrutiny and avoided inviting anyone to my house, miraculously this boy walked right in, mowing the lawn for Jocko, doing the dishes for Baa, making everything seem easy. So, two days before my birthday, when I hit fourteen years and 363 days, before we moved from the Libbit house and before he departed without a word, Jocko allowed me to go to the movies with Steve.

Steven Craig Bloomfield was born in Fargo, North Dakota, a year and a half before my birth. His father abandoned his family when Steve was only a few months old, never initiating any contact with his son again. Steve then grew up under the scrutinizing eye of his mother, Glory Rose, who was a hard-edged, exacting businesswoman, perhaps because she had to be. And maybe she placed her four-year-old son in a military boarding school because she felt she had to, felt it was the only option she had. Maybe that's true. But at four?

When Steve was thirteen he no longer went to a military school but attended Birmingham High School in Van Nuys, which at that time was both junior and senior high. Finally free from scratchy wool uniforms, he joined up with a little band of Valley guys who got their kicks from pushing parked cars over whatever cliff was available, occasionally getting lucky when the car landed in someone's swimming pool. On a smaller scale, they'd fold wads of dog shit into the daily newspaper, set it on fire, then leave it on a stranger's doorstep after repeatedly ringing the bell. You can imagine what happened when the victim answered the door and began stomping on the package hoping to extinguish the flames.

Never comfortable being one of the gang, Steve split off from that band of merrymakers and started breaking into houses. But not to do any harm. He would find an unlocked window or crawl through the dog door and walk around the home, never actually stealing anything but looking in people's drawers and closets, or rearranging the furniture the way he thought it should be, then sitting in the house for a while, as if he lived there, always departing through the front door. It was a home, with a family, something Steve didn't have.

When he was finally caught, Glory found a way to keep her son from being sent to Juvie Hall (a juvenile correctional facility) by agreeing to have him imprisoned in a different institution for a year: a boarding school for children with learning disabilities. Maybe that too was the only option she had, I don't know. But at the time, the term *learning disability* could include a whole range of things, so among the students were kids with varying forms of autism and borderline mental health issues, like the overweight fourteen-year-old boy who felt compelled to save all his bodily fluids. There were kids with different degrees of brain damage along with a few whose parents were simply too busy to deal with them.

Luckily, one of the counselors at the facility recognized Steve's bright mind—which must have been like spotting an orange jellybean in a bowl of green ones. He ordered Steve to go to the small library every morning, find a book, then take it outside and sit under a tree on the big lawn the rest of the day. For one solid year, day in and day out, Steve sat under that tree and read. From Dickens to Hemingway, Steinbeck to Twain and Tolstoy. Devouring book after book.

Steve had spent much of his childhood in institutions, not unlike my grandmother. And whether in a military school or a facility for the mentally challenged, there was always a list of rules, a strict set of enforced boundaries, walls that held him in and doors that locked him out. Steve refused to surrender, refused to play by those rules wherever they were. He went in the door that said *Exit* and left through the door that said *Enter*. Forever in deep revolt against the world that tried to tell him in what tempo he had to march, starting when he was only four.

A year or so after being released from the facility, he intercepted me at a school football game, jumped right into step as I walked to the snack bar to get drinks for the girls, who were waving at me from the bleachers. Steve began the conversation by saying that his friend wanted to meet me, then pointed to a boy waiting in the stands, but since that sounded like the prelude to a humiliating prank, I shied away. He kept right on talking, and by the time we'd completed fifteen laps around the snack bar, he'd forgotten about his friend's attributes altogether and focused entirely on his own. Long after halftime was over, I continued to sit on an empty bench—snackless—with persistent, determined, gentle Steve.

I didn't know any boys, other than my brother—had never been friends with a single one. There had been the awkward

Steve's grad night 1962.

parties in the seventh and eighth grade, gatherings where everyone danced to Paul Anka singing "Put Your Head on My Shoulder" as the parents hovered in the kitchen. Times when we actually played "Spin the Bottle" and everyone smelled of Hershey's Kisses, not human ones. Even the distanced flirtations in the ninth grade never included having an actual conversation. Every boy's hand felt sweaty and sex was described using baseball terms, as though reaching home base was more for the bragging rights than anything else. But not Steve. We talked and talked because he wanted to know me and needed to tell me how filled with feeling he was. He seemed like someone who knew his way through the woods and whether he did or not, I felt safe to wander out beyond where I had been before. If my mother was my backup generator, then Steve was my flashlight, illuminating what was right in front of me.

He instantly became a member of my family—not because they invited him in; they weren't like that. He simply made room for himself, forming a solid friendship with my brother, who also didn't have many friends; performing athletic antics with my little sister; staying up late in the night to talk philosophy and literature with my mother—later on getting drunk right along with her. Jocko seemed to get a kick out of Steve, although he still tried to belittle him, like he did the rest of us. But to survive his complicated life, Steve had developed a wily, honest charm that even Jocko couldn't penetrate. He was going to find a way into my life, no matter what. If the door was locked, he'd climb in my window or crawl through the dog door. He wanted a family and I was it.

And for the first time I heard myself verbalize my feelings, an endless stream of verbiage about Dick and Baa, Ricky, and slowly, bit by bit, about Jocko. Steve never backed away from emotion; to the contrary, he thrived on it, would push to find it—in everyone. He had an intuitive sense of anyone's despair and like a hound dog on the trail of fugitive feelings, he'd root them out, lock his focus on the injury, then comfort and soothe. I had never told anyone anything, convincing myself my life wasn't any different from any other little girl's. But Steve's concern told me it *was* different and since his own childhood had not been a skate in the park, I trusted his perspective. Because he was with me, I began to feel what I had been afraid to feel alone. And by helping me, he, in turn, felt stronger himself.

I was fifteen and a half when Jocko returned and saw the tract home we now owned, an obvious demotion in the world. The El Caballero house was compact, a one-story place that had very little yard in the front and even less in the back, but Jocko took one look at it and immediately started building a swimming pool. I mean, he literally started shoveling dirt, and only after many days of shirtless digging did he finally decide to hire a professional pool contractor to complete the job. When the dust settled, we had a swimming pool that practically butted up against the sliding glass doors to the backyard. You could almost jump into the pool from the living room, without ever stepping outside. But since I had my own bedroom—which was connected to my sister's by a small bathroom—I thought it was perfect.

Not long after his return, when I was sound asleep in bed, lying on my side under the window I always kept open, I was suddenly pulled awake by the smell of booze oozing from someone's pores. It was Jocko, trying to worm his body next to mine, fumbling with the blanket I had tightly wrapped around me. We were no longer in the Libbit house; the upstairs bedroom was gone (though it has never left my life), and I'd lived for months without the on-edge feeling of his presence. But now, instantly it was back and I couldn't move. I gripped the covers, holding them in place while I played possum, and as I pretended to be asleep, he wiggled up close, whispering something I couldn't understand. I held my breath—not only out of fear but to avoid the sickening smell of his drunkenness.

And then one night some piece of me that had been quietly, wordlessly growing in my brain finally ripped out of my self-imposed fog and took center stage. Rage. Jocko and I met nose-to-nose, just as we had when he swept me off my feet at the age of four.

It had all begun innocently when I'd asked permission to go out, something that by then hardly needed clearance, and as Steve waited for me in the small foyer off to the side, talking softly to my brother, Jocko began to flare.

"I have the ability," he slurred at me. "I have the ability to see your Achilles' heel, little lady, everyone's Achilles' heel. That one thing about people...about you...and if I told you, it would destroy you."

"What are you talking about? What does that mean?" I tepidly threw back after enduring twenty minutes of his incoherent rant while sitting quietly on the sunken-in sectional. Across from me sat my mother, cross-legged on the floor with her swaying torso propped against the coffee table, barely able to keep her head up. I wanted to look at her, but I didn't want to see how repulsive she was, so I didn't.

"You little smart-ass, listen to me. You think I can't tell you things you don't want to hear? Things you *can't* hear! Things that you could not *bear* to hear! You think you know anything? ANYTHING?!" He stood up over me in a familiar stance of power and intimidation as my mind frantically searched for what it was that could destroy me.

"I have the ability to tell you what you could not stand to know about yourself."

Without thinking or even believing my words, I blurted, "That's not true!" And then, said it louder: "That's not true!" Suddenly, I felt like a cuckoo clock whose hands hit midnight and all the cogs and gears automatically fell into place.

"You don't know anything about me," I dared. "You don't have any abilities…to do anything. You are a fool and a failure."

The room turned red, bright blazing red. I rose from where I sat perched on the edge of my childhood, rose up through the years of fear, fury, and longing, of confusion and love. I stepped onto the coffee table and there we were again, eye-to-eye, nose-to-nose.

"I hate you! YOU'RE the liar! Not ME! And you know NOTHING!" From my mouth came a voice, but it didn't belong to me, and from a faraway place I watched as this little person who looked like me stood up until she seemed to tower over this man.

"You don't know who I am!" This guttural voice, filled with loathing, vomited forth as she peered into his eyes. But it *was* me. I was still there, somewhere. And while she stood, I held my breath—for a minute? An hour? And a stunning realization hit me: He was frightened of her. He was frightened of me.

In one quick slash, he grabbed me by the neck, lunging with me in his meaty fist toward the sliding glass door that opened to the pool, now dark and covered with leaves. My shoeless feet fluttered in midair as he pounded my doll-like body against the glass again and again. Baa sobered enough to rise as Steve and Ricky haltingly moved toward the clumsy dance, but never made it far enough to cut in.

I didn't roar, or kick, or cry. I hung in his overpowering, massive grasp and knew. I had won. Somehow, some part of me that wasn't afraid, that didn't care if I was loved, or if I lived or died, had beaten him. He knew it too.

6

That Summer

IN THE SPRING of 1962, right before Rick graduated from high school, my brother pulled me into the back door/service porch area where his room was located. We leaned against the wall, whispering with our heads bowed, our foreheads almost touching, feeling slightly awkward with each other. He wanted me to know that I could count on seeing him at Christmas and perhaps for a short time each summer and that was it. He spoke curtly, without emotion, then fumbled the next sentence as if he wasn't sure what he wanted to say. "I wish I could take you with me, Sal" were the words that came out. After a beat of silence, we both laughed, knowing that wasn't true. "I'll be okay," I said, but when I looked at him, I saw the face of the little boy who had come to rescue me from Dick's house and I felt my eyes burn. I knew Ricky was going to college, this wasn't news, but until that moment the fact that my big brother wouldn't be living in the house with me anymore had never registered in my brain. He was leaving.

At some point along the way, Ricky had stopped crying, had swallowed his tears and quietly begun propelling himself to beat Jocko at his own game. Knowing that there would be no financial support from our parents, my brother had worked toward and received a gymnastics scholarship to the University of California at Berkeley—eventually ranking second all-around in the nation. But when he was a junior his left biceps pulled away from the elbow, taking part of the bone with it, forcing him to quit. Rick then went on to become a high-energy elementary particle physicist. A first-class athlete and a world-renowned scientist, two things Jocko would never be.

By the time my own graduation rolled around, Ricky had been in college for two years and yet I never saw him as an example, never thought to make any plans of my own for the following September—or any day after that. All thoughts of my future were shoved out in the mist that vaporized everything I couldn't deal with, while I floated around in a cloud, seeing only the few things that were manageable. I was a seventeen-year-old varsity cheerleader—or songleader, as we called it—and queen of the drama department. That was pretty much it.

Everywhere else in school, I felt slightly shy with a strong baseline anxiety, either unconscious of or uncomfortable with most people and always wary of the girls. Too many times in my middle school years, eighth and ninth grade, I was the one they decided "needed to go" and I'd be kicked out of the club (there actually was a club, the Shondells). Once, during an eighth-grade slumber party, after the girls had TP'ed a neighbor's lawn, then turned on the sprinklers, they decided it would be fun to rub peanut butter all over my underdeveloped body, throw me into the swimming pool, lock all the doors, and wait for me to panic. I wasn't sure if I hated being treated that way or liked it. I was somehow an integral part of everyone's good time—though uncomfortably gooey—and being thrown in a swimming pool was nothing new. I didn't enjoy being humiliated but at least I was familiar with it. And maybe this was the price I had to pay to be liked, to have friends.

These were the girls who became the heart of the A group, the three or four supremely popular girls who were certain to break through to safety in any playground game of life, or that's how it felt. And the biggest jewel in the crown, for any of the girls, was to become a songleader—a feat that had always seemed like a foregone conclusion for the A's, as if they didn't even need to try out. For me, it was the first thing I remember deeply wanting, and I—not shrouded with foregone conclusions—was thought to have zero chance. But I'd already spent a fair amount of time onstage by then, and knew what it was like to stand in front of an audience, to risk failure, and to fall into a place that meant more to me than popularity. Without hesitation, I reached out to Lynn, a tall, sweetly awkward girl who hovered on the edges of the A group, exactly where I hovered. And after practicing day in and day out for weeks, we found we had kicked and pranced and laughed our way into becoming best friends—certainly the best I'd ever had. We also became songleaders for the following year. Whereas the others did not.

Jumping up and down on the sidelines of a football field was never-endingly fulfilling, but it was the drama department where I felt most alive. Inside that school auditorium I

Varsity songleader.

was clearheaded and focused on the task in front of me, or the pages in my hand, or the performance coming up. It wasn't that I was particularly good. I don't think I was. But when I was onstage, I could hear my own voice talking to me, asking me questions, forcing me to be present at that moment: aware of my hands, my mouth, my heart rate. And at the same time, I would watch the other actors, meet them fully in the eyes, react to them in whatever way they affected me—ultimately behaving in ways I was unable to do offstage.

But just because I could lock eyes with my fellow actors didn't mean I wanted to work with them. The term play, which we performed each semester, was the teacher's responsibility;

he chose the text, then directed and cast it. But throughout the semester each student had to select several scenes to work on: scene study. Like a thirsty person needs a glass of water, I needed to explore this world of acting in every way I could. I never thought about being nice, never spent an ounce of energy concerned about other students' feelings. Which meant that if I felt no one in class was serious enough or even good enough to join me in a scene, then I'd choose to do a monologue. If I couldn't find a monologue, I'd pick a scene and cut out all the other characters, resulting in some very long monologues.

Midway through my junior year, the teacher, Mr. Kulp, called me to his office, not to praise me for my efforts but to ask if I would please be more sensitive to the other students. I remember feeling stunned, ashamed to see myself as being blindly ambitious and hungry, embarrassed as though I'd been caught with my hand in the cookie jar. After that, I started doing scenes with more than one character, but even though I tried to be friendly and appreciative of the other students, my gnawing appetite kept me at the head of the class table. And like it or not, my reign continued. I wanted to do theater in the round, so we did theater in the round. I wanted to do children's theater and we did that too. The auditorium was my spot. It's where I went for lunch, during every break or free period, and often when I should have been in another class, like Algebra.

At the beginning of my senior year, the school counselor informed me that if I didn't go to night school to make up for the classes I'd either missed or done too poorly in to be counted, I wouldn't be graduating in June with the rest of my class. That was all he said. He had never called me to his office in the eleventh grade to suggest I take the SAT, never inquired if I was planning to go to college or helped me to see what options I might have, and through my foggy brain the thought never penetrated. Certainly, it wasn't a topic of conversation around the family dinner table, where the ongoing drama had nothing to do with continuing my education and everything to do with finding the money to put food on the table. Jocko had been cast in two back-to-back *Tarzan* movies, no longer playing the bad guy but now portraying the ape man himself. In 1962 there was *Tarzan Goes to India* and in 1963 *Tarzan's Three Challenges,* which was shot in Thailand— a harrowing location where Jocko almost died. But despite a case of dengue fever and dysentery, losing over fifty pounds and looking like a hairless cat, he kept shooting, breathing through an oxygen mask between takes, which was either heroic or stupid. Or maybe the man was fighting to hold on to his career the only way he knew how.

Whatever money he'd made from those movies couldn't have been much because the endless anxiety over how to make ends meet never seemed to ease and much of the time the proverbial cupboards were bare—literally. I remember looking for something to eat one morning before driving my mother's car to school and finding nothing but a white Styrofoam box containing half of a sandwich that Jocko had brought back from the Screen Actors Guild board meeting, where Ronald Reagan was the president—not of the USA but of the SAG. I cut the half in half again and shared it with Princess, who then walked to the corner where the school bus would pick her up.

In all this family stress and scramble, I felt slightly separate, safe because I had someone to talk to, someone to take me to the movies or to get a hamburger when there was nothing in the house, many times bringing Princess along. Steve had graduated from Birmingham the same year as Ricky, and by the time I was a senior he'd finished a year at Pierce Junior College and received a scholarship of his own, a track scholarship to USC. But even with classes and workouts, he somehow managed to spend more time at my house than I did. He was woven into my family, everyone's confidant, aware of every argument and all the problems.

But he wasn't there for them. He was there because of me, because of the bond we had with each other. From the beginning the sexuality between us had felt both exhilarating and frightening. But as the sensations grew, I could feel myself pulling back, hanging on the shore, disconnected but performing, as if I were repeating the pattern I'd learned with my stepfather. Steve could feel my hesitance and thought it was simply who I was. Slightly asexual. I didn't know that some part of me, some important part, would not allow herself to be seen. She simply never showed up in Steve's presence, and since I'd never been on a date with anyone else, I was not aware of her existence either. My body was out of my reach as well.

Then, in the middle of the twelfth grade, something inside me began to simmer, eventually coming to a boil in the last weeks of high school when I abruptly pushed Steve away, told him I needed to break up, maybe see other people even. After that, for very short, shocking bits of time, someone completely new would be standing in my shoes. I'd find a boy I barely knew, a boy who wouldn't notice the drastic difference between the reticent, sexually passive girl I had always been with Steve and the playful, if not downright aggressive, person I became. Nowhere in sight was the careful part of me with her cautionary advice. Maybe that's how every adolescent brain works. Maybe. But I've never been able to remember these episodes clearly, only a distinct feeling of changing gears. After they occurred, I felt so ashamed I'd force them out of my head, lock them out of sight in my brain's attic, like Rochester's mad wife. Slowly I would lose the memories, and with them the opportunity to get any distance, maybe even a little perspective from which to look at this young, sexual side of myself. I was afraid of my "mad-woman in the attic." The pinched face of my grandmother, wordless messages from my mother, and the constant shadow of my stepfather had built a maze around my healthy sexuality, which was lost somewhere in the center. But there was more to it than that and at the time, I couldn't see what it was.

As if I were imitating the gobbledygook going on in my head, I put together a slapstick performance of "The Walrus and the Carpenter" from Lewis Carroll's *Through the Looking-Glass* for the senior assembly. My best friend, Lynn, whom I'd convinced to join the drama department, played Alice, while another theater student and I waddled around the stage, falling and smacking into each other playing Tweedledee and Tweedledum. As a result, I was named "Funniest in the Class" in the 1964 *Tomahawk*, the school yearbook.

But when the curtain came down and the pom-poms were dumped in the trash, when the last notes of "Pomp and Circumstance" faded away into that June day, the reality of what lay ahead of me began to penetrate the fog. I had no stage. Without that I didn't exist. I had to find a place where I could act.

*   *   *

The Film Industry Workshop was a small organization located on the lot of what was then Columbia Pictures, in the heart of Hollywood, and one night a week the group was allowed to hold classes on a soundstage. FIW was not well known in the acting community and I can't imagine it was well regarded. Its classes primarily focused on teaching students how to hit their mark, which was a piece of colored tape stuck to the floor. You were expected to find that smidgen of tape without looking down to see where it was located, while at the same time performing in front of a make-believe camera, simulating close-ups and over-shoulder shots. The scenes were handed out at the beginning of each class, material taken from an episode of one of last season's television shows. Not exactly Ibsen.

I'd never heard of the workshop but then I hadn't heard of anything. It was Jocko who stepped up, saying that he knew someone who knew someone, which was enough for him to tout the workshop, suggesting I audition to see if they'd accept me. Unfortunately, the workshop charged a twenty-five-dollar fee for the opportunity to perform in front of its panel of experts, and that was twenty-five dollars which Baa didn't have. This meant that I either had to give up the idea or force myself to call and ask my father—whom I was still visiting, though less frequently. For all of Dick's shortcomings, he had always found a way to show up for an evening performance of my term plays, sometimes driving an hour to get there. And when I surprised him with my request, he surprised me by immediately sending a check.

A week later, in front of a half dozen people sitting at a long table, I performed a two-character scene from Lillian Hellman's *Toys in the Attic,* with my mother playing opposite me.

I hadn't bothered to read the play, stopped after finding the one scene, so I don't know what the hell I thought I was portraying. But whatever it was, I was admitted to the workshop. And on the following Thursday evening, after my first—oddly unchallenging—class, I stood on the corner just outside the gates of Columbia waiting for Ricky to pick me up, since I wasn't allowed to drive at night.

Just as my brother had promised two years earlier, every June he came home from Berkeley for a few weeks, though that summer I'd hardly seen him. Most of the time he was with a girl whom he had met years before while competing in a gymnastics match against Garfield High. Beautiful, slightly shy Jimmie was the student who held the scorecards in the air after every event, cards that always had my brother on top. After graduating, he reconnected with her and that fall, Ricky would take Jimmie back to the Bay Area with him, where she was to be a freshman at the University of San Francisco. Eventually Jimmie would become his wife, which she is to this day, devotedly.

As I waited on the corner, watching all the cars whiz by on busy Sunset Boulevard, I noticed a man heading toward me with such purpose he made me wonder if I'd left something behind.

"Excuse me," he said. "Are you Jock Mahoney's daughter?"

"Yes," I said meekly, then reconsidered. "Well, no. Actually, I'm his stepdaughter."

The man smiled, then continued quickly, as if trying to keep me from running off like a scared rabbit. "I know your stepdad. I know Jock. I'm Eddie Foy the Third. I saw your audition last week. Tried to catch you in class tonight but just missed you."

"Hi," I said with as much ease as I could muster.

"I work here," he continued. "I'm head of casting for Screen

Gems, the television division of Columbia, and I'd like you to come on an interview tomorrow."

I just stood there with my teeth hanging out, saying nothing. I couldn't believe this was real. Mr. Foy watched me searching for something to say, then handed me a little card with his name and the Screen Gems logo on it, asking if I had an agent he could contact. When I shook my head with an incredulous *no*, he told me to show the card to Jock and to come to his office tomorrow at eleven.

"Can you do that?" he asked, as if I were a five-year-old.

I reached for the card like I was afraid it might bite me and said in a voice so high only dogs could hear it, "Okay..."

"Great." And as he began to walk away, he stopped, then turned back. "Tell me your name again."

With eyes as big as pie pans, I answered, "Sally. Sally Field."

"Okay, Sally. See you tomorrow," and he walked away.

Something had reached out of nowhere to change my life, just as it had for my mother and even my grandmother before her. For one moment, I could see out of the fog and into my future, then it was gone again, and the only thing I knew for sure was that Ricky was very late.

If there was a tiny part of me that felt relieved when Jocko insisted on accompanying me to that meeting the next day, it quickly vanished along with any hope I might've had of sitting quietly in the corner, unnoticed. When he sauntered in with a protective swagger, then immediately treated the receptionist as if they were intimate friends, loudly laughing at some remark he whispered in her ear, I wanted to crawl under one of the sofas lining the reception area. I tried to act as if

I didn't know the man, smiling nonchalantly at a few of the young women who filled the room. Most of them were holding eight-by-ten photos of themselves; some even had zippered portfolios, which I presumed were stuffed with pictures and résumés of their vast experience. All I had was a wallet containing a few snapshots of God knows what, which was lost somewhere in the tangle of stuff crammed into the big straw bag I held at my side.

When I was finally asked to step inside Mr. Foy's office, Jocko walked in before me, shaking hands with everyone and blasting a baritone greeting in such an alpha male display he might as well have lifted his leg on the furniture. But after a moment, he reluctantly backed out, closing the door behind him, leaving me to face four men dressed in suits—two on a sofa, one in a large chair, and one in a smaller desk chair. After an awkward beat, they began asking me questions: How was graduation? Where had I been acting? Did I have any plans for the summer? And even though they were watching me, I knew they weren't really interested in my answers, I knew it was about something else. Like flipping a switch, I began to bubble. I told them about going to the beach later that day, that I had my bathing suit with me, that Jocko was dropping me off at my friend Lynn's house so she could drive us in the old beat-up Ford she'd been given for graduation—the car that would soon be sitting in Lynn's family garage as she headed off to her freshman year at San Jose State College and slowly moved out of my life.

A little later, I sat perched on the chair opposite one of the men, Bob Claver, who was my reading partner, and we ran the three-page scene they had given me to study for a few minutes in an adjacent office. Rarely looking down at the slightly crumpled pages, I recited all the dialogue with an avalanche of raw energy—not knowing how to contain it, or even that it needed to be contained. And as I said the last line, I looked at Bob, then crossed my eyes—actually used the facial expression as a punctuation mark. I don't remember ever doing that in a conversation before. I mean, yes, I was a champion eye crosser. I could cross them, then move one eye at a time, as if one was crossed and the other was watching a tennis match. This time I performed a simple cross, hold, and release. And they laughed. Effortlessly friendly and entertaining, I radiated pure delight, because that's all I felt. The slivers of me that were nervous or unsure watched from a great distance, until they seemed to vanish altogether and I was without fog or fear.

I lost track of how many times I walked into that waiting room, because from that point on, the entire summer of 1964 was sprinkled with meetings. And with each meeting, more and more people would crowd into the room to watch whatever I was asked to do, while there were fewer and fewer hopeful young women pacing the waiting room floor, listening for their names to be called. Finally, the group was down to eight and I was asked to do a "personality test," which consisted of sitting, then standing, in front of a camera while answering random questions asked by Bob—my reading partner in every previous meeting. By August, when it was down to three—and I was lucky enough to be one of them—we were asked to do a screen test.

On that day, after having greasy dark makeup applied to my face and my hair put in pigtails, I was led through one of the huge soundstages and into the middle of a bedroom that had only two walls. Where the other half of the room should have been were big pieces of equipment, most of them on wheels, all being pushed and pulled into place by busy, bustling guys. With genuine curiosity, I turned to Bob, who was standing at my side, and asked, "Which one is the camera?" I had visited a set only once before, one of Jocko's when I was about eleven, and five-year-old Princess had come with me. But we hadn't seen much because we sat squished together on one canvas chair, hidden away in a darkened corner.

Jocko is behind us, covered with oil from the scene he was filming.

In reality, most of any soundstage—a huge airplane hangar of a space—is nothing but darkened corners. Only the center, the actual stage, radiates with light. People move around on the rim of it or in the shadows or on the wooden walkways suspended from the high ceilings above, but their focus is always on the light's center, even if they aren't looking at it. And for the first time, I was standing inside that light where it was loud and bright, so searingly bright it was hard not to squint as you looked around the two-walled room. Someone asked me to move to the side, out of the dangerous hustle, so I walked off the set and waited, standing in the dark. I have learned to love the darkness on the edges of that bright world. In those dark safe seconds, before stepping into the glow, I've lived and relived every moment of my life, the good ones and the bad ones—over and over.

In 2004, I received a large manila envelope from my manager, Judy Hofflund, with a note saying: *This was sent to me in hopes that I would send it on to you. You probably don't know this person but he says he knows you and wanted you to have them… so I'm sending it on just in case.* Thinking it was nothing, I casually ripped it open, dumped out the contents, and immediately felt as if I'd jumped into an icy pool while holding exposed electrical wires. It was filled with letters written by a seventeen-year-old me to a boy I'd met that summer, and all these years later he was sending them back. A very kind thing to do. I looked at the letters from my young self and did what I have done my whole life—I hid them in a plastic box out of my sight. But again, I didn't throw them away. I have to admit I still haven't read them, don't know that I ever will.

That summer was the first time—though not the last—that my life went into spin cycle. Things began to come at me all at once, situations I couldn't see until they flew into my face, until I was overwhelmed with events. Sometime shortly after graduation, right before I started the Film Industry Workshop and when Steve was out of the picture, I met a boy who was a few years older than me. And although I remember precisely what the Screen Gems lobby looked like, I can't remember where I met this young man, can't even see his face in my mind. But that summer, in '64, as I was going from meeting to meeting at Screen Gems, each audition more important than the last, I was also spending time with him. Most of it I don't remember; some of it I will never forget.

I remember sitting in the back seat of a car, blankly watching the landscape of Los Angeles roll by, then San Diego, though I felt no movement at all. We must have been in that car many hours, but I had no sense of time. I didn't know where we were going and I didn't ask. I just sat—suspended—with my mother by my side. We didn't touch. I never met her eyes.

Directly in front of me sat Patti, with her short curly hair, dark but not black like Baa's. And next to her, in the driver's seat, sat Dr. Duke, her mega-masculine husband, silently driving his new state-of-the-art baby-blue Cadillac. Duke and Patti were family friends, or at least friends of my stepfather. Baa didn't seem to be truly close to anyone who came to the occasional gatherings they had, evenings when four or five couples would sit crammed together on the big purple-and-green sectional, plunging cubes of bread into the bubbling cheese fondue and constantly refilling their drinks.

I had only seen Dr. Duke outside of my own house twice. Once, in the eleventh grade, I had gone to his office in Tarzana to have him painfully remove the plantar warts from my right foot. Then, in September of 1964, just as I was waiting anxiously to hear the final decision from Screen Gems, I sat in his office as he told me I was pregnant.

I couldn't look at him when he announced the urinalysis results or when he gave me the first injection, with clear instructions to come back for another the following day, and then one more the day after that. I just numbly nodded my head as he said maybe this would solve the problem and maybe it wouldn't. The only thing I felt was the glare of the summer sun bouncing off the parked cars, slapping me in the face as I walked toward the roasting interior of my mother's blue Corvair, which I had borrowed under some false pretense. But this trusted family doctor had neglected to tell me that in approximately five minutes, while I was driving cautiously on the Ventura freeway, my vision would blur, or that by the time I miraculously drove the car safely into our driveway, my tongue would become so swollen, it would be difficult to talk. He also forgot to inform me that my whole body would then convulse. It took all the concentration I could muster to somehow get from the car, past my mother, and into my room without allowing her to register my condition or without collapsing in a total panic. And that was day one.

After each of the panic-laced injections, I held my breath and waited, even prayed...but there was no change in my condition. I couldn't lie or invent another world or push it out of my mind, couldn't run away because I had nowhere to go. I was locked into a nightmare and couldn't wake up.

The life-changing ramifications of my situation were painful enough, but my deepest dread was in the knowledge that I'd have to explain my disgrace to Jocko.

Even now, I wonder why I didn't just pull my mother aside to talk to her alone, but I didn't, and one evening I asked if I could talk to them together. As if it were yesterday, I remember sitting on the purple shag rug with my legs folded beneath me, staring at my shaking hands, unable to speak as tears dripped into my lap. I can still hear my mother's voice, usually so unchangingly sweet, now sounding panicked and shrill as she sat on the sofa next to Jocko. "What? What is it? Jock, what's happened? What?" she kept repeating over and over until he sternly commanded her to shut up, taking over like it was the helm of the *Caine* and only he could steer the ship out of the storm. I couldn't look at him as he began talking to me softly, saying, "I know, Sal, I know. Doodle, I know. You don't have to say anything." Was he telling me that I didn't have to utter the words? Was I being rescued, airlifted off the battlefield? He motioned for me to move to his big lap with a "Come here, baby."

I'd been "called to him" countless times since he first entered my life thirteen years earlier, but I hadn't stepped into my stepfather's shirtless embrace since I was fourteen, and we'd been locked in battle ever since. Feeling the familiar clawing on my insides, I climbed into his arms, hiding my face in the musky smell of his neck. And more than anything, I wanted my mother, wanted her to talk to me from under the closet door, wanted to be held by her, not by him. Why did I have to go through Jocko to have my mother?

I don't know what words I was able to get out, but he knew,

somehow he knew and started cooing, "It's okay, baby. Don't talk. I'm going to make it okay, my little Doodle. Your ol' Jock is here." I didn't want to hear, couldn't stand his imperceptible note of triumph. If he'd been hoping for my downfall, and I felt sure he had, then this was it. I wasn't aware of anything else but that. No right or wrong, no other living being involved in this catastrophe, only me and defeat.

When I got up the next morning he was gone—a casually mentioned personal appearance somewhere. Maybe that's how he got the money. I'll never know.

Less than a week later, I sat in the back seat of Duke's hermetically sealed four-door with my mind safely tucked in a blank fog. Eventually, the Cadillac pulled over on the edge of a roughly paved, treeless road. Instantly, Patti's incessant chatter stopped and my mother's eyes went to her lap. Dr. Duke hooked his arm around the back of the seat and turned to look at me, carefully explaining that he couldn't go in, that I had to go alone. He told me that they knew I was coming and gave me a large envelope with instructions to hand it to the people at the desk. "When you're finished, get back here to me as soon as you can. Do you understand?"

I met his eyes for the first time and flatly told him, "Yes."

Across the street—which smelled slightly rancid, like the odor coming from the men's bathroom at the beach—stood the low brick building that Dr. Duke had pointed out, and when I stepped from the bright midday sun into the dimly lit waiting room, with its flickering fluorescent lights, my eyes needed a moment to adjust. I don't recall if anyone greeted me or how I got from the door to the chair where I sat, but during an acting exercise years later, I did remember how I stared at the large fish tank that stood in the center of the dim room. I remembered the sound of the bubbles pumping tiny amounts of oxygen to a family of ordinary little fish gliding through their murky glass world, remembered so clearly watching those fish as if they mattered, until a man appeared speaking thickly accented English. He led me to a room with big dirty windows and a long metal table positioned in the center, then pointed to a small alcove in the corner, partially hidden by a limp curtain. Inside I found a cot where a folded dingy-white gown waited, obviously for me. The man then handed me a paper cup and a white pill, which I washed down with the tiny amount of water held in the cup. It was barely enough to moisten my mouth—but since this was Tijuana in 1964, drinking the water was probably not a good idea anyway. I removed my clothes in a hurry, not wanting to be caught in between; out of my clothes and not completely in theirs.

I can see myself climbing up onto the shiny table, feel the cold slap on my bare bottom, remember awkwardly lying down and looking up at the ceiling. And even though I remember everything, I know that part of me wasn't in the room anymore. I had left rooms many times before, and the transition between being present and being gone was a familiar glide away. Some piece of me was there, responding to their instructions, and the rest of me went off somewhere else, somewhere I wasn't in danger anymore, even though the girl on the table probably was.

I'm sure it was all terrifying, but she didn't feel afraid. She just lay still as a mask was periodically placed over her mouth and nose, emitting the unmistakably noxious fumes of ether, which she remembered from when she'd had her tonsils taken out at the age of five. She tried to pull the numbing gas into her lungs, gulping as much as she could, but each time the mask would be removed before she could inhale enough to ease the tearing, scraping pain that was impossible to get away from. She could take in only enough to make her head spin, only enough to disconnect her from her arms and legs, leaving her unable to move. And always she felt the pain, a dangerous deep invasion.

Then something else. She felt something else and tried to focus, to turn her mind to that "something else." What was it? The ether was being administered by the man she had followed from the waiting room and as he stood at her side, hoarding the anesthetic with one hand, with his other he had shoved aside her gown, exposing her right breast, and he was now in the process of rubbing and fumbling with it.

The realization blew a whistle in my dizzy head and the taskmaster in me woke up. *Move, Sally, move!* the voice in my head said over and over. *Move your arm. You can do it! Think, move your right arm. Move it!* Gathering as much force as I could, I batted his hand off, then turned my face away from the ether. I was done with that. I didn't want any more. There was obviously a price to pay for relief and I would not pay it.

When all the nameless equipment was finally removed, I tried to curl into a ball, wrapping my arms around myself as best I could, but the two men wanted me to get down, aggressively helping me from the table. With tiny steps I walked back to sit on the flimsy cot, then vomited in a pan on the floor, and as I slowly started to dress, one of the men pulled the curtain aside, telling me to leave. I couldn't stay any longer. I must go, now. So I did.

I didn't lay my head down on my mother as the day faded into night. I don't know why. She was sitting right next to me in the car, but I didn't. I sat up straight, leaning my head on the clean, automatically powered window. If I slept, it didn't give comfort, and where there had been Patti's mindless gay chatter on the drive down, there was a heavy silence the whole way back.

I couldn't possibly see the lifelong path that was opening up before me that summer and early fall of 1964, just as I couldn't see the 405 freeway during the long trip home on that day in September. I don't remember saying goodbye or thanking anyone when I pulled myself from the air-conditioned back seat, stepping dazed onto the summer-thrashed Bermuda grass. I most certainly should have said something, because at that time, Dr. Duke had been risking his profession for me. Maybe my mother made up for my neglect when she climbed out behind me, though I have no memory of her walking into the house at all. I guess she must have, probably looking for the comfort only vodka seemed to give her.

When I finally looked toward the door, longing to be inside and away from the day, there was Steve, sitting on the front step, waiting. My heart split open as he stood and wordlessly enfolded me. Had I told him? I don't know. But I didn't expect he would be there and I instantly hid my face in his chest, feeling safe as he led me into the house, opened the door to my room, and carefully put me to bed. When I cried, it was not my mother who held me. It was Steve. I felt I was changed, forever tainted, and I grieved deeply for the loss of something I couldn't name.

*   *   *

Six weeks later, in early November, three days before my eighteenth birthday, I began my career. Wearing a dreadful pink swimsuit, I stood on a cold Malibu beach, looked directly into the camera, and said my first line of dialogue. "You see before you, me. Gidget."

PART TWO

Who knows anyway what it is, that wild, silky
part of ourselves without which no poem can live?

—Mary Oliver, *A Poetry Handbook*

I promise there will always be
a little place no one will see
a tiny part deep in my heart
that stays in love with you

—"Where Do You Start," Alan Bergman,
Marilyn Bergman, Johnny Mandel

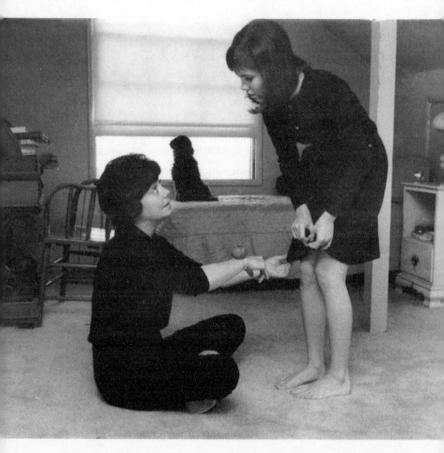

Photo from TV Star Parade *fan magazine of Baa shortening my skirt.*

7

Gidget

A PILOT IS ONLY a pilot. It means next to nothing unless the network decides they want it on their schedule for the following season, and since countless pilots are made every year, resulting in very few "pickups," it's probably not a good idea to count on it. But until the network makes their decision, you can't walk away and forget about it either. This was my first big lesson as a professional actor: "Learn to labor and to wait," in the words of Longfellow. And so, with one foot in my childhood and one unsteady foot on a path under construction, I waited . . . off-balance.

Actually, there was nothing sturdy to stand on, anywhere. Jocko's career was going downhill fast, with the deadweight of his marriage to my mother not far behind, and by early 1965 he was hardly working at all. Plus, it seemed that my mother had gradually stopped, never even occasionally going out on an audition—or interview, as they were called back then. Years later when I asked her why, she told me she'd given it up to be with her children, and maybe that was true, but it made no sense. We weren't little kids anymore—Ricky wasn't even living with us—and at that point we needed all the money we could get. When we were forced to sell our home in Tarzana, this time moving into a rented house on the cusp of Encino, I know Baa felt silently disgraced. But whatever feelings of loss or fear might have been running through her, they never showed. She energetically, and almost single-handedly, loaded everything we owned into boxes we'd gathered from the market, then unloaded it all into a lightless, musty-smelling place that always felt like it belonged to someone else—probably because it did. And though he never said anything either, I know that this house, with its empty, pool-less backyard, was another demotion for Jocko. But since my bedroom was separate from the rest of the house—an awkward add-on above the garage with lots of windows and a lock on the door—it was all fine with me.

Ricky was in his third year at Berkeley, Steve in his second at USC, and I was waiting by the phone. But happily, my one and only boyfriend was back in my life, and at night, I was the recipient of shadow classes in history, literature, and philosophy, hearing about the books Steve was reading, listening to him passionately pore over passages or to his long explanations of Kierkegaard and Nietzsche, as close to a formal education as I would ever get (something I long for to this day). Steve's appetite for learning was endless but he could never find a place to actually put all that education, except in my lap.

Not knowing what else to do, I bought a stack of spiral notebooks, sharpened a handful of pencils, and with the best of half-hearted intentions, signed up for a few classes at San Fernando Valley State College—which at the time didn't even have a theater arts department. And who knows what I might have discovered there had it not been for that one morning in early May when the phone rang just as I was leaving for classes. The voice on the other end of the line said, "Pack your bags, Sally, ABC picked up the show and they want you in New York by the end of the week." All at once, I took both feet out of my childhood and stepped onto that new path.

Five days later, I was sitting in the first-class section of a TWA Boeing 707 heading for New York City, the Plaza hotel, and the ABC Upfronts. I'd never been on an airplane before, never traveled outside of California (not really), and it was such a major moment in my life that I remember exactly what I was wearing: a little white hat with blue cloth forget-me-nots pinned to one side and a new baby-blue suit, purchased with the money I'd saved from the pilot. It had large white buttons down the front of the cropped jacket, worn over a matching, slightly A-line skirt, a skirt that Baa had shortened the night before. She was now buckled up in the aisle seat beside me, and as the plane began to lift off, away from the life I had always known, I took my mother's hand. Radiating with the same excitement that I was feeling, she said, "Here we go, Sal," and I knew she meant more than just the trip to New York.

No one bothered to tell me what the Upfronts were and I didn't ask. I didn't know I'd have one day of rehearsal before finding myself onstage at Radio City Music Hall in front of hundreds of station owners from across the country, all affiliated with the network—the affiliates. Advertising representatives from companies like Procter & Gamble, Westinghouse, and the Ford Motor Company were also sprinkled through the crowd, giving them the opportunity to purchase airtime on the season's new shows up front—thus the name. I went from a suspended daze to performing skits with Barbara Parkins from *Peyton Place*, David Janssen of *The Fugitive,* and the cast of *The Big Valley,* including the brilliant Barbara Stanwyck— whom I must have met, though that part hasn't stayed in my head. I'm sure I was respectful but vague. Ms. Stanwyck was an actress I greatly admired, and despite the fact that I'd grown up in a show business family, I'd met very few actors in my life and never anyone I admired—except Beulah Bondi, whom I was thrilled to find sitting alone in the living room

Onstage with lovely Barbara Parkins.

of the Libbit house one day when I was about eleven, though what she was doing there, I still don't know. But now I was eighteen, in New York City, the star of a new television series, and about to walk onto the enormous stage at Radio City Music Hall. Awe was something I couldn't allow myself to feel, not in the slightest. My carefully learned survival system was securely in place so I wasn't fragile or unsure, wasn't quaking in my boots—which would have been completely understandable. I saw what I needed to see, did what I needed to do, and blocked from my brain anything that felt overwhelming, which unfortunately included Barbara Stanwyck.

Approximately eight weeks and a handful of surfing lessons later, production began and I walked through the looking glass. On one side was my life, my real life as it existed, and on the other side was a greatly altered world. And my God, how I loved the girl on that side of the glass, loved her ease around people, her trust in them. She was pure and untarnished. My twin sister, who looked very much like me, was a part of me, and yet was not me. For thirty-two episodes—and many more weeks than that—her house, her friends, her family, and her perfect pink-and-yellow bedroom were mine.

What Gidget did during the day, I did during the day; her life was my life and the pages of that life would come to me in advance so I could read where my life was going. I knew next week I would have a crush on a handsome schoolteacher, or be thrust into auto shop at school, showing a group of adorable boys that I was as good as they were, while being appealingly inept. Or I'd be caught in a misunderstanding with my family—her family, not mine.

The truth is, Gidget's "other side of the glass" world was a one-dimensional illusion with laugh tracks, dealing only superficially with the life of a teenage girl and her widowed father—a world where his wife, Gidget's mother, remained curiously unmentioned. But it didn't matter to me. It was like feeding a three-course meal to a starving person, and the main course of that meal was Frances (aka Gidget) Lawrence's father, Russell. A father who was safe and caring, a father whom she felt so completely comfortable being near she could actually ignore, whereas he never ignored her—very different from either of the fathers on my side of the glass. Whenever I stepped through, there he was: Gidget's father, played by Don Porter.

From the first moment we met, Don put his protective arm around me, while at the same time always treating me with respect as if I were a weathered professional, which he was and I wasn't. He never seemed upset that I, a rank new-comer, had most of the page count in every episode, and if he had a problem with the lack of interesting story lines for his character, I never felt his dissatisfaction. He just quietly watched out for me. And in return, I never tuned out, never had a foggy moment. Well, not many. Occasionally we'd have a table read for the next episode to be shot, which meant that all the actors—plus the writers, producers, and director—would sit around a long table and read out loud that "hot off the presses" screenplay. It was the only time the fog rolled in, making my mind a total blank. I'd look at words I used every day, simple words, and not be able to remember what they were. How Don did it, I don't know—maybe I was easier to read than the script—but he always made sure we sat together so that he could whisper the word to me before I fumbled or stumbled or mispronounced it so badly that everyone roared with laughter. The laughs that came out of the show were great, Gidget's laughs, but this laughter felt as though it came from the other side of the looking glass, aimed directly at little Doodle. Don was my safety net, a constant and quiet friend. And in this new territory I could barely react. I never thanked him, not really. I wish I had.

Most of the day I was so joyously buoyant that I couldn't sit down, and whether she was rummaging through the kitchen or running up the stairs or pacing around while talking on her pink princess phone, Gidget never sat still either. Occasionally she'd flop down on her bed, sticking her feet in the air, but other than that, she and I were constantly on the move. As I look back on it now, I see my eighteen-year-old self soaking in the information that everyone had to give: the other actors, the director, and the ubiquitous crew, who for me have always been an important part of acting in front of a camera—something I was just learning at the time. I was enveloped in the feeling of not being alone, of being surrounded by people all working toward the same goal, which really was as simple as getting through the day's work with enough skill to be asked back the following day. We were all on the same team.

From the barely dawn morning, when I'd drive onto the Columbia lot, until long after the sun had set, I lived in Gidget's world. Then I'd climb back into my newly purchased yellow MGB, carefully work the frighteningly unfamiliar stick shift, and drive back through the looking glass into Sally's world—where my feet hurt so bad I thought of putting them in a pan of hot water and Epsom salts, the way Aunt Gladys always did.

Unlike Gidget's bright, cheery home with a welcoming father, I lived in a dank, unfamiliar house with a family who didn't look like themselves anymore. My sister towered over me, giving the impression of a soon-to-be-gorgeous sixteen-year-old, rather than the bewildered twelve-year-old she really was. Jocko seemed less physically changed, other than his hair thinning on top and graying on the sides, although if he was not off doing a personal appearance at a fair or rodeo or God knows what, then he moved through the house like he weighed four hundred pounds, as opposed to his lithe two-hundred-something. But when I flip through the photos of that time, it's the changes in my mother that are hard to look at, that hurt to see, even now. The combination of vodka and swallowed emotions had thickened her body and bloated her delicate face, making her look like a biscuit rising in the hot oven. I always wondered if unconsciously she didn't want to be beautiful anymore and had just closed up shop.

When I was thirteen I read T. S. Eliot's "The Hollow Men" while lying on the floor next to the bookshelves in the Libbit house and one line, "rats' feet over broken glass" has gone round and round in my head ever since. That was the feeling hovering throughout this house, as if there were something horrific hidden in the basement, perhaps a dead body; except we had no basement. And it was to this "rats' feet over broken glass" house—long before the show went on the air—that fan magazine photographers started showing up on prearranged Saturdays with assignment editors in tow. Screen Gems needed publicity for the unknown actor starring in their new ABC series, and whether for *Screenland* or *Photoplay* or *Teen Talk*, the task was to create a cute two- or three-page story, loosely based on the interview I was required to do during the week. Still wearing the wardrobe, I'd drive from the studio to Scandia or the Brown Derby for lunch and in Gidget's lime-green pedal pushers I'd proceed to have an overly animated conversation with the weary, uninterested writer who'd been given the assignment. But no matter how I had answered their questions, always careful to paint an appropriate home life, what was ultimately printed barely resembled anything I'd said, resulting in stories entitled "Gidget at the Crossroads," or "The Night Sally Field Proved She Was a Woman," or "Do It If You Must but He'll Hate You in the Morning."

As I look at the faded, brownish pictures of my family scattered through these magazines it makes me almost physically ill. We're all walking toward the camera with our arms around each other and Jocko is in the middle, smiling like he doesn't have a care

A happy family, fan magazine style.

in the world, or we're leaning on a fence and he's looking down at me while I hold his hand as though it were my idea. In all of them my sweet sister floats around the edges, just wanting to be included, and if Baa is in the picture, then she looks uninvolved and blank-eyed. In one awkward shot, Jocko is lying on the floor with his knees bent, but instead of demanding that I stand in his hands so he can lift me over his head, he wants me to stand on his knees, though for what reason, I don't know. Princess, trying to be helpful, is standing next to me, bracing my unsteady attempt, and we're all laughing—or what looks like laughing. They're the same kind of stiffly posed photos that were taken of our "happy little group" when I was six, except Ricky's not present and—as hard as he may try—Jocko's not the focus anymore. I am.

Then early Monday morning, off to the other side of the looking glass I'd go.

If you were an actor working on the Columbia lot in 1965, whether in a feature film or on a new or returning television series, you went upstairs to the makeup and hair department located on the second floor of a three-story building directly across from most of the soundstages. Instead of every show having its own separate expandable makeup trailer—like it is today—at that time, all the actors with morning calls, from all the different shows, went "through the works" together. Every morning as the sun was inching out of night, I entered the department, where it was brightly lit, buzzing with activity, and smelling like bacon and eggs from the local coffee shop. Scurrying around were eager young people with the lowly title of second second assistant director who patiently took the orders, then delivered the food.

Since Gidget needed very little time in the chair, other actors were always there before me. Barbara Eden—who was working on *I Dream of Jeannie*—seemed to live there, because every time I stepped in, there she was, in exactly the same chair, singing most of the time, and I never saw her anywhere else. Wonderful Elizabeth Montgomery from *Bewitched* was usually there, sitting quietly in the corner, not singing. But then Elizabeth didn't need to do anything, not sing or even talk. To me, she was perfect without doing one single thing and remained that way. (Later the cast of *The Partridge Family* and *The Monkees* would be moving in and out of the big barbershop-type chairs, but I was on a different show by then and don't want to get ahead of myself.) Everyone would eventually depart to their separate soundstages, which were lined up in a row opposite the building. Only *Gidget*'s set was located away from the others on one of the two stages across from the drive-on gate, next to the parking lot. And that's where we spent most of the day, Gidget and I. Except for the day or two each week when we'd shoot on location.

The majority of the days off the lot were spent working at the Columbia Ranch, a huge parcel of land sitting in the heart of Burbank and filled with various faux neighborhoods and city streets. It also had a dreadful fake beach called the Berm, consisting of a man-made lake filled with dark, stagnant water and surrounded by tons of coarse brown sand—not like the sand on a real Malibu beach, more like the stuff they use to make cement. As we'd sit in the dirt with the cameras rolling, acting as though it were another happy day at the beach, it felt slightly ridiculous to be looking out at the flat, lifeless sludge and yelling "Surf's up," then grabbing our boards and running off camera where everyone would pile up out of view of the lens, desperately trying to keep from stepping into the water, which seriously did not smell right.

The reverse shots, the ones revealing where we were running—toward the ocean—were filmed during the few days when we actually went to one of the beaches in Santa Monica or Malibu where I'd spent so much of my life. On those days—as few as they might have been—I'd vibrate with the same excitement I felt when I was a kid, knowing we were going to spend the day frolicking in the ocean. But the ocean I'd always known in the Augusts of my childhood was very different from the one I met that November day when we first filmed on the beach. It was freezing, both the water and the air. Everyone was wearing gloves, ski hats, and heavy down jackets. Everyone except for me, that is, and of course the handful of surfers—real surfers—who clustered around totally unfazed by the weather, the cold water, or the waves. While I clung to the large terry-cloth robe that had been placed over my shoulders, most of the true surfers were so eager to jump in the water that they'd barely registered theirs, abandoning them immediately. White terry-cloth piles ended up scattered around the sand.

I can't say the swell was especially big—three to five feet— but to me the waves looked huge. Adding insult to injury, this was not a "point break" like the easy rolling waves of Mondos Beach above Oxnard, where I'd been taken many times by Darryl, the surfing coach. This was a "beach break," and Zuma, for God's sake. Notoriously difficult to ride. While I stood there shivering, hoping they'd decide to shoot something else, the assistant director held up his bullhorn and screeched, "EVERYONE IN THE WATER." And since all the other surfers were either paddling out or standing knee-deep already, he basically meant me. Let's be honest: Even though I'd become a strong, confident swimmer and was one hell of a boogie boarder, surfing was never going to be my sport, with or without Darryl's instructions. I didn't even have a car before I began to work, and the huge board, which weighed more than I did, was the same size as my new MGB, so how would I have gotten the thing to the beach?

Just in case someone on earth had missed his last message, the assistant director blasted another "IN THE WATER!" So off went the robe and into the icy water went the girl. Since it was supposed to look like a sunny summer day, no one wore wet suits of any kind, and the water was so cold the lower half of my body instantly went numb. There I was in the water, sitting on a board the size of the *PT-109*, trying to power a stiff blue body that barely knew how to maneuver this craft under the best of circumstances. I mean, really, what the hell were they thinking? Were they just testing to see if I was serious about this whole acting thing? Then again, was this acting or a study in humiliation? Or is acting always walking on the edge, always flirting with the possibility of falling flat on your face, or of wiping out and losing the top of your bathing suit? I know that the latter option was going through my mind when I heard the faint but unmistakable bullhorn voice shriek, "TAKE THE NEXT WAVE!" and before I could even look to see if there was indeed a wave to take, I heard the heart-stopping word: "ROLLING!"

Even now, as I remember this moment in the cold Pacific so long ago, it's not the sound of the waves I hear, or the screeching bullhorn; it's the sound of Jocko's mocking laugh when I'd fail to dive into the water or flip over the pole as he demanded. I hear his repeated shouts, "Do it! Arms straight, toes pointed. Don't think! GO!" And I'd stand there, with my toes gripping the pine platform, frozen, feeling worthless and afraid. Though frozen for sure, I was no longer on that high dive, my toes gripping nothing but the edge of yesterday.

Without hesitation, I put my forehead on the board and began paddling furiously, pumping my legs up and down at the same time, trying to inch my big board forward, now aware of the wave forming behind me. Just when I thought I'd failed, had missed the wave and the shot would continue on without me, Mickey Dora, the champion surfer who was by my side, pushed my gigantic board in front of the wave, exactly where I needed to be. When I tentatively started to stand, Mickey grabbed my hand as he expertly maneuvered his board beside me. Small though it might have been, we rode the entire wave until finally we slid gently to the shore and the flabbergasted crew began to cheer. I don't know how many more waves I caught, or Mickey tossed me into—it didn't matter. I'd found something new. I was terrified, yes, but instead of letting some other part of myself perform the task while the rest of me floated away, I had held the reins and fearlessly, without thinking, told myself to just *go*.

Right before *Gidget* went on the air in September of 1965, when Steve still thought it was all a fluke and Rick was too busy to even notice, I was sent on a promotional tour, which meant flying to seven different cities in six days, working one day in each city and flying to another every evening, where

I'd then spend the night. For a week, I visited local television and radio stations, going on air live, giving interviews to the regional newspapers, then spending the rest of the time doing whatever ridiculous thing the publicity people could dig up before I'd dash to the airport and head to the next city.

Baa went with me. Except for that one quick trip to New York, I had never spent days and days with my mother... alone. And I remember how we laughed. Everything we came across during the day, she'd cram into the big purse she carried on her arm: half-eaten sandwiches wrapped in a cloth napkin swiped from the restaurant, fruit out of the complimentary basket, dinner rolls and pats of butter wrapped in gold foil, plus every tiny bottle of vodka the airline stewardess offered. "You wait and see. We're going to need this," she'd say. I'd roll my eyes at her, halfway worried that if anyone saw, they'd think we were poor white trash, San Fernando Valley style. But when we'd get into Tulsa, Oklahoma, or St. Louis, Missouri, late at night, long after room service had closed, we'd sit on our twin beds as she dumped out that day's stashed goods. We dined on bread and butter, bananas and booze. Actually, I had a Coke from the vending machine—wishing to God they had ginger ale.

Whenever I was near my mother I felt giddy, thrilled to be in her presence, a jolt of electricity shooting through me when her eyes met mine. And now, as we sat cross-legged on our beds, laughing at nothing and everything, the Christmas-morning excitement of my life was magnified because Baa was somehow a part of it. So much of what was happening belonged to her. All the many times she had patiently watched me in whatever living room, in whatever house, always glowing like honey in a glass jar as she sat laughing at my pantomimes, listening to the monologues, handing me something she loved and slowly backing away, as though she'd carried the load as far as she could and it was up to me to complete the journey. Even in the seventh grade I felt it, something unspoken, an intangible bargain between us. And after a performance I'd look for her, wanting to meet her eyes first, to see her see me, waiting for her nod, her recognition of my end of the bargain. But what was in this bargain? Where was the deal memo? And as we sat in this hotel room, late at night, I felt the first inkling of something different. Was it because I was now helping to support everyone with my whopping $500 a week, or because I had suddenly become the gift giver at Christmas, that the family cast was starting to shift, to change roles? I'm sure that was part of it, but only part. At the time I felt a tiny pull, a part of me that wanted to turn, to deny her my eyes, a feeling that grew over time like a minute splinter slowly festering. And I never knew where the wound was located.

After many months of safely exploring the dimensions of my newly constructed acting envelope, I was given a scene to play that stepped—if only a toenail—outside of the mild emotional landscape of situation comedy. In the scene, Gidget's father has refused to speak to her, marching angrily off to his room, which sends our girl into a complete tizzy. Hoping to be forgiven for something that only midsixties television could define as a problem, she goes to his room to confront the situation and her father.

When we were ready to film the scene, I stood behind the flats of the set, waiting to hear someone say "Action." And as

I looked down at my hand gripping the knob, preparing to enter the bedroom of Gidget's father, one part of my brain was rehearsing the lines, "Please, Daddy, please..." while another part of my brain went somewhere else. When action was called, I opened the door, stepped into the room, then looked at my father—her father—and began to cry with such force I couldn't speak, except in hiccupping spurts, while a constant ribbon of snot rolled out of my nose. I moved across the set to sit on the bed—next to Don—just as the scene had been blocked out, saying everything, doing everything we had rehearsed, but suddenly I was trying to control a borderline case of hysteria. Don, looking deeply concerned, began running his hands up and down my arms as though he wasn't sure if he wanted to continue the scene or stop to comfort me. He continued the scene and I was grateful—still am. Someone in the dark finally whispered "Cut" as though not wanting to wake the baby, and after a long beat the crew began to applaud, while Don held me tight in his arms, rhythmically patting my back, saying without words that he was proud of me. I didn't know where the emotion had come from, much less how I got to it.

Unfortunately, that first take was in a wide "master" shot, like looking at the scene with the binoculars backward. When we moved tighter, into over-shoulders and finally into close-ups—when the camera can practically see inside your brain—I was unable to find any real emotion at all. I was dry, as they say. But the moment stayed with me. I didn't know what I had learned, didn't know if it had been about the scene or about Don, or if it belonged somewhere in Sally. I didn't realize it then that that's what acting really is. Any and all of that, mixed together.

*   *   *

Toward the end of production and after the show had been on the air for about five months, I was asked to fly to San Francisco one Saturday to do a haphazard personal appearance. Whenever the studio or the network wanted me to appear somewhere, it was always Bill Sackheim (the "showrunner," or producer of the series) who did the asking. When I was first hired—the fresh-off-the-turnip-truck newcomer—Bill looked me in the face and sternly said, "You know, Sally, you can't change your mind." I couldn't imagine what on earth he meant, though it did give me a jolt. Bill always seemed friendly and was endlessly avuncular, but everything coming from him felt very little like a request and very much like a demand.

Gidget even made an appearance at one of Ricky's gymnastics meets in Berkeley. That trip I loved.

Because I was so new, I never thought to ask how giving up my precious weekend, my few days of sleeping past sunup, to host a fashion show in San Francisco for an auditorium filled with high school girls would actually benefit the show. I wish I had.

Nevertheless, a few days later, there I was, standing onstage describing outfits very similar to the clothes Gidget wore on the show. Since I wasn't good at cold readings, I didn't use the script I'd been handed right before stepping on the stage. Instead, I tried to point out what each young model was wearing as she walked out, just as I saw it—which needed no explanation at all. In between, I filled in with snippets from my day on the set, told the audience about the cute boys hired as extras, confided in them about watching all the kids leave together as I stayed to work through the rest of the day. Which in reality, I never noticed...I don't think. I shared with everyone the amazing loop-de-loop ride I was on, felt comfortable talking to these young women, something I had rarely felt when talking to the girls I'd gone to school with. And the young women in the audience seemed to accept me, like it was a whole room made up of my friend Lynn, whom I was losing sight of as we traveled in different directions. After the fashion show had ended, I lingered onstage, answering questions, genuinely wanting to talk to everyone.

Slowly they started to move out of the audience, climbing onto the stage with me, chatting at first, then asking me to sign things. They'd hand me scraps of paper or programs, and since I hadn't signed many autographs, I didn't know what to write to each of them. When they ran out of paper, they wanted me to sign their clothes or even their arms. As more and more came onto the stage, I felt their friendliness turning into a hunger for something I didn't have, and as their urgency began to overwhelm me, I tried to push away from them. But instead of moving back they crowded around me, frantically pulling at my clothes and hair, like they were playing a game of "Red Rover," only now the arms were locking me in, not out. As I bent down, covering my face with my hands, I suddenly felt a huge presence pick me up, effortlessly hoisting me over his head and holding me high in the air. "I gotcha, Gidg," beamed the big man as we waded through the crowd, which now looked more like a flock of evil birds than a group of high school girls. I've always thought that perhaps this guardian angel was the school janitor because he wore a uniform, but I'll never know for sure. After he set me down in a utility closet and flipped on the light, he left.

For a moment, I stood at the door, listening to the commotion outside, then turned a small wastepaper basket upside down and sat, my hands still shaking, feeling deeply alone but oddly thrilled. Never again would I walk down the street or push my cart through the produce aisle without being aware of people when they recognize me—and when they don't recognize me. Either way, I was no longer a member of the club anymore. The Human Club. I was a celebrity.

8

Get Thee to a Nunnery

WHEN I WALKED onto the set—a classroom containing ten or twelve children of varying ages—everyone stopped dead in their tracks and stared at me. Gidget's happy-go-lucky clothes were gone, and in their place I wore several layers of ankle-length ecru wool, starting with a long-sleeved dress. Over the dress, with its Peter Pan collar, was placed an apron-like panel called a scapular, the front section loosely belted at the waist, leaving the back to flap in the breeze—layer number two. After my long hair had been bound to my head with countless bobby pins, a nylon sock—which looked as though it had once been attached to a pair of panty hose—was pulled down over the top and anchored in place with long straight hairpins. Covering the whole wad was one of my two hat choices, and since this was an interior scene, I wore the smaller, scarf-like head covering with its shoulder-length veil attached to the back.

The camera had already been set up and the assistant director was in the process of placing the children into positions. There was a rote feeling to it all, probably because the scene had already been filmed the week before and they were planning to do it exactly the same. Only one thing would be different: This time I was playing the lead. The director—whom I'd worked with on several *Gidget* episodes and adored—put his arm around my shoulder with an easy smile and started to explain the shot. Before he could finish, however, the cameraman—whom I had not worked with before—butted in to introduce himself and at the same time began inspecting my appearance. Moving close, then pulling back, he flatly stated that I needed to cut my eyelashes. They were too long.

Mind you, these were not fake, glued-on eyelashes, but the things that grew out of my lids, for God's sake, the same as my mother's and grandmother's. Trying to make light, I laughingly begged him to please let me keep them, saying that I was proud of them and it would be weird to *cut them off*! Joining the discussion at that point was the Catholic technical advisor, who took her job very seriously. Luckily, she didn't remain for many episodes, at least not on the set. After giving my face an impersonal examination—everyone leaning in like they were looking at a painting on the wall—they walked to the edge of the set, then huddled together to discuss the serious situation while the crew waited, watching the unfolding drama. When a few uncomfortable moments had passed, it was announced: My eyelashes could stay. Praise be to God. Everyone quickly moved into their positions as the assistant director yelled an unnecessary "Quiet on the set." Swack, as the director was called, suggested we run it once—then roll film. I was fine with that, and that's what we did.

Even with my eyelashes in place, I felt defeated before I said my first line.

*　　*　　*

When *Gidget* was canceled after that one blur of a season, I felt only one quick painful stab and then it was gone. I'd never read the reviews, wouldn't have known where to find the Nielsen ratings even if I'd wanted to know what they were, which I didn't. I was only slightly aware that the show had been a product at all, bought and sold by an industry that needed to see an immediate profit (or the likelihood of one soon), something they didn't see from *Gidget*. Maybe the fact that I had lived in a fogbank so long was keeping me from projecting ahead, forcing me to live one day at a time with very few expectations. I don't know. But when I walked away from the girl I loved so much, I didn't feel crushed. Gidget was still with me, *was* me. And living with her so relentlessly that year had given me things I hadn't owned before: a tiny sliver of her confidence, her willingness to be optimistic, and her daring ability to look toward the future.

I hadn't had an agent when I was initially cast as Gidget, so Jocko introduced me to Herb Tobias, who seemed like a nice man, though befuddled by the fact that I'd landed the starring role in a television series without any representation at all. And although Mr. Tobias visited the set during that first year of my career, maybe even asked me to lunch—something I have only a vague memory of—I always felt that he thought of me as an energetic flash in the pan. However, when I was asked to meet on two projects immediately after *Gidget*'s demise, and when those meetings resulted in two very different offers, Herb started calling with regularity, if only to say hi.

The first offer was for the lead in a play being produced at the Valley Music Theater—a short-lived but well-intentioned theater in the round, located in Tarzana...or was it Woodland Hills? Clearly not Broadway, where the play had first been produced in 1961, and later adapted into a film starring James Stewart and Sandra Dee. *Take Her, She's Mine* is the story of a feisty teenage girl and her anxious, loving father, very *Gidget*-like territory. But this would be a stage production, like going back to the familiar drama department, and the father was to be played by the great Walter Pidgeon. I was thrilled. The other project was a movie entitled *The Way West,* starring Richard Widmark, Kirk Douglas, and Robert Mitchum, to be shot in Oregon all that summer, now 1966. I was to play a feisty teenage girl with an anxious loving father, which sounds painfully familiar, but this time everyone is stuck on a wagon train heading west and when this daughter finds herself pregnant by a creepy older guy, she jumps off the back of her covered wagon, rolling head over teakettle down the hill. This prompts the sweet redheaded boy—who has always loved her—to leap to her rescue, somehow running down the hill faster than she can bounce. Miraculously, he catches her, then marries her, even though he knows she is damaged goods. I chose to do that one.

I'd never been away from home for more than a week, and then it had been to happily stay at Joy's house in Pasadena. Now I was to spend three months in the dusty Oregon wilderness, not knowing how to occupy myself, stupefied with loneliness if Steve wasn't beside me. And since he remained in Los Angeles, I was alone. Most of the cast was made up of wonderful character actors, like Jack Elam, Stubby Kaye, Harry Carey Jr., and Peggy Stewart, all people who knew Jocko and my mother,

On location in Oregon with Bob Mitchum.

some having worked with one or both. But joining this cluster of actors as they sat around on their canvas chairs between
shots, chairs that seemed to magically appear out of nowhere
no matter how remote our location, would have felt awkward,
like I was sitting in on one of Baa's fondue gatherings. So I'd
smile when they made room for me, sit for a moment, then
slowly back away unnoticed, preferring to find a place sitting
in the dirt, without their company or a canvas chair.

Once, Robert Mitchum, who rarely sat with the group
either, made a sandwich for me, which unfortunately was
smothered in yellow mustard—the one food that made me

want to retch. He handed it to me grinning from ear to ear, then plopped down, making a dusty spot for himself next to mine—me in my gunnysack dress, Bob wearing nothing but his buckskin pants. I ate every smackerel of it while he joyfully watched, and actually, since we were holding up production—something he liked to do—the whole company watched me eat the revolting thing. But I didn't care. I would have eaten a whole jar of mustard, one spoonful at a time, because I was crazy about Bob Mitchum, even though I could barely understand a word he said—and he talked to me a lot. I'd listen intently, catching a word or two, sometimes enough to get the gist of what he was saying. If not, I'd smile and nod with a little chuckle, not having a clue how to respond. He once told me I was the real thing, reassuring me softly that I was one of the gang, his gang, and that like him, I'd be around a long time. I would have been overwhelmed to hear Robert Mitchum say that to me, but I wasn't sure he'd actually said that and I couldn't make myself say, "I beg your pardon," or even "What?" I only know that some twenty years later, somewhere in the eighties, I was being presented with a People's Choice Award and found myself seated at Mr. Mitchum's table. Without hesitation, he stood, took my hand with both of his, and said in his Bob Mitchum gravel, "I told you so." Or at least, I think that's what he said.

Then there was the day that Kirk Douglas read *The Little Prince* to me as we walked the twenty-minute journey back to base camp after wrap. I always suspected he did that only because Mitchum had made me that sandwich a few days before. I mean, honestly, who carries a hardback copy of *The*

Little Prince with them out into the Oregon plains? I wasn't quite sure how to respond to that either, though I remember to this day the passage he read and how much it affected me. It was about the Little Prince tending his rose and after he had planted it, watered and fed it, he found himself caring for it deeply. He had helped it grow and therefore to him it was "unique in all the world." How that fit into my life, I can't tell you.

Michael McGreevey, who played Brownie to my Mercy, was fun and easy to be with, and the only one who appeared to be close to my age—though we acted more like bratty ten-year-old boys than two people in their late teens, which is what we actually were. I had never been a mischief maker, never thought it would be fun, didn't even have a clear idea of what "fun" was. But at that moment, dropping water balloons out of my hotel window onto the unsuspecting folks below, then ducking down to avoid being caught, seemed a perfect way to spend the afternoon.

All of that is well and good, but what makes this movie important had nothing to do with water balloons or mustard sandwiches. I don't need to look at the photos or even, God forbid, the film. All I need to do is close my eyes and instantly I can smell the dusty heat with a hint of sage, hear the clunking sound of the wooden wagon as it rolled next to me. I'm dressed in a potato sack with sleeves; there's a rope tied around my middle and a pair of huge clodhoppers, without laces, on my feet. When you put that all together and add the thick bushy fall, or half wig, anchored to the crown of my head, I look like a bagged squirrel with big feet, walking in the midst of the Armada.

You need to know that the Armada, which was spread across a wide prairie-like field outside of Eugene, consisted of eight to ten covered wagons being pulled either by four horses, called a four-up, or by six horses, a six-up. The only exceptions were the two enormous oxen pulling the wagon that I now walked beside—the one belonging to my movie family—and on most days, I found myself sitting in this wagon, staring at their dung-covered hindquarters—not my family's but the oxen's. Some of the other actors were walking beside the wagons, as were most of the fifty or so extras—young and old— while several dogs ran around barking at the few scrawny cows being led by an extra or tied behind a wagon. A handful of stunt guys on horses were weaving in and out, looking for disruptive animals or panicked participants. The whole Armada was about half a mile long, give or take a mule or two.

It was one of my big scenes in the film—and I had a few— but this one worried me. In the front room of my memory, I can see the two of us, Brownie and Mercy, walking along, my focus locked onto the big brown stick about a hundred yards away, visible only by the red dot painted on its edge. This is my mark. The camera, mounted on a big arm connected to the crane, is slowly moving down from high above, overlooking the progress of the settlers, and when it reaches its proper position—about fifteen to twenty feet in front of my big stick—it will stop. At the moment the camera stops, I will hopefully reach the red smudge, step into the medium two-shot, and start crying. If, perchance, when I land on said stick, I am unable to remember my lines or happen to have an aneurysm, then everything in the Armada—whether on wheels or legs—will have to turn around and slowly return to its original position, leaving in its wake an overwhelming trail of manure, not to mention deep grooves in the supposedly virgin land. That's when an army of "greens men"—or whoever can hold a rake—will scurry around in a frenzied attempt to erase all traces of mankind's presence and, at the same time, my agonizing inability to *act*!!!

I'm walking alongside Brownie, sensing the camera's movement, seeing from the edge of my eye the red dot. *There it is, getting closer.* I am almost at the red dot. I clench my hands. I hunch my shoulders. I'd jam a pencil in my eye if I thought it would help me land on that evil red dot and produce any kind of moisture in my eyes. *Think, Sally, think. When was the last time you cried?* Nothing. Crickets in my head. I am so benumbed by loneliness I feel nothing. Nothing! And I'm horrified by the realization—I don't know how to deliver. Some people have menthol blown in their eyes by the makeup artist. I'd do that, sweet Jesus in heaven, if I knew where the makeup person was—which I don't—and the red dot is getting closer. *Why can't I do it?* The script says, "Mercy's eyes well." *Okay, "well" your eyes, Field!* My eyes don't well. *How does anyone "well" their eyes? You either cry or you don't and you, Miss Field, are getting horribly, painfully close to* don't, *and your eyes will remain well-less.*

I hit my mark dead on—that I can do. I stop. The camera stops. Brownie stops. I say my dialogue with my shoulders touching my ears, and a look on my face like I'm about to join the oxen in producing a huge pile for the rakes to quickly hide before we can begin again.

In the middle of the Armada, well-less.

I don't know how many takes there were. Not many. The director seemed happy, or at least we printed something and moved on, but I did not move on. I had hit a wall. It was agonizingly apparent to me; I was not good enough. And that discovery, coupled with the unforgettable pressure of that godforsaken Armada, lit a bonfire in the sweet place I'd created for myself—my acting bubble. I wanted to be better. And more than that, I never ever wanted to feel that helpless drowning panic of not knowing how.

*   *   *

Somewhere in my stomach a feeling starts, like a moth bashing itself over and over against a hot light bulb, and if I get this feeling while reading a script it means: Walk away, this one's not for you. Every time I've ignored this fluttering advice I've struggled, sometimes learning hard lessons, sometimes wishing I could find a lesson to learn. At that point, my experience with reading screenplays was rather limited so it wasn't a feeling I instantly understood, but from the minute I sat down in my newly rented apartment and began reading the pilot script waiting for me when I returned from Oregon, that kamikaze moth revved up and by the time I finished the last page, I knew.

The word *no* was almost impossible for me to say, but somehow, I managed to convey to my agent that the show was not my cup of tea. He was astonished, but kindly said he understood and hung up. He then called again to tell me, less kindly, that he thought I should do it. I could never clearly articulate why I so vehemently did *not* want to do the project, couldn't clearly see that I wanted to be a part of my generation or at least not declare my allegiance to the establishment, especially a religious one. More than that was the bottom-line fact that I didn't want to play a cutesy version of a Catholic nun, wearing nothing but beige with never a thought of sex or a flirt with madness, two things that seemed much more interesting.

Fifteen minutes after I'd talked to my agent, Bill Sackheim called—now the producer on this show as well. He began in a friendly, chatty way, reminiscing about our *Gidget* days together, then asked if he'd heard my response to the offer correctly. When I confirmed that he had indeed heard correctly, he was flabbergasted that I would consider walking away from this series, sounding personally injured, disclosing the confidential fact that the project had been written especially for me. Feeling proudly confident, I stuck to my guns, telling him I was sorry, it just wasn't something I wanted to do. And with resigned understanding he hung up—then called back three more times, the last sounding impatient as he explained that he was only looking out for me and I SHOULD DO IT!

How did this even happen? *Gidget* had been an unmitigated flop, with weak ratings for most of the 1965–66 season. Yes, true. But when the show went into its summer reruns, the kids—who were then out of school—found it and *Gidget* suddenly became a hit (of sorts). At that time, the networks rarely moved a show to a different time slot in search of a bigger audience and never picked it up again after letting it go. So ABC wanted to find another show for Sally Field, and they asked *Gidget*'s executive producer, Harry Ackerman, to help. Mr. Situation Comedy of the fifties, sixties, and seventies, Harry was responsible for *Bewitched*, *I Dream of Jeannie*, *Father Knows Best*, *The Donna Reed Show*, *The Monkees*, *The Partridge Family*, and many others. As luck would have it, he'd recently developed a show adapted from a thin children's book called *The Fifteenth Pelican* and he wanted me to play that fifteenth pelican.

I remember clearly when Mr. Ackerman finally called. My armpits began to sweat but I stood straight, clenched my jaw, thanked him for his offer, apologized profusely, and ultimately stuttered a final no. After that, all went quiet on the Screen Gems front and the phone stopped ringing.

Two weeks later, Jocko appeared at my front door. I hadn't

seen him since I'd packed all my things into boxes and, with Steve's help, had practically thrown them into my Encino apartment before locking the door and leaving for my first movie location. Hadn't been around over that summer to watch my ever-declining family move again, this time into a tiny, shabby house that I can't describe because I never set foot inside. And now, suddenly here he was, my stepfather, waltzing around my sparsely furnished one-bedroom and bath, wearing a forced smile as though he was proud of my new independence, while I stood awkwardly caught off guard.

I remember watching him plop down on the cheap, unpainted bar stool I'd purchased for the kitchen counter, worrying that it would snap as he leaned back and casually suggested I make some coffee so we could talk. Quietly, I scooped and poured and pushed the appropriate buttons, willing my new percolator to hurry, until finally, holding his freshly made cup of Folgers, Jocko began. Harry Ackerman had called him, he told me. Which was a huge surprise because I had only recently told Baa about the offer and as far as I knew, Jocko and Mr. Ackerman had never met. But now he acted as if they were old friends, telling me that Harry wanted his help, wanted him to talk to me before it was too late. Looking at me as if I had four flat tires and he owned the only jack, he said, "I'm here to help you, Sal. Do the show." Or something to that effect.

I was unprepared, had to scramble to find the confidence that wavered whenever my stepfather came near. Feeling my face flush with heat, I told him (with a definite whine) that I didn't like the show. But Jocko started talking over me, saying he thought I was lost, that I was feeling like hot shit because

I'd just had my first movie experience. I could feel my insides frantically searching for the new strength I'd found, wanting desperately to stand firm. Instead I opted for the truth and haltingly confessed that I wanted to do better work, that I wanted to be a better actor. He paused for a moment as if taking in my words, then said solemnly, "They've already started shooting this...with someone else. Do you know that?"

I hadn't known, and for the first time a smack of doubt hit me. Thoughts flew through my head: *Maybe I've given up something that other actors actually want, or maybe I don't know enough to know what's good, or maybe I have too many voices in my head to have any clear opinions at all.* Then Jocko—the man who had told me he knew me better than I knew myself— reminded me that I'd earned very little money doing *Gidget* and even less making the movie, that I didn't know the business like he did, and finally said something that I'll never, *ever* forget. "If you don't do this show, Sally, you may never work again." And with that, one of the water balloons tossed from the Eugene hotel window landed on my head, drenching me with icy-cold fear. I was afraid.

Because of that, for three years I was the Flying Nun.

15¢ Local Programs May 3-9

TV GUIDE

The President's Skillful
Approach To Television
by Ray Scherer
Page 8

Madeleine Sherwood,
Sally Field
of 'The Flying Nun'

9

Wired

THE FLYING NUN was an instant hit. Everywhere I looked someone was telling a nun joke: on talk shows, variety shows, street corners. I couldn't tell if the Flying Nun was the joke or I was, couldn't distinguish between the bell of my past and the chimes of the present. I felt deeply disgraced, as if everyone were laughing at me.

When we first meet her, she is stepping off the boat in San Juan, Puerto Rico, having been transferred from San Francisco to the Convent San Tanco. Born Elsie Ethrington and given the name Sister Bertrille upon entering the convent, she is still a novice, not a full-fledged nun—a petite little slip of a girl who finds that when the trade winds come in contact with her wide-winged cornette, she has the startling ability to become airborne. "When lift plus thrust is greater than load plus drag, anything can fly" was the piece of scientific information that Sister Bertrille would repeat at the drop of a hat, though hopefully not her own. And trust me, her petite body—the load part of the equation—fluctuated radically throughout her stay at the Convent San Tanco.

It was all gibberish. Not inspired comedic nonsense like *I Love Lucy* or *Fawlty Towers*, but meaningless twaddle with nothing real to relate to. Most of the time the little bundle of ecru spent the half hour trying to convince agnostic Carlos—Argentinian actor Alejandro Rey—to change his playboy ways by manipulating him into helping her accomplish some good deed, usually teaming up with either Sister Sixto (Shelley Morrison), Sister Ana (Linda Dangcil), or Sister Jacqueline (the formidable Marge Redmond). And whatever well-meaning mischief the little nun and her cohorts got into, it always ended with a disapproving, though secretly charmed, reaction from the mother superior, played by the imposing, enigmatic Madeleine Sherwood.

The only episode I can remember actually being about something was the one where Sister Bertrille had to deal with Irving, a lovesick pelican, explaining gently that while she was very fond of him, she was not ready to settle down yet. Other than that, every episode was pretty much the same, every day pretty much the same. Including the day or two in each episode that was different, because they were always different in the same way. On those days I would have to fly. That meant I'd be wearing the harness, which was a cross between a corseted one-piece bathing suit and a straitjacket, with one large screw sticking out of each hip. After I got it on and tightly laced to my body, a specially made habit with corresponding holes on either side was placed over the torturous contraption, allowing the screws to poke through where two thin wires were then attached. They were called piano wires, but I doubt that they were the same fine strands of steel used to create music. Not while I was attached, at least.

During the pilot and early in production, I was required to do all the flying. Not only the tight shots—where you could actually see my face—but also the wider ones shot from a distance, when you couldn't tell if it was me or Baby Huey thirty-five feet in the air. On these exterior days, mostly spent at the Columbia Ranch—so close and yet so far from Gidget's neighborhood—I'd be connected to an enormous building crane by my nonmusical wires, then hoisted up over the façade of a large town square containing a brownish-gray convent. Operating this heavy piece of machinery was a bleary-eyed special effects man who usually smelled as though he would have failed a Breathalyzer test. This guy would then proceed to fly me smack into building after building, while the whole time I'd be screaming for him to watch where I was going. Luckily, I'd have time to prepare myself and as I watched the convent speeding toward me—or me toward the convent—I'd raise my legs and extend my arms, then plant myself on the wall—looking like Spider-Man in a nun's habit. Halfway through production a blessed saint of a stuntwoman was hired, and Ralph, or whatever his name was, would then splat her all over the convent wall instead. I guess she was expendable.

I continued to do all of the closer flying shots, which were mostly filmed on Stage 2 at Screen Gems, where our sets were located. Wearing the same dreaded harness, I'd be cranked up ten or twelve feet off the ground in front of a blue or a green screen with two big fans standing just off camera to blow a steady gale in my face—the whole thing aptly called "poor man's" process. I can't say the days on the outside were more fun, but they were less painful for sure. Once the camera was in place, and the wires painted the color of the screen, and the wind blowing at just the right angle, I'd have to dangle there for what seemed like hours, leaning on or over a ladder between shots—usually supplied by a thoughtful grip.

When I was asked to surf for *Gidget*, the studio had provided me with a lesson or two, but no one gave me any pointers on how to perform in the air and no one thought I might benefit from a singing lesson or two... or four hundred. Because not only did Sister Bertrille fly, she also sang, something that didn't come naturally to me—not that flying did. I'd always wanted to sing, and knew every musical by heart, but damn, I could not sing. And, as much as that tormented me, the studio didn't see it as a problem. Every weekend they'd drag me into a recording studio, then place a pair of padded headphones over my ears and tell me to sing. I remember waiting, early one Saturday morning, on a bench outside one of the stages, filled with dread because I was going to have to stand up straight and do something I had no idea how to do. I'd been exactly on time to the Capitol Records Tower just off Hollywood Boulevard, but the stage I'd been assigned to was still occupied, so I sat there. For hours.

Finally, the door flew open and Grace Slick—along with much of Jefferson Airplane—stumbled out after having been ensconced for days, leaving me to fill their marijuana-infused stage with my zippy little tunes. My hair in braids, hands in my pockets, I stood on the worn wooden floor surrounded by abandoned music stands while the producers moved into place behind the glass wall of the booth. Finally, the sound mixer put his hand on the enormous instrument board, I slipped the earphones over my head, then stepped under the huge hanging mic, and we were rolling. Yes, I could clearly hear the prerecorded track through the headset, but for Christ's sake, I had no idea when to begin. Whatever pride I had was swallowed when the composer/producer stood and pointed at me, as though it were my turn to jump out of the airplane. His finger shot my way and without a parachute, off I went, singing the unforgettable lyrics of "Optimize, optimize and you'll cut your troubles down to size..." Matters not that the notes

The Flying Nun sings, or wishes she did.

were flat, that I didn't have a clue how to sharpen the pitch; they all smiled, knowing they would fix it in the booth when I wasn't around. They'd play my voice on top of itself three times, crank up the echo, and presto: humiliation at thirty-three and a third.

In February of 1968, after the show had been on the air for a few months, I was asked to be a presenter at that year's Golden Globes ceremony. I was thrilled to be included with people whom I admired, real actors. But there was one little caveat: They wanted me to fly across the Cocoanut Grove, where the ceremony was being held, and then present the award. The Golden Globes were only interested in me as the Nun, not as Sally Field. I didn't know which edge of that sword to feel. I wanted to be invited to the party but I didn't want to have to be a laughingstock in order to be included. The publicity department, plus Bill Sackheim, repeatedly told me how much they—the studio—wanted me to do it, saying it would be great for the show.

Why was that word, that tiny word, so hard for me to utter? NO. It was a frightening, dangerous word, like the pin in my personal hand grenade, and if I pulled it, I could explode myself, plus everyone around me. And when I'd feel the power of the pin between my fingers, I'd hear the words my mother repeated to me every time I faced a dreaded weekend with my father; they were stitched into my life. "We all have to do things we don't want to do."

I was stuck. I desperately did not want to be the joke of the Golden Globes but I was unable to pull the pin and toss out a big fat no. So I finally said, "Okay, I'll do it...but I won't wear the habit." By God, if I had to fly across the Cocoanut Grove, it would be as Sally Field, not the Flying Nun. Which basically made no sense at all.

With my hair in Shirley Temple ringlets and Steve holding my hand, I went to the ceremony wearing a dress that Baa had made for me at the last minute. Then in the midst of the show, and without any rehearsal, I was connected to the damn wires by a man who assured me that he'd flown Mary Martin in *Peter Pan* billions of times, and without warning, he nonchalantly hoisted me up like a flag on the Fourth of July. And off I went.

Suddenly I was sailing across the historic grove wearing a pink taffeta culottes outfit and heading toward the stage doing what felt like forty-five miles an hour. Directly in front of me, the man onstage widened his stance, bracing for the catch, and at that moment, I realized I was about to make physical contact with John Wayne, one of the most legendary actors who has ever lived. As I got closer to the Duke, I began nodding a polite hello, like we were entering an elevator together. *Holy Mother of God, let this night be over.* After the catch was accomplished with a thud, he held me in midair while I opened the envelope to read that the best newcomer of the year was Dustin Hoffman for *The Graduate*. Big applause. Dustin comes to the stage to give his speech of appreciation, as Mr. Wayne steps awkwardly to the side with an armful of smiling me. The happy winner leaves the stage to return to his seat, at which time Mr. Wayne proceeds to put me on the ground (or what would have been the ground if my feet could have touched it, which they could not). Thinking our work together is done, he turns to leave while I begin to dog-paddle my feet. Foolishly, I then look out at the forest of faces, the entire industry, and quickly grab the back of his tuxedo jacket to hitch a ride, pleading, "Oh, Mr. Wayne, Mr. Wayne." If I'd had a gun I would've shot myself, but with the way things were going, it would've bounced off the harness and hit some innocent bystander.

And waiting for me at our table in the back sat Steve, smiling sweetly through it all, looking like a young Steve McQueen to my insane Baby Jane.

Right after *The Flying Nun* pilot was picked up, I'd moved from my first apartment in Encino to one in Malibu, just down from the Colony. It was in a twelve-unit complex standing on tall wooden stilts, like telephone poles, allowing the waves to roll under the building at high tide, vibrating the floor and tingling your feet. When production started in June of '67 my MGB started racking up mileage as I drove to and from work every day—PCH before the sun came up and PCH long after it went down.

I remember dragging myself home one night, relieved to be out of the scratchy wool for a few hours, and when I opened the door to my apartment there on the sofa sat Steve, happily sifting a large brick of grass through the sieve I used to drain spaghetti. Like most of our generation, he had found marijuana, and on the coffee table before him was a small mountain of freshly cleaned weed, waiting to eventually be dumped into the two-foot-tall Brach's candy jar standing empty on the floor. He'd push and plead and criticize, but I rarely participated in either the cleaning or the smoking of it. I told myself it was because I had so little time and that frolicking through the night, eating Hostess Ding Dongs with abandon, was something I didn't need. That I had a job. Which was all true but in reality, I didn't know how to frolic and Steve did.

During the day while I was at work, Steve would often rescue Princess from her life in the Valley, bringing her to the Malibu apartment to get her away from our incoherent mother, who was in the process of falling apart, and her father, with his freak show of false posturing. Jocko's career was down to an occasional low-paying personal appearance, and soon he disappeared, abruptly departing with one of the many women in his life, leaving me to pay the rent on a small apartment in the Valley for my broken mother and little sister.

Now fourteen, and almost six feet tall, Princess ran wild like an escaped puppy frantically sniffing and peeing everywhere with no one to grab her collar. One moment she seemed like my comrade, and the next she felt like a responsibility I didn't know how to accept. But unless I took her to work with me—which I did frequently—I wouldn't see her. Too often I'd drag myself into the apartment late in the evening, and everywhere I looked would be the remnants of the fun-filled day that Steve and my sister had enjoyed. Sand still on their feet, they'd sit on the balcony smoking a joint, and no matter what I said—or didn't say—my "adult supervisor" tone always gave me away. I began to feel like the boring grumpy ant to their happy-go-lucky grasshoppers.

Steve really needed to have a life of his own, separate from mine, with his own identity. But how do two people grow up together, build strength in their own legs, when they're always leaning on each other? How could he find his place in the world when my life kept sucking him in, making it hard for him to take those first wobbly steps to begin a craft or career? Maybe that's part of the reason why he'd lose interest in everything after his initial burst of enthusiasm. He'd won a track scholarship and though he had real talent, he was impatient with the coaches, aggravated by their rules and the mindless, repetitive tasks he was forced to do, so he stopped going to practice.

As I look back right now, I realize that it was all of those mindless, repetitive tasks I was forced to endure day after day, the getting up and doing every scene the best I could, over and over, that gave me a kind of "miles in the saddle." They strengthened muscles not located in my body but in my heart—muscles not easy to access and certainly not fun. But easy is overrated and fun is extremely relative.

As that year crawled away, month after month, summer somehow becoming fall, I began to change for reasons I couldn't name, other than the fact that I was working all day then coming home and instantly turning into Ebenezer Scrooge. And when, in a moment of anger, Steve told me with a dismissive air that this "acting stuff" was nothing, that anyone could do it, that he could do it too if he wanted, the self-righteous out I needed presented itself. Midway through that first year of the *Nun*, I found myself alone. I was without Steve and my brother and my mother. I didn't drink, as Baa did, so I ate. And for the first time in my life I wanted food, over all else.

I would drive to work early in the morning, work all day, drive home at night, eat, and go to sleep. Next day, I would wake up before it was light, drive to work, work all day, drive home, eat, sleep. And on Saturdays, I would go into the recording studio or do a photo layout, then fill the rest of the day cooking and eating, trying to drown my loneliness in a vat of spaghetti with gobs of meat sauce and a whole chocolate cake, unable to stop eating even when I was in physical pain. And always I was alone, hiding in a closet of food.

I'd stick my fingers down my throat, longing for the relief of puking, but get nothing except a hacking, impotent gag. Maybe that belongs under the category of "God works in mysterious ways." I'd never heard of an eating disorder—no one talked about such things in the late sixties. But if I'd found the ability to regurgitate all the self-loathing I'd shoveled into myself, perhaps I would have continued down that destructive highway. Luckily, I didn't.

Instead, I suffered for days after each binge, the following morning being the worst. After sleeping ten or eleven hours, I would wake in agony, my entire body swollen and inflamed, actually sore to the touch. On Mondays, I'd go on a starvation diet of grapefruit and eggs or would eat nothing but cucumbers for a week. And when that wasn't enough, I started visiting the famous Louise Long as well. I'm not sure what Ms. Long's technique was called, but massage it wasn't. In the wee hours, before my 6:30 or 7 a.m. call, I'd drive to her place in the Valley, which was always overflowing with actresses (some famous, most not) all looking to get the crap pulverized out of them before heading off to work. In the overly heated little house, Louise or one of her trained associates would move from one sheet-covered table to another and violently pound on the naked bodies of all the women who had come looking for instant slenderizing or atonement—or both. For months, my black-and-blue anatomy looked like it had been in an automobile accident, so I guess it was a good thing I wasn't wearing Gidget's bathing suits anymore. But it didn't matter how much I got smacked around, or how many days I lived on hard-boiled eggs. My weekend benders were winning, and soon the press started reporting on my "baby fat," visible to every columnist I plopped down next to during lunch. My face was so round that my bangs looked shorter.

Finally, I called the one doctor I knew, Dr. Duke, who gave me a prescription for the only solution he had to offer—diet pills. Straight Dexedrine. Now, that was a horse of a different color. I was told to take one every morning, accompanied by a maximum-strength diuretic, wait thirty minutes, and lo and behold—a jubilant, cotton-mouthed, babbling idiot who had to pee every two seconds. Hot damn...summer in the city! Nirvana. I'd found true happiness. It didn't matter that by the end of the day I was so exhausted I could barely drive home, or that the happiness was by then nowhere in sight. Every morning I'd jump out of bed, still fuzzy from a night when my eyes never closed, and dutifully take the mud-green capsule waiting on my night table. Then I'd wait to feel the rockets fire. Five minutes and counting, four, three, two, one, and liftoff. On to the set, ready to film the day's work.

One day, when I was doing a scene with all the other nuns, my hands were shaking so badly that I could barely think. All my focus was on the fact that I couldn't lift the teacup from its saucer, take a sip, then put the cup back down without noticeably fumbling around. I found myself having to use both hands to lift the saucer and cup together as a unit, which made everyone look at me as though I'd lost my mind (and at that moment I *had* lost my mind). I couldn't concentrate on the work, on anything except my hands. I had most definitely lost weight, because with the chemical jet fuel coursing through me all day I ate nothing, not even cucumbers. Nevertheless, I knew I had to stop. Acting wouldn't let me travel down that road. It reached in and grabbed me, steering me away from cliffs I couldn't see. I was an actor and that had always given me more than these chemicals ever could. It had given me a language with myself, which unfortunately at this time I was not speaking.

The Monkees television show was being shot on the same lot as *The Flying Nun*—on *Gidget*'s old stage, actually. I didn't watch the show, but I knew who they were and the enormous appetite the country seemed to have for them. Many times, I'd spot a couple of them wandering onto my set, or I'd look up to see two of their faces grinning down as they sat on the wooden catwalk high above, legs swinging off the edge. They never seemed to be befriending me or even flirting. They treated me like I was a private joke between them, as if they knew something I didn't, like perhaps I had a *Kick Me* sign pinned to my back. But I wanted them to like me, wanted to be comrades, maybe more. I wanted to feel as I did when Elizabeth Montgomery would visit, stepping through the padded vault-like door that separated our two stages, pulling up a chair and watching for a while. Or the way I did the few times I ventured into her *Bewitched* world, her beautiful face lighting up when she saw me coming.

One day, three of the Monkees suddenly crammed into my tiny, round-domed camper of a dressing room, located on the stage only steps from the set. Their unexpected visit must have made the two-wheeler look like a clown car, loaded to the brim with a bunch of colorfully dressed guys and a nun. They sat there staring at me, making jokes among themselves, egging each other on. Then, with his British twang, Davy said, "I'll bet you give good head." Uproarious laughter shook the tin room, while I sat on my hands, a stupid grin glued to my face.

Somewhere inside I had an inkling that these guys were trying to fit into the cocky suit of clothes handed to them when *The Monkees* went on the air, but I couldn't see who they might be underneath. Instead I felt red in the face and began to sweat, not because of what Davy had said, but because I had no idea what it meant. I knew what a blowjob was, but I'd never heard it called "giving head." I simply didn't know what they were talking about. I did know I was being humiliated—or that seemed to be the desired effect, and *that* vocabulary I understood.

This very moment, I believe, is why I began to talk like the proverbial truck driver, slowly learning how to out-pottymouth anyone who tried to embarrass me with sexual words or innuendos. Eventually I was able to take vulgar to a whole new level, thus winning the game of "let's corner the girl." But at twenty, sitting with these guys, I went blank. Couldn't have found a witty reply if my life depended on it. So, I laughingly tried to fake it by saying, "Yes, sir. You bet," sounding like my version of Marjorie Main. Where was the easy, funny, capable part of me? The girl I was on the set all day. I despised this stuttering, anxious person now sinking into the shabby love seat, loathed her sadness and fumbling inability, which made me sick to my stomach. It never occurred to me then that it might be their behavior that made me want to retch, not my own.

Luckily, there was a sharp bang on the door, followed by a muffled voice saying, "Hey, guys, we need you," and off they went, asking me to visit their set, conspiratorially adding that they wanted to show me something. "You bet," I repeated, the only two words I could get out.

During a break the following day, I boldly told the assistant director that I was going visiting, ignoring the immediate rise of his eyebrows. I wanted to take my cornette off, to let my hair down and just be the girl I was, but I knew that if I did, the hairdresser would have to twist it up again while the company waited to continue the day's work, so I walked across the lot looking very much like the Flying Nun.

Stage 6 had been transformed from the conservative upper-middle-class home of the midsixties—*Gidget*'s set—to the multicolored, pseudo-psychedelic world of the late sixties—the *Monkees*'. And as I stood awkwardly in the back, half-hidden in the clouds of "bee's smoke" being puffed out by several machines, I recognized former members of the *Gidget* crew, until one by one, heads began to turn in my direction, greeting me with a smile or a "long time no see" expression. When Davy, who was standing on the set, noticed the minor hubbub, he moved to me, took my hand, and led me through the side door to the parking lot outside, telling the assistant director to get him when the shot was ready.

Butted up against the stage, taking up four or five parking spots, was a windowless concrete-block vault with a meat-locker door, and as Davy pulled the handle it snapped open with a pop, releasing a blast of cold air, bright pink lights, and a fog of pot smoke. Choosing not to walk through the entrance sideways, I took hold of the edges of my hat, pulled them down under my chin, and stepped into the bunker to find a smiling Peter Tork leaning back on several of the brightly colored pillows that were piled on the ground everywhere.

I wanted to look nonchalant, like this was no big deal, so I plopped down on the extra-large pillow in the middle of the square room, and after a beat, Peter (I think) asked if I wanted a hit off the joint being passed around. When I declined, they came back, almost in unison, "Ah, come on. You're the Flying Nun, aren't you?" Uproarious laughter again. My God, they certainly enjoyed one another's company.

While the two boys seemed to be talking in code to each other, I sat there, frozen, unable to speak. Were they sending me signals that I was just too stupid to read? Was I expected to do something, say something funny or smart or biting? If I could, maybe then they'd like me. Maybe they already liked me and this was how you were supposed to show it. Was this how people flirted with each other? Perched on my big pillow, I looked around, smiling but in agony, desperately wanting out of this concrete cell, unable to make my mouth move. Finally, the vault door was yanked open and Jon, *The Monkees'* AD (who'd also been *Gidget's*) stepped inside. He took one look at me perched on my big pillow and immediately burst out laughing, then moved in for a hug—hard to do with my hat always in the way. After taking a long pull off the joint, he held the smoke in his lungs while letting me know that I was needed back at the convent, ASAP. Glory hallelujah.

Since the *Nun* was considered a bona fide hit, which *Gidget* had not been, the amount of focus—not to mention energy—the studio directed toward me had significantly increased. They pushed me to do more publicity and for the first time to appear on talk shows, which I tried to do, but when I did them I was visibly terrified and sounded like a blithering idiot.

Afterward, the studio was quick to let me know that they thought I'd been dreadful—something I already knew. They began to casually suggest I stop wearing "mod" short skirts and bright colors when out in public, even though I, like every other twenty-year-old female, wanted to look like Twiggy—which was never going to happen, no matter what I wore.

Not long after my visit to the Monkees' bong shelter, I received word on the set that Jackie Cooper—vice president of program development for Screen Gems—wanted to see me in his office, a five-minute walk from my stage. The moment his secretary announced my arrival into the intercom, the adjacent door flew open and Mr. Cooper—who was now in his late forties but still looked like the nine-year-old boy starring opposite Wallace Beery in *The Champ*—came striding through with his hand extended. I didn't know it at the time, but Jackie had been instrumental in the studio's decision to hire me as Gidget, ultimately launching my career. Yet I'd never met him, nor had I ever been asked to dash over to the executive building between shots. In my heart, I worried that this meeting was a reaction to my being seen hanging out with the Monkees and, while it was okay for the guys to inspire some bad-boy gossip, it was not okay for me, the Flying Nun.

After we were seated—Jackie behind his desk and me in the leather chair in front—after I said no thanks to an offer of something to drink, and after some meaningless chitchat, he settled into the heart of the matter. I don't remember our conversation exactly, but it went something like this:

"Sally, I'm so glad you decided to do this show after all. We wouldn't be here if you hadn't. I really mean it. You're doing a wonderful job, and I wanted you to hear that. Not only from me but from the studio. We would like to show our appreciation in some way. What can we do?"

"Do?" A million things raced through my head at that moment, all vaguely having to do with getting out of the convent. But I looked at him sweetly and said, "Nothing."

"No, really," he continued earnestly. "We want to give you something. Come on...there must be something: a boat, a piece of jewelry, down payment on a house?"

Now, I am not stupid, but I could not comprehend what was being said. I'd been gearing myself up for a scolding, but instead I sat there, speechless, stunned to be offered things I couldn't even visualize when all I really wanted were better story lines and maybe a new outfit from Judy's clothes store. In lieu of revealing my deepest desires or my suspicion that something was not being said, I stuttered a shy "Ummm...I don't know."

"Wouldn't you like a new car?" Jackie blurted, getting excited about the idea as soon as he said it. "How about a Ferrari! You want a Ferrari?" Clearly, *he* wanted a Ferrari and wouldn't let up until I got as excited as he was. I wasn't even sure what a Ferrari was and I sure as hell didn't want one, but I desperately wanted to leave this uncomfortably energetic meeting, so I said, "Sure. That'd be great."

A week later, during my lunch hour, Jackie Cooper took me to the Ferrari dealership on Sunset Boulevard and bought me a blue Pininfarina convertible, and I sold my beloved yellow MGB. Neither Mr. Cooper nor anyone else at the studio explicitly told me to dress more nunlike, nor did they demand that I keep a squeaky-clean image, but I couldn't help feeling that this gift was some kind of bribe, a tool to keep me in place. Though why they thought a flashy sports car would do the trick, I do not know. And when I drove onto the lot the following week in my new blue prize—which felt like a horse I wasn't skilled enough to ride—I felt both proud and skeptical. But most of all I felt embarrassed. I didn't want this machine that made everyone turn and look when I drove by. And where were the gifts for everyone else on the show?

I spent every day with those actors, laughing and easy. I knew I was the star, but I didn't want to stand out any more than necessary. I wanted to be a part of the team—though not necessarily friends with anyone. Even when I went with Alejandro to the Factory, a club located in Hollywood—and

The nuns discuss the facts of life with Irving, the pelican.

the only club I'd ever been to—I spent most of the time submerged in the dark herd of gyrating bodies, completely lost in the thunderous music, never actually talking to Alejandro. Whenever any of the cast made a move toward me, I felt myself lean back, wondering if it was a genuine offer of friendship or if they saw me as a coin they all wanted in their pocket. I was suspicious, always, of everyone, no matter how hard I tried not to be. I'm sure that everyone thought I was friendly and open, because part of me was, while a more significant part wanted to hide in a dark, safe closet with the door closed, waiting for my mother to talk to me.

The most difficult task of all was simply getting through the day, every day. Even in my high school drama class, whether in scene study or a term play, I'd been sublimely lost in the work, connected to myself, completely unaware of time as it slid by. But now every minute seemed to repeat itself, never ticking away as minutes are supposed to do but ticking up and down in the same place. To stay alive, not to mention awake, I created little games for myself, just as I'd done at the racetrack with Dick. I stopped reading the scripts beforehand, would wait until I was called to the set, then stand beside the script supervisor to look at the current scene and try to memorize my dialogue instantly. The game was to see if I could do it all in one take, then it evolved into seeing if I could do it in one breath. Both are valuable exercises for an actor, but I sure as hell didn't know it.

Many of the directors we had on the show—a different one for each episode—literally pushed and pulled me into place, like I was a bowl of fruit, and by then I'd gained so much weight I looked like a bowl of fruit. After they'd yank me to my spot, I'd take a lungful of air and play the game, saying every line in one breath, give or take a paraphrase or two. I would do other takes if they wanted—and they usually did—which meant the distraction of my games would wear off, and I'd be thrust headlong into deadly boredom.

I couldn't make myself numb no matter how much I ate, which ultimately made it worse. Then I was bored, ashamed, *and* fat: the poster child for self-loathing. Maybe I was only feeling the young adult in me pushing to emerge. Maybe I would have been struggling no matter where I was or what I was doing. Certainly, I was earning a living, and I can't imagine what I would've done if I hadn't been. Maybe it takes the distance of so many years to feel grateful. At the time, all I could see was this character, a one-dimensional girl whom I was embarrassed to be playing, and an endless string of days in which I was powerlessly trapped inside her.

One afternoon toward the end of that first year, I was standing in the mother superior's office surrounded by all the other nuns—something I had done countless times before. Just like every other day, I started to say Sister Bertrille's chirpy words, when suddenly I hit a wall, stopped midsentence, and flat-out couldn't continue. I put my face in my hands and sat down, begging the feeling to pass so I could jump to my feet, dust myself off, and start all over again with a big plastered-on grin. But I couldn't. A tiny voice inside my head whispered, then pleaded, *Suck it up and get on with it.* I just couldn't. I was stuck behind my fingers like they were glued to my face, couldn't look up, couldn't look at everyone looking at me, couldn't even release enough to begin crying. I sat on the floor in front of the mother superior's big desk with my legs crossed and my body bent into my lap. As if I didn't really want to be heard, I quietly mumbled, "Please let me go home. Please let me go home. I'll do better tomorrow. Please let me go home." I kept repeating it, rocking forward with my palms mashed into my eyes. I don't know what the rest of the actors were doing or how they reacted to this sight. I only know I felt a strong, unapologetic hand grab hold of my arm, seeking not to look in my face but to guide me. It was Madeleine, the mother superior. I wasn't completely sure she was my friend. Then I heard her quiet, clear demand, never raising her voice but stating with a kind of force that no one questioned, "Get her a car and a driver. She's finished for the day. Now."

If anyone said anything in reply I didn't hear it, and I couldn't force myself to look for fear I would see the dismay or disapproval on their faces. Madeleine placed her whole body around me—though not really in a hug. She didn't make cooing sounds or try to be reassuring, she simply encased me as I walked blindly forward. And as she guided me toward the huge sliding stage doors, I heard the loud honking sound announcing their movement, heard the clacking as they parted, and felt the sunlight when she led me through. I never took my hands from my face as she pressed my head down, only slid onto the front seat of some vehicle—I have no idea what—and was silently driven home.

The next day, I energetically propelled myself through the work as if nothing had happened, while fleeting looks of sympathy and out-and-out bewilderment shot from everyone, including the crew. Late in the afternoon, Madeleine took hold of my arm, pulling me into a dark corner. She lowered her head to mine and whispered, "You're going to meet me at this address after work next Tuesday," and stuffed a folded scrap of paper into my pocket. "You're doing it. It's not far from here. You can go right from work." I looked at her, not knowing whether I felt warmed or repelled.

"It's the Actors Studio. Have you heard of it?"

"Yes," I muttered.

"Well, you're coming. I'll meet you there." She stopped and stood back, watching me.

Registering the challenge I saw in her face, I replied, "I'll be there."

10

Together

IT WAS JUST an ordinary-looking house in an ordinary-looking Hollywood neighborhood a few blocks south of the Sunset Strip, twenty minutes from Columbia. After parking on the street, I walked up the steep driveway with my heart pushing against my shirt, hoping that Madeleine's would be the first face I saw. At the top of the drive was a small building that perhaps had been the garage at one point; now, where the wide car-size opening might have been was a long white clapboard wall with an ordinary door standing open at the end. A cluster of people gathered under the yellow glare of the naked light bulb mounted above the door, while a swarm of moths danced around the glow.

Still looking for Madeleine, I stepped through the back door of what appeared to be the main house, sliding awkwardly between those waiting at the coffee machine, nodding at everyone who met my eyes. These were all actors and as I scanned the small group, I recognized several faces, though I couldn't pinpoint from where. At the same time, I felt the energy of being recognized myself, if for no other reason than the fact that I was new and nervous. And there she was, lost in an animated conversation with a tall woman who wore her frizzy gray hair pulled back in a long ponytail. When she saw me, Madeleine's pixie face crinkled into a relieved smile, as though she had half-expected that I wouldn't show up. She moved forward, calmly introducing me to everyone while pulling me out the door and up the path to that onetime garage, where everyone eventually headed. Inside was a mini theater with gradually elevated rows of chairs facing a curtainless stage. People were taking their seats, moving with a kind of certainty that indicated they'd done this before and had a preferred spot. Madeleine chose two chairs, not in the back but not in the front where force of habit had been pulling her.

A longtime member of this historic acting workshop, Madeleine had done her studying in New York, which had resulted in a remarkable stage career. She had originated the roles of Abigail in Arthur Miller's *The Crucible* as well as "Sister Woman" in *Cat on a Hot Tin Roof* and Miss Lucy in *Sweet Bird of Youth*, both by Tennessee Williams. She was a force, that's for sure: She had been blacklisted in the McCarthy era, had worked with Martin Luther King Jr. during the civil rights movement, was arrested while participating in a freedom walk, then jailed and sentenced to six months' hard labor for "endangering the customs and mores of the people of Alabama" until her lawyer, the first African American to represent a white woman south of the Mason-Dixon Line, secured her release. She rarely talked about any of this, but you could feel it in her, like something lashing around, unwilling to settle down. A dust devil looking for loose dirt.

Two scenes were up that night: The first was from *A Moon for the Misbegotten*, by Eugene O'Neill with two characters, and the second was a monologue from Euripides's *Medea*, adapted by Jean Anouilh. As everyone was filing in, Madeleine explained to me what I was to see, and how I should see it. The performers were to pick one or two very specific things they wanted to work on, and the scene was in no way to be considered a finished performance. Everything was a work in progress. It was study. She also told me that during the winter months the position of moderator would rotate according to whoever was available. Veterans and longtime members like Ellen Burstyn, Bruce Dern, Shelley Winters, and even Madeleine herself would show up on different nights, always actors who had studied closely with the guru—the acting teacher who had made the Actors Studio so famous and infamous, Lee Strasberg. But during the spring and throughout the summer Lee lived in L.A., and for those months it was the master himself who taught at this little neighborhood residence.

The lights went down and the first scene was up. I wasn't familiar with *A Moon for the Misbegotten*, but even if I'd known it well, I wouldn't have completely understood what was happening because whatever the two actors were working on, being heard wasn't one of them. It didn't matter. Their focus made it worth holding my breath to catch whatever words I could, as if we, the audience, were eavesdropping on something personal happening between these two people, something that they would hide if our presence were known.

After the scene, the actors gathered their things and adjusted their clothes, never looking out at the watchers, talking only to each other, as if allowing themselves the few moments it takes to leave the privacy of concentration. Tucking their emotions out of sight, just as they tucked in their shirts and tied their shoes. Eventually they sat on the edge of the stage with varying degrees of awkward composure until the moderator (I'm sorry to say I don't remember who it was that night) asked them what they'd been working on. After the actors explained their tasks, the moderator gave comments and finally asked for comments from the audience—all actors and members or, like me, invited observers.

When the short break ended, everyone took their seats again and quieted as a tall, striking woman, a character actor I vaguely recognized, moved to center stage, keeping her eyes down. She stood still for what seemed to be a long time, then began to speak as Medea. Slowly, she raised her eyes and searched the audience, meeting one face, then another. And with a booming voice, she began to wail while strutting across the stage, then laughed insanely with her mouth open wide, looking toward the rafters. It was periodically mesmerizing, boldly unafraid, and at the same time hovered constantly on the edge of embarrassing. At the end of the long spew of words, she screamed with fierce abandon, ripping the bodice of her dress open, yanking it with the most authentic behavior thus far, and finally stood in the middle of the stage, breathless and bare chested. No one moved. I must admit, I admired her freedom, though perhaps not her sense of economy. After a moment, Madeleine leaned in to me, whispering a little too loudly, "She finds a way to do that in every scene, no matter what the play." But I couldn't take my eyes off of this exposed actor as she gathered her things just like the others had done, pulling herself back, transitioning from the place where she had been to look at the people sitting in front of her.

I can't say I learned anything that night, or at least not anything I could take to the set with me the next day—God forbid—but I was totally compelled. I wanted to tell the actors what I thought, how at times I was confused and then completely transfixed, wanted to ask them why they chose to work on things that were so complicated to explain. I walked away with a new hunger, and not for chocolate cake. I wanted to get up there, wanted to work, really work—not the kind of work I'd been doing. I wanted to learn the break-it-down, bit-by-bit, layer-by-layer craft of it.

There's a saying that actors have: "Life is what happens in between jobs." Then there's the riddle: "What is the worst time in an actor's life?" Answer: "When they're not working and when they're working." Both of these apply. During the months that *The Flying Nun* was in production, I had zero time off because I was in every scene of every script, so when hiatus arrived at the end of the first season, I tried to fill my life with everything I wouldn't be able to do after the second season began.

Immediately, I started seeing a therapist once a week, even though I didn't stay with him for long. I remember shuffling into his office for my session and sitting on the edge of his hard leather sofa, feeling just as stiff as the furniture. It was perhaps our second meeting, so I'm sure I looked terrified, because I was, and deeply sad, trying to hide myself in layers of baggy clothes, looking slightly childlike. Without even registering my appearance, he opened the session by scolding me for being fifteen minutes late, telling me I was acting disrespectfully to us both. I felt ambushed, tears dripping off my chin as I tried to defend myself, explaining how every day the clock was relentlessly on me and I was never late, admitting it was a luxury to allow myself a little tardiness, something I didn't know I felt until I heard it come out of my mouth. I wish I could have said, "Thank you for your time, you're not the right person for me," and left. But I couldn't find that part of myself, and as the session continued I fell back into my familiar cell, locked behind my face, unable to speak.

This same doctor insisted that I attend a torturous, weekend-long group marathon as well as his weekly group therapy sessions, when a knot of strangers, usually years older, would burst out laughing when one of the members asked if I'd driven there or had I flown over, one of a hundred unfunny jokes thrown in my direction while inside my head a voice pleaded for me to speak. *Please speak.* But I sat with my head down, a little ragamuffin girl, mute and now with a pounding headache.

Then on Tuesday and Thursday evenings, scene nights at the Actors Studio, I'd step out of the ragamuffin's wordless world and become an entirely different person. And on Wednesday nights, when Lou Antonio, the charismatic New York actor, conducted his popular exercise class, I could hear my voice again and I could open my mouth and use it. This class was not an evening filled with sit-ups and push-ups—though that might have been a good idea too. These exercises had only to do with acting.

The first time I timidly stepped into his class, I hadn't even put my rear in a chair before I heard Lou shout, "I want six people up, now!" Without worrying if I was prepared or informed or qualified, I jumped onto the stage, then looked out at the theater, half-filled with actors just settling in. As soon as Lou had all his volunteers standing ready under the rudimentary work lights—making it somewhat brighter onstage than it was in the audience—the exercise began. It went something like this, give or take a few details: Lou climbed onstage with us, then one at a time whispered to each actor their own private motivations. In my ear, he informed me that I was desperately in love with the unfamiliar performer standing to my right, adding that I had an overwhelming urge to touch him. Then, he quietly told my love interest that one of his contact lenses had popped out and though he desperately needed my help to find it, an obnoxious odor seemed to be radiating from me—basically, I reeked to high heaven. After everyone onstage was given a secret drive, always a motivation in direct conflict with someone else's, Lou called "action," and what must have resembled a scene from *The Snake Pit* began. He would then move into the audience or stand in the back and yell out different locations periodically: You're on a storm-tossed boat, in a roasting desert, stuck in a crowded elevator. All of which would radically change the physicality of everyone's behavior, but not their need to get whatever it was Lou had told them they wanted.

I loved every joyful minute of it. And even though most of Lou's exercises seemed like silly party games, they were actually a kind of limbering up, stretching your imagination, strengthening your ability to act on a fleeting impulse, and challenging your concentration. The more intense exercises—sense memory, emotional memory, room, and the private moment—I wouldn't learn until later, all conducted by Lee Strasberg himself.

One Wednesday night during that first hiatus, I was heading

home from exercise class with the top down on my flashy sports car, still feeling slap-happy from the evening's improvisations. I had the *1812 Overture* playing loudly on my eight-track—yeah, go figure—when I stopped at a red light on Sunset Boulevard. Pounding on the wood steering wheel as if it were a bongo drum, I noticed a car filled with cute guys pulling up next to me, and for a moment I was just an ordinary girl… in her ordinary blue Ferrari playing the overture of 1812 full blast. So I met their eyes and smiled. Most people my age were looking at either college or the threat of Vietnam, and to them anyone over the age of thirty was under suspicion. They were listening to Jimi Hendrix or the Beatles or Buffalo Springfield, not Tchaikovsky in an ostentatious vehicle, and though I was clearly not over thirty, they immediately recognized me as a participant in that over-thirty world, and of all things, the Flying Nun herself. So to the timing of Tchaikovsky's thunderous cannon fire, they all flipped me the bird, except the one poor guy who made a wet raspberry sound. I drove the rest of the way home feeling like the ragamuffin again.

Even in the first days of my hiatus I began to prepare for what lay ahead, to smooth out some of the bumps I knew I'd be traveling over as soon as production started again. I gave up my Malibu apartment and rented a big ugly house in Hollywood, ten minutes from Columbia, eliminating the long commute that was not only a waste of my precious time but filled with anxiety, since I never knew when the temperamental Ferrari would overheat on the 101 freeway, forcing me to pull over and wait for traffic to thin before I could limp home. From Kings Road, I could almost coast to work if I had to.

My twenty-first birthday party, hosted by Screen Gems.

This time it was Princess who helped me load up the boxes, staying with me a great deal of the time, helping me unpack as if we were building a new life together.

There are no family photos taken during most of those years because there was no family to take them. The only tools I have to unearth memories are the scrapbooks Aunt Gladys devotedly kept, basically documenting my career until 1989, when she passed away, less than a year after her older sister, my grandmother Joy. In the stacks of carefully cut-out articles, clippings, and fan magazine stories (all placed in clear plastic sleeves with the date on the top) I find a paparazzi-style photo of an overweight, double-chinned Sally. With long straight hair and short blunt bangs, I'm smiling gleefully as I stand jammed against two of the Monkees, Davy and Peter. It was my twenty-first birthday party, held at the Factory, hosted by Jackie Cooper and thrown by Screen Gems. I'd hated birthday parties ever since my brother's fourth-grade no-show, and even though the whole event had been arranged by the studio and was mostly a publicity opportunity, I remember being very nervous. Shortly after the band's deafening beat started up, a few familiar faces began to appear, mostly the cast and a few executives. But when I looked up to see those two strutting guys walking toward me carrying a big ribbon-bedecked package, I felt a jolt of either dread or excitement, not certain which. (I don't remember opening that gift, which I'm sure had been put together by Screen Gems.) The contrived stories in both *TV Radio Mirror* and *Movie Mirror* dated February and March of 1968 reported that Davy was my date, but whatever it might look like in those photos, I remember that he wasn't. Behind the smiling threesome, almost unnoticeable, looms my very tall little sister with an "I want to be in the picture too" look on her face. I was turning twenty-one but looked like a chubby fifteen-year-old. Princess was fifteen but looked twenty-one. She was my date.

What my sister was feeling as she stood glowing in my shadow, a statuesque beauty who looked so much like her father—with the same mannerisms, the same gliding gait—I'll never really know. At the time, I couldn't see far enough out of my own blur to ask her, and since she tended to balk at the suggestion of introspection, even if I had asked I don't think she would've answered. As I look back now, I can see how excluded she must have felt from the original Ricky/Sally team. Not only was she the baby of the group but she also had a different father. A father whom she adored, whose very presence would turn her ordinary day into a celebration. A wise and supportive man she'd painted in her imagination, then plastered like a billboard over the father she actually had. She never talked about Jocko's cruelty or neglect and remembered only the times when he had paid her any attention at all. When he had encouraged her to ride down steep hills on her skateboard, watching her careen dangerously around turns, then praising her for the scabs and scars she received, treating her like a chip off the old block because they were gathered without tears. She was long-legged and gracefully athletic, with the same kind of fearless physical prowess as her father. But when her brother began to blaze his way into the science world and her sister was catapulted into the arts, Princess wandered around feeling deficient, like she'd been born without thumbs. By the time she was fifteen, her adored father had escaped into his new life and Baa had hit a depressed, drunken bottom. Princess stopped attending public high school, was in and out of various alternative schools, then finally dropped out altogether, dabbling occasionally in the world of sex, drugs, and rock and roll. Her life had been a constant slide down without anyone she could hold on to... except me, and I wasn't exactly stationary either.

We had grown up together, often in the same room. We had never been apart for long, but as close as we were, there was always something thorny between us, something that neither of us could pick our way out of, something we couldn't even begin to talk about or admit. There were the basic childhood rivalries, and the fact that she was in the heart of her teenage years, that she felt judged by the taskmaster in me and I felt threatened by her free spirit. And the minute I stepped into the spotlight of show biz, our already complicated sisterhood changed in ways that began to define us, to deepen the designated family roles we'd already been cast in. I often became her parent, frowning at her behavior, criticizing and lecturing her about how to fix her life—even though I had absolutely no idea how to fix my own. And everything was muddled with the reality that I now held the purse strings. Whether gifts or hand-me-downs, it all came with a mixed bag of emotions for both of us.

Yet she was my dearest friend. I missed her when she was gone and felt a lift when she walked into the house, sometimes arriving unannounced, dropped off by friends I didn't know, people I never met. We'd put a Laura Nyro album on the stereo, turn it up so loud that the windows vibrated, and singing at the top of our lungs, we'd dance around the living room until we were drenched with sweat. We may have held each other at arm's length but our hands were always locked together. She was my family, and I needed her as much as she needed me and we both needed Baa.

So, with an unconscious desire to fix the messy unit that we'd become, I took the three of us on a small vacation before I was sent back to the front lines of work. There we were: my drunken mother, my adolescent sister, and me, sunburned and waterlogged from the day at the pool, sitting in the living area of my room in one of Palm Springs' small midcentury hotels. Each of us with so much bottled up inside, stuffed to the brim with words that pleaded to be spoken but unable to get the first word out. Like a jar of pickles so packed you can't pry loose a single pickle.

Princess and I sat on the floor around a small coffee table with our room service order, while Baa sat on the sofa drinking. For most of the meal we laughed; we were good at that. Laughing till our stomach muscles cramped. Laughing at God knows what, something someone said, or someone we knew. Laughter that felt like holding each other, that felt like loving each other. And out of that safe place, I started casually trying to figure out how we had all ended up as we were, right at that moment. Which, of course, led to childhood moments, and slowly, unwittingly, I stumbled into feelings. I heard myself complaining about Jocko's treatment of Rick and his attitude toward me, and as I edged closer to the visions in my mind, my insides started to tremble, filled with unexpected emotion. I'd never tried to reveal what was at the heart of my relationship with Jocko and was unable to say the exact words. I inched myself toward something I didn't want to see, wanting them to get the picture without actually having to paint it, deeply wanting to remove some undiagnosed malignancy from our bond. I don't know what I said, but suddenly Princess reared up, defending her helpless father against my self-righteous, self-absorbed woes (as she called them) while my mother, who was past the slurring stage, started talking about "the little pixie people."

In an uncontainable blazing flash, I picked up Baa's drink and threw it in her face. "I can't stand this!" I seethed. "I hate you like this. I can't look at you." And with that the pickle was out of the jar. Everyone was crying and I was the cause of it. Princess put her arm around our mother, led her to her room and away from me. I was the monster who had caused the pain and had ruined the trip. In some weird way, I felt as though I was filling the space that Jocko had just vacated.

After that weekend, I reached out to my father for the first time in my life, asking him if I could come to dinner. I don't know what was going through my mind when I climbed into the Ferrari, or how I felt driving for that hour. I only remember that when I finally found his house, one I'd never visited before, and pulled into the driveway behind what I presumed to be Dick's car, it began to drizzle. My eleven-year-old half sister, Shirley, was the first one out the door to greet me, followed closely by Dick, while his third wife, Peggy, stood quietly in the doorway, watching as I said hello to her pretty blond daughter.

Dick had remarried twice since he and my mother divorced, his second marriage lasting only a few months. Then when I was nine, he married Peggy Walker, a kind but uninvolved British woman whom I was always happy to see but felt no emotional connection with—not from me to her, not from her to me. Soon after they were married, Shirley was born and I became their every-other-weekend babysitter, always assuring them that I loved getting up in the morning with the new arrival. But I didn't love it. I was already spending a lot of time looking after my other half sister, who was four at the time. And whatever they might think, Shirley was not a playmate for a ten-year-old, she was a baby. I couldn't say any of that, couldn't ever tell my father what I was feeling. I could barely tell myself.

But right then, I wanted things to be different, and when I gave Dick a quick hug, I was flooded with how he smelled: not good, not bad, but familiar and safe. Instantly, my throat began to burn, so I put my head down to keep from looking in his eyes, to hide my longing while I followed Peggy into the house. And there, standing in the middle of the bland living room, were six or seven people, adults and children all smiling broadly as they watched me enter. A few had cameras; others carried little leather-bound autograph books or fan magazines with my picture on the cover. Dick was beaming when he introduced his neighbors, making me wonder whether he was proud of them or of me.

After signing everything there was to sign and smiling sweetly during their endless departure, after listening to Dick's comments about the price of fame and wasn't that a nice group of folks, after dutifully touring the new house and inspecting the small shrine that Shirley had created in her room with photos and clippings of the big sister she would never really get to know, I finally sat down with Dick and Shirley to watch a golf match on TV. When at last we were called into the dining area, which opened into the kitchen, Peggy was in the midst of delivering plates of food to each of the table's four place mats with a pleasant "service with a smile" look on her face.

Dick sat on my left, carefully putting the paper napkin on his lap, while Shirley—on my right—never took her eyes off my face. I sat at the head of the table, locked in again, wanting something I couldn't ask for because I was unable to find my voice. I wonder if my father could feel emotion radiating from me, because he began to talk a mile a minute, telling me how he and another man had purchased a pharmacy, a full drugstore, how it was a great deal, even though he wasn't sure that he could make ends meet before it was up and running. After taking a few bites of the chicken baked in cream of mushroom soup, he began again. Maybe I'm paraphrasing, but not much.

"I read you made four thousand an episode. How many episodes were there?"

"We made thirty-one, but I only make a thousand per episode, and then my agent takes out his ten percent, so it's not even that. It goes up to twelve hundred next season, I think."

"Your car must have set you back some, I bet."

"No... actually, no... They sort of gave it to me."

"Well, well. Pretty snazzy, huh, Peg?"

As we sat, mercifully but awkwardly quiet, a pressure began to build inside my mind; maybe I could just whisper how sad I was feeling, maybe he would ask me why, maybe then I'd know how to answer. *Go, Sally, go.* I opened my mouth to start, and Dick cut me off.

"Sally, I have to tell you," he said quickly, using his wadded napkin to wipe the grease off his mouth and the tears from his eyes, "I will always miss my children. Do you have any idea how much it hurt me to lose you? You and Rick? I never got over it... never." He took a sip of water and looked at me. If only I could have said, *I'm right here... You never lost me... You never saw me, but I'VE BEEN RIGHT HERE!* But I couldn't. Instead, I put my hand on his shoulder, patted him just as I had when I was four, and instantly turned into the village idiot. "Hey, it's fine. We're all fine. Come on, Dick, tell me, who flung gum in Grandpa's whiskers?"

When the meal was over, the dishes were in the sink, and my promise to return was repeated to everyone, Dick walked me to the front door, stopping at the entrance, where he stood with his arms folded, legs apart as though bracing himself against a strong wind.

"Sal," he began nervously, "you remember when you asked me to give you the twenty-five dollars you needed to join that workshop? The one where you got noticed? None of this would have happened if I hadn't given you that money. Your mother didn't have it. Do you remember?"

"Yes, I remember. I hope I thanked you."

"Well, you can thank me now. I need to borrow some money. Just five thousand. Of course, I'll pay you back. I just need it for a short loan."

"I don't think I have five thousand dollars. I don't know. I...I just got a business manager...a few weeks ago, just to help me with taxes and stuff."

"That's great. Just great. If you give me his number, I'll call him. Then I don't have to bother you."

"I don't remember his number," I said quickly, wishing this would stop. Knowing what it was like to be broke had made me afraid of money—or the lack of it. So much so that I couldn't look at it, didn't even know how much I had. But however much it was, I sure as hell didn't want to give it away.

Dick pushed on. "That's okay, what's his name? Tell me his name and I'll find the number. Then I don't have to bother you," he repeated.

I longed to see the interior of my dreaded Ferrari, to feel the safe isolation of my dreary rented home, but I nodded, then jotted the name on the notepad Dick quickly produced, one that still had NATIONAL DRUG CO. printed on the top. As I turned to go, Dick slung his arm over my sagging shoulder, pulling me toward a small bathroom.

"Listen, Sal, I'm your father. I want you to come here

anytime, okay? Let me give you some things to take home."
He dashed toward the kitchen, returning instantly with a
brown paper bag.

"I got some stuff here that you might need," he said, opening a cabinet to reveal row after row of stacked boxes and
bottles. "Here, some aspirin," he said, tossing a large bottle of
Bayer into the bag. "And Vicks VapoRub, large jar. Stick some
in your nose when it gets stuffy. Works wonders." He continued to toss items into the bag with a running commentary:
"Decongestant spray? Diuretics? Peggy loves these, gets rid
of all the puffies. How about some mood elevators? I use 'em
when I play golf. Helps me with my game." From a large jar
he removed a dark green oblong capsule. It was either the twin
or a very close relative of the green bombers I'd been given to
lose weight, except now it was being called a "mood elevator."

"How 'bout some laxatives? Here, these are great. Stool
softeners?"

I nodded my head at everything, bewilderingly pleased and
grateful for each added ingredient, like a kid who couldn't get
enough sprinkles on her ice cream.

I drove back in the pouring rain, blurry and dazed but
knowing I had a father who cared enough to make sure my
stools were soft. What the hell, it was better than nothing.

Looming on the horizon, like a funnel cloud coming my way,
was the *Nun's* second season, and I couldn't find the tools to
board up my brain, or the safety of a cellar to withstand the
twister of another nine months of colorless nonsense. I felt
hopeless, futureless. I desperately wanted to believe that I'd
find my way through this, that something was possible on the

other side, that someday I'd be offered roles that I'd be proud to play. I wanted at least to be considered for other projects, to have a chance—even if I wasn't available. But in those days, there was a pronounced class system between the artists of films and the crude laborers of the small screen, especially situation comedy. And I was the Flying Nun, right at the top of the "don't call us, we'll call you" list.

I had hardly thought about the fact that months earlier I'd signed up to do a scene at the Actors Studio, had almost forgotten that the only date I could get was right before production was to begin again. Only now did it dawn on me how close that day really was. I hoped that Madeleine would be back from New York and sitting in the audience, because it would be my first scene performed at the Studio and the moderator would be Lee Strasberg.

I remember feeling dark and depressed, dressed in my ragamuffin clothes as I sat on the floor of the theater arts section at the public library. Flipping through play after play, though not necessarily reading them, I was looking for scenes between two characters when I stumbled upon a long one from Jean-Paul Sartre's *The Respectful Prostitute*. Without knowing what the play was about, I knew I'd found it: a scene, a character to create, and my rag doll body came to life. Immediately, I asked Paul, one of the actors I'd worked with in exercise class, to play the rich southern bigot, Fred, to my Lizzie the prostitute.

To accommodate the many actors who wanted to perform for him, Mr. Strasberg had handed down an edict declaring that no scene would run longer than fifteen minutes, at which time he would stop it. In the classes that I had attended since Lee's arrival for his six-month L.A. stint, I'd realized it was not unusual for him to halt a scene long before the fifteen-minute cutoff, which made everyone in the room flinch with the implied blow.

When Lee was the moderator, every scene night was standing room only, and the night I was to perform it seemed especially packed, every chair taken, with the overflow sitting on the floor or leaning against the back wall. I don't remember watching the first scene that night because mine was up second, and I was only slightly aware of Lee commenting after that scene finished, speaking sharply to one actor and dismissively to the other. All I knew was, we were up.

I was standing on the cheese end of a mousetrap, unafraid or unaware that I could be crushed. I saw it only as a way to lift off the ground, to be catapulted into space, to feel alive. The grubby, worn boards of the stage became the grubby, cheap room where Lizzie lived. The filthy twin mattress, usually stored in a side room filled with props and bits of random furniture, became Lizzie's unmade bed. I buried my nose in the sheets, into the smell of humans, fully the madwoman down from the attic, and said my dialogue: " 'It smells of sin!' What do you know about that? You know, it's *your* sin, honey. Yes, of course, it's mine too. But then, I've got so many on my conscience. Come on. Sit on our sin. A pretty nice sin, wasn't it?"

As my fellow actor began to grope me, rubbing his hands intimately over my body, the madwoman part of me stayed present, and when he began to choke me—truly lost in the task—the red rage of me pushed him away, while I jumped to my feet crying ragamuffin's tears, and the rock-solid piece of me said the required dialogue. All the pieces, the voices, the parts of me came together. Worked together. Lived for that moment... together.

Then the scene was over. Lee had not stopped us when our allotted fifteen minutes were up, like he had done with all the other scenes. Our *Respectful Prostitute* had taken forty-five minutes. As I had seen the other actors do after completing their work, I gathered my things and sat on the edge of the stage, not wanting to meet anyone's eyes. My partner pulled up a chair, took out a notepad and pen, then sat poised, ready to jot down important instructions and words of wisdom from Lee, while I sat with my legs crossed and my hands in my lap. Lee asked Paul what he had been working on and received a long explanation, which I didn't listen to because only then did I realize with a jolt that Lee would soon turn to me, asking the very same question, and I had no answer. I wasn't working on anything. And, sure enough, after commenting briefly and rather blandly to Paul, Lee turned and looked at me. But he didn't ask me what I'd been working on. He asked, "Why are you here?"

My heart stalled in my chest, and I braced myself to hear him say that I didn't belong, that I shouldn't be there.

"You work," he continued. "A lot of people here don't and you do. You're doing very well. Why are you here?"

"Because I want to be good," I said.

"You are good," he said. "Good enough to work all the time."

"Yes, I do work. But... not the way I want. I'm not good enough. I want to know how."

Never taking his eyes off mine, he sat back in his chair while making little clicking sounds, as though he had a popcorn kernel stuck in the back of his throat. After a moment that felt like an hour, he leaned forward and very softly said, "I let this scene continue. I wanted to watch you. You were quite brilliant."

My stalled heart would have exploded, but he spoke so softly I wasn't sure that's what he had said. He held my look, clicked the back of his throat, and repeated nonchalantly, "Quite brilliant."

Instantly the room became vacuum-packed, airless and still. No one moved. No one raised a hand to offer comments, as I had seen happen in the past. And my eyes, which had been fastened to Lee's, began to search the room for Madeleine.

11

Second Season

WHEN FILMING BEGAN on the *Nun*'s second season—leaving me with no time to attend classes—Lee's words became fuel, a verbal elixir I would drink over and over in my memory. At the Actors Studio, I felt inside my body. Without that space, without that kind of exploration, I lost the ability to hear parts of myself, as though half of me just vacated the premises. But on the edge of my brain I could still feel that one moment of coexistence, like an echo of harmonizing voices, and one day, after we'd been in production about a week, I surprised myself.

Except for the phone call in which I had initially passed on the show, I'd never had a real conversation with Harry Ackerman, the executive producer on both *Gidget* and *The Flying Nun*. I remember seeing him on the *Gidget* set once or twice and in the convent for short, infrequent visits that sent tense "Big Daddy's watching" ripples through the entire company. After a few moments of stiff chitchat, I would always find a reason to back away. But when production on the *Nun*'s second year started up, Mr. Ackerman invited me to lunch in the windowless, hard-to-find conference room known as the Executive Dining Room. It was an hour of forced smiling from me, of pushing the food around my plate while I counted the moments until I could leave. Then, as I was preparing to scurry back to the set, relieved to be finally free, I sat back down. Without knowing I was going to, I asked Harry if it might be possible to have one show written that season about an honest human problem, or even one scene every now and again, adding that it would give me something to look forward to. I hadn't rolled every word around in my head four thousand times, hadn't begged myself to speak. I just made a request, plain and simple. And when he replied, "That might be good for you, Sally; however, your audience doesn't want to be surprised or touched or taught or have to think too much," I silently nodded my head. Yet, as I walked back to Stage 2, I felt oddly triumphant. Without feeling blazing rage or fear or sadness, I had asked for what I wanted. Getting it seemed secondary.

I never told anyone in production about my dissatisfaction with the show and struggled hard to keep it from showing, except when I was with Baa. If she wasn't drunk, she was my sounding board, my pillow to scream into, patiently listening to my endless stream of frustrations. Since the first days of *Gidget* she was always advising me to get to know the camera, to make friends with it—which, instinctually, I had. Sometimes I felt more intimately connected with that mechanical device than with anything breathing on the set. But in that friendship, she warned me, I had better be careful of what I was feeling. She repeatedly drilled it into my head that if I was irritated or impatient or bored or just fed up with the work, the camera could and would see it, implying that those colors were unappealing and would paint me as unlikable. I scoffed at her advice, not because it wasn't right, but because it seemed as if she was telling me to erase my true feelings, to swallow them, to settle for what I had and never want more.

I have a little square snapshot of my mother taken around 1936, when she was fourteen or fifteen. She peers over the shoulder of an unnamed young man, with an open joyous laugh on her face and a spark in her eyes like a challenge to anyone who thinks they can stop her. She's alive and going to take a big bite out of life. Either that or a big bite out of the boy standing next to her, and maybe at that moment, they were one and the same.

Fifteen-year-old Baa with her infectious laugh.

It goes without saying that my mother's generation had a more confining set of boundaries dictating their behavior than the one I grew up in. And she had been a bit of a renegade in her way, had challenged those parameters, behavior that must have given the women of her family some worrisome, hand-wringing moments. Before taking the career opportunity that had landed in her lap, before earning a living in the foreign world of show business, she'd spent two years in a city college, and quietly knew so much about so many things. Certainly, literature: I could hardly name a book she hadn't read, and she remembered them all, could summarize the story and talk about the author's other works. She had read Freud and Jung, had seen a psychiatrist in the early fifties, could spout the theories of most of the important philosophers, studied art history on her own, practiced painting with oils all her life, was proficient in quilt making, knitting, and sewing. And when I tried to learn French in my early sixties, then foolishly attempted to speak to her using my shaky skills, she maddeningly filled in all the words I couldn't remember, using the correct and exact pronunciation.

What happened? Why was the confidence of her youth so ephemeral? Why is mine? As my mother approached the end of her life, I began to feel a frantic need to know more about her. I pestered and pushed, wanting her to reveal stories and secrets as if that would somehow answer the questions I had about myself, or would heal the wound between us, a wound that only I seemed to feel and pick at. One night she told me how much she had adored her father, loved being near him and felt proud to be the apple of his eye. But when Joy had found her sitting on his lap one day, she'd been furious, wordlessly accusing the little girl of trying to steal his affections. She told me that Joy had always been angry with her because of how much Baa and her father loved each other. It was because of that, my mother continued, that she couldn't be friends with women. Women always wanted to compete with her, she said, and she refused to compete, she wouldn't compete anywhere, and to some extent, that had ruined her career.

These tiny slivers of information didn't quite add up for me, and even though I was in my sixties when I heard this story, I couldn't yet use it to connect the dots, to connect the daughters. Baa finally ended the conversation by deadening her eyes and reporting that she never thought Joy had loved her, tossing it off by saying that it was a good thing. "How," I asked her, "could that possibly be a good thing?" And flatly she said, "Because I stopped looking for it. I just accepted it wasn't there and moved on." But I know that wasn't the truth. My mother had devotedly taken care of Joy during the last, difficult years of my grandmother's life, and I could see how much she loved her, how they loved each other through a barbed-wire fence. And all my mother's life, she ached to be loved. We all do. But Baa would lose herself in that ache. It became bigger than the rest of her, would eclipse her creativity, her love of words, her strength, and for a time, her children.

Tossed carelessly in a box of memorabilia—treated with disregard but kept all the same—I found a few disjointed pages of a journal that my mother had written when she was newly single and I was working on the *Nun*. After piecing it together, I read about one tiny, intimate encounter that happened when she'd been invited to a party in Malibu. At that gathering she met a writer whose work she respected, and like a young girl, she confesses that she was in awe of him, thrilled that he had talked to her as though she had something of value to say. Because of that, she admits to feeling nervous around him and says, "I had too much to drink," something she never would have admitted to me. When the two of them sat in the sand together, unseen in the dark, she writes, he kissed her.

I realize now that my mother at forty-six, and I at twenty-one, were separately feeling the same thing: alone.

When I was on the set every day with the people I worked with, I could be funny and capable, cocky with my position of leadership. But I had continued to push Steve away, so on the weekends if Princess wasn't with me, I'd pace back and forth in front of the big sliding glass door of my rented house like a caged tiger, longing to have friends and to meet people, but not knowing how. I wasn't writing in a journal at this time, disjointed or otherwise. But according to Aunt Gladys's scrapbooks, on Memorial Day 1968, Screen Gems put together a press junket that included actors from their current shows and journalists working for various publications. We were then sent, in one large group, to Mexico City for a weekend of sightseeing and nonstop interviews. I know from the September issues of *TV Radio Talk, Modern Screen,* and *TV Picture Life* that I was besieged with idiotic questions about dating Davy Jones, or was I secretly married to him or dating my co-star Alejandro Rey: nothing that was remotely true. Ultimately, I told them that I'd just met someone, that I'd gone out with him before I left to attend the junket, and that I was looking forward to seeing him again. His name was Jimmy Webb, and he was the young songwriter who had become an overnight sensation after composing such songs as "By the Time I Get to Phoenix," "Up, Up and Away," and "MacArthur Park." When they asked me how we met, I can read the same answer in each of the publications, which leads me to think it must be true: His press agent called my press agent to ask if I would accompany Mr. Webb to a composer's banquet. I don't remember having a press agent at the time, so maybe it was someone in the Screen Gems publicity department, and even though I have only a dim memory of attending a banquet, I obviously agreed to go. According to one story, when Jimmy called to say hello, I told him to be prepared because I was very shy. To that he replied, "Fine, we'll be shy together." I vaguely recall that tidbit, but only after reading it in the crumbling tabloids.

What I remember clearly is waiting for Jimmy to call after I returned from Mexico City. If I wasn't on the set working, then I was home waiting breathlessly, in proper girl fashion. He must have phoned me again, but if we ever went on an actual date somewhere, I don't recall.

I have only one clear memory of us being together. Crystal clear. I was in Jimmy's rented Hollywood house, about five miles from mine, sitting next to him on his piano stool while he played on and on. There I sat, beside that talented boy who was just as young and probably just as lonely as I was. We never spoke. I just sat there listening to him sing his songs as he smoked a joint filled with hash. I rarely smoked pot, which drained me of energy and not only reinforced my inability to speak but left me unable to remember what I wanted to say even if I *could*. And I had never smoked hash. At that moment I wanted to be someone I wasn't, someone Jimmy would like, so when he handed me the joint, I smoked it.

I don't know how long we sat there—it seemed like an eternity—but slowly the colors in the room got vibrant and bright, slightly fuzzy on the edges, and I started to feel disoriented. I stood up, asking for the bathroom, then wandered through his empty bedroom, trying to put one foot in front of the other. I found the room, locked the door, then sat down to pee—even though I wasn't sure I had to. Suddenly, everything began to tilt, and a black dot appeared in the center of my vision, like a flashbulb had just exploded. Feeling panicky, I curled up on the cold tile floor, wishing I could go home, and passed out. When I woke up, I couldn't remember where I was, had no idea how long I'd been facedown on the floor, and even worse, I couldn't feel my arms and legs, couldn't locate them on my body, couldn't locate my body. It seemed to take a massive amount of time to finally connect with my limbs, pull myself up, gather my wits enough to move out of the bathroom and into the bedroom, where I could lie down again, perhaps snap out of this horrifying condition. I felt like the child I once was, terrified in the night and afraid to call for help. Very softly, I called out for Jimmy to please come help me, then slid into darkness again. I don't know what signal he thought I was giving, or if he didn't need one, or if he was in the same half-conscious dreamlike state as I was (which quite possibly was the case) but when I woke again—an undetermined amount of time later—Jimmy was no longer singing but on top of me, grinding away to another melody. Even though I was barely conscious, thoughts rolled in my head: Maybe I had asked for this by lying on his bed, maybe I hadn't pulled my pants all the way up so what was he to think, maybe this meant he liked me. Then I couldn't think anymore.

I woke before it was light, gathered my things but couldn't find my shoes or my car, until I remembered that he had picked me up at my house so I had no car. With that realization, I walked home barefoot. The sun hadn't yet warmed the asphalt streets as my feet pounded down numbly, speaking the words my mouth couldn't, leaving the soles of my feet covered in a thick, solid blister.

When Steve appeared at my front door, slightly out of breath and almost instantly after he called asking if we could talk, I felt like smiling. Here was my best friend, my fingers-crossed, King's X spot in the world, standing in front of me. We'd been filming the second season for weeks and I hadn't seen him in all that time. Nor had I seen him during my hiatus, spent mostly at the Actors Studio. In reality, I hadn't seen him in almost a year, except for the few times I'd come home to find that he had broken into my house and was waiting, wanting to talk to me—something he did no matter how completely I tried to lock him out. This time he'd called.

Without any catching-up words or "how've you been" chatter, we moved directly into the living room to sit on my new green velvet couch, purchased at Bullock's department store, and looked at each other. Then, as if preparing to give me the results of a biopsy, he carefully told me that he'd met someone at a Sigma Chi party, that she was a wonderful person, and that he was going to marry her. All the blood went out of my body.

It was the last thing on earth I thought he was going to say, and in a state of stunned confusion I asked him, "Why?" over and over. It made no sense. He was going to school, living in a house with a bunch of other guys. Where was he going to

live with his new wife? How were they going to live? I didn't
know what made me more upset, the fact that he was going to
attach himself so completely to someone else, or that he was
forcing me to deal with something completely removed from
all the things I was actually dealing with. And no matter what
I said, no matter how logical I was, he kept repeating that he
wanted to get married and simply wanted me to know. "She
and I have discussed it; nothing's decided yet," he continued.
"But I told her I had to talk to you first and that's hard on her.
She's a little sensitive about you."

He then went on to tell me that, oddly enough, he was going
to marry the actress Screen Gems had hired to play the Flying
Nun after I'd originally turned the part down. Unbeknownst to
him when he met her, she was the same person who had shot for
two days on the pilot before being abruptly fired when I suddenly
changed my mind. As mind-boggling as that was, I could barely
hear him, much less register how Steve's new girlfriend must be
feeling now, knowing that he was in the midst of meeting with
me. I was rapidly flipping through all the stages of grief: disbelief,
then anger, then haggling, then sadness. Finally, after mindlessly
arguing back and forth, trying to convince him that this was a
ridiculous idea, that he hardly knew her, that he shouldn't be getting married at all, there was a long heavy silence before he said,
"Then you marry me. I may not know her very well, but I do
know you, and you know me. We belong together. Marry me."

I'd always kept the thought of Steve tucked safely in my
back pocket, like a return-trip ticket if I ever needed to go
home. I loved Steve, was comforted by his presence, and I was
waterlogged with loneliness. But I didn't want to get married. I needed away from his passions and emphatic opinions

No family photos of the trip, only a picture from a 1968 issue of TV Radio Mirror, *another fan magazine.*

that would send mine into hiding. Plus, there was a sliver of me that felt like he was breaking into my house again, determined to be in my life whether I wanted him there or not.

"Marry me, Sally, or I'll marry someone else."

When Jocko threatened that I might not work again if I didn't do *The Flying Nun,* I agreed to do the show not because I wanted to, but because I was afraid. When Steve told me that if I didn't marry him then he'd marry someone else, I accepted for the same reason. I was afraid.

*   *   *

The year before, I'd been the maid of honor at my friend Lynn's big fairy-tale church wedding—a memory I will always cherish. Everything was white lace and pink rosebuds, with a gaggle of bridesmaids covered in lavender tulle floating around, and Lynn's mother dressed head to toe in mauve satin, her eyes overflowing with tears. All of it an elaborate celebration of my friend's marriage to a man she'd met during her first year of college.

I've always loved ceremony and tradition (except birthday parties), but I never even considered planning some kind of wedding event. I felt uncomfortable, underplaying everything. Don't worry about an engagement ring. Who cares. It's no big deal. I wasn't feeling celebratory or excited about building a life with the man I loved, only glad that Steve would be waiting for me when I got home from work, and that was enough. I didn't even bother to tell my father or Joy about our decision. And even though my brother and Steve had always been best friends, I felt awkward when I called Rick, never expecting more from him than a distracted, half-hearted congratulations, which is what I got. Steve's relationship with Princess hadn't changed one bit over the past year—if anything they were closer. She had grown up with him in the family, so the idea of my marrying him didn't change a thing.

But nothing felt real until I told Baa. Her opinion was so important, affected my own so powerfully, that many times I was afraid to hear what she had to say, afraid that if she disagreed, I'd begin to equivocate on something I had felt certain about moments before.

I don't know why my voice turned into a defensive plea,

don't know why I felt embarrassed or ashamed or what the difference is between them. I only know I felt relieved after telling her of my decision and then tried to dismiss my disappointment when she reacted with understanding instead of joy. Did I want my mother to feel excited? Was I hoping she would make me feel something that I did not?

A few days later, I was sitting in my bubble of a dressing room waiting to be called to the set when I heard a soft knock on the door, followed by a sweet "May I come in?" Because she rarely visited the set, and never without a plan, an electric jolt of *oh no* ran through me. As Baa stepped into my cramped, overheated space she fumbled her words, instantly revealing to me that she was nervous, which made me nervous. Quickly scooping up the pile of stuff stacked on the worn upholstered chair, I stashed it on the floor, and as I was sitting back down on the equally worn love seat, she handed me a needlepoint kit she'd purchased. She was always getting me little gifts, poetry books or rose-scented hand cream, but needlepoint had become my secret weapon against the lure of the craft service table. After a moment of silence, she said, "I miss you, Sal."

"I miss you too," I answered, but suddenly wasn't sure if I did. Since Steve had been back in my life, my need for her had dissipated.

"Sally, listen. I don't want to butt into your life... but I'm your mother and I love you... and have to tell you what I feel... even if you don't want to hear it. I couldn't live with myself if I didn't. You can't marry Steve. You can't."

I felt smacked in the face. I'd made a decision, thought she'd agreed with me. I had felt comforted by her acceptance.

"How can you be saying this? You've known him since we were kids...you love him. What are you saying to me?"

"I'm sorry, Sal. But he's just not right for you."

"How do you know? How do you know what's right for me?"

"Because I just do. I know this makes you mad at me. I wish you wouldn't be...but I just have to tell you what I think."

"I don't want to hear what you think. I don't want to know."

"You can't marry him. I had to tell you."

If she had suggested that we wait awhile, that it wasn't the right time for me, for either of us to get married, I might have agreed, might have even felt relieved. But she was saying that Steve was not the right person, that after all these years she could see that he was not the man I should marry. Why? Was there something she knew about him that I didn't? Why wasn't she asking me about what I was feeling, about my loneliness? Why didn't I ask her to tell me precisely what was causing her to say this? I asked her nothing. I pushed away from her, filling in the blanks with my own answers as clearly as if I'd heard the words: She feared that if I married Steve I would no longer need her. She needed me to need her and I always had, turning to her instead of making friends, so ultimately I had no friends. She wanted my allegiance. But was that really the truth? Why didn't I ask any of this, ever? Neither of us ever asked the questions that needed to be asked.

I felt bewildered and betrayed by my mother.

Steve and I got married on September 16, 1968, in Las Vegas. No one from my family was there. No one I knew was there, except Steve. Ten days later the second season aired.

12

Peter

I KNEW HE WAS there before I actually knew. Even before I could register any changes in my body, I knew. I didn't try to be pregnant. Then again, I didn't try not to be pregnant. I just didn't think about it. Perhaps all thoughts of conceiving stayed locked in the attic along with everything else sexual or erotic, the part of me that stayed out of Steve's sight. Be that as it may, six months after driving to Las Vegas, then returning the next day as a married woman, just as filming on the second season was wrapping up, I realized that I was with child and everything changed.

It seemed as if I'd gone to sleep in a cave and woken up on a mountaintop with a view of the whole world. I felt honored, proud to be female, powerfully capable of miracles. But the thought of having to tell anyone at the studio, who would then inform the horrified network, made me feel protective not only of the baby but of myself. Or maybe, protective of the baby, and therefore myself. My soon-to-be baby was nobody's business but my own. I didn't want to hear their qualified words of congratulations said through clenched teeth or take the chance that I would sound apologetic or ashamed. Steve made all the appropriate calls, becoming a real partner as he alerted those who needed to know in a businesslike fashion, while I sat listening from a safe distance, feeling cared for. And after many calls back and forth, plus a few days of tearing their hair out, the producers came up with a plan. We would shorten our hiatus, go back into production earlier than planned, and—if the scripts could be written in time—we'd have almost the entire season in the can before mid-October, my ninth month. At that time, I'd be given maternity leave.

When Lucille Ball discovered she was pregnant in the midst of filming *I Love Lucy*, her condition was written into the series, creating a television event in 1953 when she gave birth to little Ricky on the show and Desi Arnaz Jr. in real life. When Elizabeth Montgomery found out she was expecting her second child, an entire season of *Bewitched* was developed around the impending arrival of the little witch, Tabitha. But sadly, there were no story lines that could be woven into *The Flying Nun* to accommodate my condition—at least not in 1969. Instead, I'd have to hide my nonimmaculate conception.

It helped that the habit I wore was already a shapeless sack, but when filming began on season three, the loose belt around my middle was no longer loose and soon became an elastic-backed, expandable item, growing as it moved higher and higher up my body with each episode. Before long, I started carrying bulky objects in every scene: a stack of books or a vase filled with flowers, flowers that went from daisies to gladiolus as my girth became more and more difficult to hide. Finally, there was nothing big enough I could carry, since a refrigerator was out of the question. From that point on, I had to be shot in close-ups.

Also, new methods of flying, without wires and that god-forsaken harness, had to be invented. Luckily the stunt person had been doing all the wider outside shots since halfway through the first year. It was only the closer ones where I was needed. But it couldn't have taken much thought to change the position of the camera and shoot me from below instead of straight on. I'd stand on a platform, then lean over the wide, specially built railing, and with the green screen behind and slightly above me, Sister Bertrille could be sent anywhere. A quicker, less torturous way to achieve the same half-assed illusions. Hallelujah.

And as that year moved along, hitting my marks while holding an armful of purposeless props, reciting meaningless dialogue—all the monotonous moments that for two years had made me feel powerless and trapped—became background noise to a larger symphony inside me. I didn't even care what I looked like, waddling around the lot dressed as a nun. If I hadn't been a walking sight gag before, I sure as hell was now.

One afternoon, when they were setting up a shot onstage, I went outside to get a glimpse of daylight and a 7UP from the vending machine. It must have been early October because I was so round my habit was getting tight. And as I walked duck-like down the wide ramp—counting change in my hand—I collided with a tall man walking up, deep in conversation with a heavyset woman. The coins flew in the air every which way, and when I heard the instantly recognizable voice say, "Oh my," I looked up into the face of Cary Grant. All I could say was "Oh God." Without missing a beat, he said,

"Oh God is right," then gestured toward my bulging midsection, adding, "Does he know about this, Sister?"

"Yes, sir."

"Good. Always important to keep him in the loop," he replied, then picked up all the coins, carefully placed them in the palm of my hand, flashed me that Grant grin, and walked on. I'll never forget it.

With Steve handling our finances, I purchased a home in Bel Air and for the fourth time in three and a half years, I moved. It wasn't a mansion behind iron gates, not like the houses that Bel Air is famous for, but a smaller one way at the top, past all the grand estates. I had no idea of its cost because I was still too frightened of money to look. I knew only that it was a small midcentury-style house situated in an area reminiscent of my first Tarzana neighborhood and *felt* like something I could afford. But unlike my childhood home, it was bright, with lots of glass and a view looking out on the Santa Monica Mountains. A perfect place to launch a new life.

And every piece of me felt him, a foot sliding down, an elbow poking out, and I'd want to shout, "WOW." I knew what side he preferred I sleep on and how he calmed with my touch. I rested when I was tired and ate when I was hungry because he needed me to. With my childhood soulmate at my side, and the constant assurance of the future pushing against my rib cage, I felt...contentment. And only now do I realize that that is what I felt.

Once, I woke in the night unable to get comfortable and fall back to sleep. I poked Steve in the side, then watched him shoot out of bed in a panic, thinking something was wrong.

But no, I just couldn't sleep. We got up and I perched on the kitchen stool watching him make banana pancakes, something I kept saying I didn't want. With a big tray of food between us, we sat in bed, watching an old black-and-white movie, and I know nothing will ever taste as good as that syrupy mess. Maybe it was hormonal, but I've had three children and it never felt quite like that again. Everything quieted in me and I let myself need someone, allowed myself to be dependent on this one person and never doubted that he would be there. Steve. I had that once in my life. Maybe that's enough.

Early on in this nine-month journey, I began having war dreams. Terrifying, hard to shake, Technicolor dreams that would invade my contentment, growing more intense with each visit. In the dream there was always a war; that much stayed the same. It was the enemy that varied; either the Germans, or the Japanese, or the Mongols wearing pointed helmets and riding massive black horses. I was always separated from my family—not sure who, other than Steve—and desperately trying to find them, when I'd hear the bombs beginning to fall off in the distance (though how the Mongols had bombs I cannot tell you). At first, the battles were very far away, but with each dream the enemy got closer, until finally I could actually see their faces. I'd be lost, alone and watching their approach, frantically looking for a place to hide.

One night in late October, I dreamed that the battle was on top of me, with the German soldiers so close I could see their uniforms, hear their voices speaking a foreign language. Feeling trapped, I quickly scurried under a bush and held my breath as I watched their boots step up to the shrub while they stood over me talking. And then the unthinkable happened. They caught me, pulled me out of my hiding place, shoved me along the path, then raised their rifles and shot me. I remember thinking, *Oh my God, I'm going to die*. As I started to fall, the action began to slow, and while moving in slow motion, I thought, *Boy, oh boy, this is good. They're really going to love this*. A feeling of accomplishment bubbled up and when I smashed face-first into the dirt, everyone applauded. It was a scene. I'd been acting. It was self-imposed fear and not really happening. I woke not terrified but triumphant, and acting had somehow been a part of it. A feeling of strength, of solidly standing on my own two feet, stayed with me for days, even into the following week.

At two thirty in the morning on November 10, 1969, one week before the baby's projected due date and four days after my twenty-third birthday, I woke with an unmistakable yank from deep inside, accompanied by a massive cramp in the small of my back. I'd learned about Braxton-Hicks contractions, had grown used to the tight knotted-up feeling of my body rehearsing for its opening night, and with this one sharp tug, I knew rehearsals were over. The show was about to begin.

But if this was opening night, I had no idea how to play my part, didn't have a clear picture in my head of what my body was going to be doing—or how. Birth training didn't exist at that time and the only thing I'd learned, wandering around the maternity ward for an hour with the other expectant parents, was where to park, how to sign in, and what to bring. I wanted to be prepared, so I did the only thing I knew to do: I packed and repacked all the items listed on the brochure we had been given, and that was it. It's not that I wasn't nervous or curious, but the only book I could find was one written by Dr. Spock, explaining what to do with the baby after he arrived. It supplied zero information about how the little creature was going to get out in the first place.

Steve and I played our parts perfectly. We parked in the right spot, we reported to the proper desk to alert the hospital staff of our arrival, and after that I became a prop in the production. First, I was examined by a young resident who confirmed I was truly in labor, then handed to an intensely friendly nurse who said with a sweet smile, "I have to give you a little enema." She then proceeded to hang what looked like a Sparkletts water bottle over me, which—to my way of thinking—was *not* a little enema. After dressing me in a white gown, putting me in a white bed, and covering me with a white sheet, she exited stage left. I went through the various stages of labor alone and clueless, waiting for the periodic visits from either the nurse or—the true star of the show—the doctor. And since I had nothing to guide me but instinct, as the process became more intense, I began rolling from side to side, chanting loudly, putting myself into a hypnotic trance as if I were a Native American preparing to go into battle. I don't remember seeing Steve after I left him signing papers at the admissions desk, though he may have come in while I was preparing for war.

Finally, my long-lost obstetrician appeared. Jesus, where'd he been? He examined me and determined that my wonderful little bundle—who turned out to weigh eight pounds, four ounces and possessed an enormous head—was facing the wrong way. Not breech, with his feet where his head should be, but with his face turned up and not down. So, without one word, my fatherly doctor reached inside me and flipped the little fellow...over! How was that even possible? And finally, after enduring my first labor experience alone with little comforting and no medication—at least none that I was aware of—I was automatically given a spinal block. Not an epidural, as they use today, but a total block, as if I were having both legs amputated. This was the standard treatment in 1969 before the widespread use of Lamaze or natural childbirth, and before the blessed women's movement came along to break down the doors, demanding that changes be made to this demoralizing, choiceless way of doing things.

After the sensory signals from the lower half of my body had been disconnected, the pain stopped, my chanting stopped, and all feeling came to an abrupt halt. I was then rolled down a bright hallway, through swinging doors, and found myself looking up at the even brighter operating/delivery room lights. A new nurse, with a mask over her face, took one of my arms, pulled it away from my midsection—where I'd been massaging both mother and child—and strapped it to the table where I'd been transferred. She then repeated the process with the other arm. When my legs were placed into the chrome stirrups, she continued with the lockdown procedure by wrapping the two wide straps waiting there around each of my legs. "We don't want you to move around or touch yourself," she cooed. Surely I'd taken a wrong turn and accidentally entered a scene from *A Clockwork Orange*.

While I lay there, totally numb from the waist down and bolted to the lightly padded table, they casually talked amongst themselves, never to me, and when the doctor nodded to the masked nurse standing at my side, she began pushing hard on my mountain of a stomach. Every time the signal was given, this large woman started shoving with her hands, using all her weight, huffing and puffing as if she were the one giving birth. Suddenly something changed—who knew what, 'cause I couldn't feel anything. There was a moment of bustle, of masked people changing positions, moving quickly this way and that, until miraculously... there he was. My son. Peter.

The nurse held him at my side so I could lift my head to see his beautiful face—which at that moment looked like a pissed-off Inuit, apropos of my chanting, I assume. I reflexively started to reach for him, but quickly realized I was tied down. *For God's sake, people! Let me touch my baby!* "We're going to clean him up and get him all ready for his new life." I desperately wanted to reply, *Cram it up your ass. Give me my SON!!!* But no, I didn't say any of that. I let my head flop back down on the chrome table and closed my eyes.

Two days later, my breasts had become painfully engorged, either because that's the way my body works or because I was not allowed to nurse Peter except at four-hour intervals. If he got hungry in between, he was given a bottle containing water. Besides that, he had been kept in the nursery, away from me altogether for the first night, so maybe my body didn't know what the hell was happening or how on earth to adjust to it. *I* definitely didn't know what was happening or how to adjust to it.

I did know that to be released from the hospital, I had to be able to urinate, but the thought of that was not a happy one—although having a tube stuck into my bladder was not a cheerful image either. When I finally did pee, blissfully alone without a smiling nurse standing over me, I thought my

insides were falling out until I realized that what was pushing against my episiotomy stitches was not a vital organ, but a piece of surgical sponge that had been left inside me. Oops.

Finally, with my boobs packed in ice and my ass on a pillow, I sat in the back next to the baby's new car seat while Steve slowly drove us home. From then on and forever after, Peter and I would figure it out together. We would teach each other. What I didn't understand, he instinctually knew. To this day, that remains the same.

During the fourteen months since Steve and I first married, Baa had quietly hovered, worrying that I was still feeling estranged from her and not wanting to step in uninvited. She'd been working, not as an actress but as a part-time florist, learning to make festive chrysanthemum and bird-of-paradise arrangements, and while I had gestated my way through *The Flying Nun*'s third season, she hadn't been around much. But I can still see her in my mind, standing in the hospital room doorway as soon as I was out of recovery, holding her jacket closed with one hand and a bunch of flowers in the other. She stood there, not moving, until slowly we began to smile at each other. "I've been here all night," she said softly, and as I attempted to sit up for the first time, she started to cry, whispering, "Oh, Sal." Then when Peter and I were at home, away from any other supervision, I'd hear her tiptoe in through the back door every day, and feel myself exhale, letting out the breath I didn't know I'd been holding. She'd then sit on the living room sofa with her knitting, waiting to see if I needed a break. I usually did. Gratefully, I'd hand the baby to her and watch. Never spouting singsong nonsense, she'd look in his eyes and actually talk to him; telling him about her day, wondering how his was, what he had conquered so early in life? She'd walk him around the room, then eventually move outside, all the time explaining things: a leaf, a bird, details of what and why they were. I felt in awe of her, wondering if she'd been like that with me or if I was watching her become something new. Just as I was becoming something new.

I know Steve was feeling the pressure of having a son, feeling he needed to be the kind of man his child would be proud of, and at the same time feeling the absence of his own father, this man's inconceivable abandonment of him. In the twenty-four years of Steve's life, his father had never even sent him a birthday card—not that a card would have cut it. With new urgency, Steve started exploring places to put his focus. He was good at hard physical labor, building and construction, gardening and landscaping, was instinctually gifted in these areas. When we'd first moved in, Steve had completely changed the master bedroom, had knocked out walls, enlarged the master bath to include two walk-in closets. But he refused to follow the rules, so if permits or inspections were required—and they usually were—he couldn't be bothered. (God knows what happened when we sold this house and the new owners asked for an inspection, along with all the appropriate paperwork, because there wasn't any.) Next, he decided to set up a darkroom in the pseudo-poolhouse hidden in the backyard. He bought all the equipment, plus stacks of books, and began teaching himself about photography. Maybe this was it. Step by step, he could learn to become a photographer. Except he suddenly became enthralled with the idea of going back to USC to get an MFA in theater arts, focusing primarily on writing, an arena where he also had talent. And he was completely dedicated to that for a while, until that energetic burst of enthusiasm faded and he began to lose interest, as though everything he did was only a hobby. Maybe he didn't feel a pressing need to get out into the big bad world as long as I was making money. And in that way, our marriage hurt him. I wish I could have seen that at the time.

What was his role in the family, then? Steve was always an attentive, loving father, spending time with Peter, sharing in the everyday tasks, but the idea that he would stay home and take care of the baby when I returned to work never seemed to be on the table, and neither of us ever tried to put it there. Maybe it was the era, or maybe it was my own blind distrust

I'm calling from the set to check on Peter. Called a hundred times a day.

of men. I'd never been around a father-and-child relationship, not a good one anyway, so I'd never seen a man interact with his baby boy. I'd try to stand back, to observe as Steve would throw him higher and higher in the air, watch as Peter—not quite laughing—would take a deep startled breath with each toss. Many times, Steve would toss him too high, hitting the baby's head on the ceiling, or catch him painfully by an arm or a leg when he came back down. I'm sure every mother has stood on the sidelines, trying to allow the male relationship to be different from that of the female. But I began to hear a hint of mockery in Steve's laugh when Peter would start to cry, a wordless challenge that chilled my heart, and I'd instantly grab the little boy, often frightening Peter more than his bump on the head. Maybe it was uncalled for, maybe I was overreacting to something I saw through the eyes of my childhood. I don't know.

As each day passed, the inevitability of my having to resume the show was growing, like the Mongols from my dream riding closer and closer. Only a handful of episodes were left to shoot and the chances of the show being picked up for a fourth year were slim—which I couldn't help but feel was my fault. I'd never actually rebelled against anything except my bangs. As a result, a tiny strip of fake hair had been stitched to my hat, meaning that Sister Bertrille had bangs and I didn't. Where I was guilty—and consciously didn't care—was in the publicity department. When the studio began to obliquely imply that if I didn't agree to do more, they'd be forced to take my car, the blue prima donna, away from me, I thought, *Merciful heavens, please don't frow me in dat dere briar patch.*

Nevertheless, my two months of leave would soon be over and I'd have to return to work. How would that be possible? How could I ever leave Peter? I began to understand how painful it is—and always would be—to turn and walk away, even if it's just for the day. And yet, when I was out the door, back into my life without him, how relieved I'd feel to be free, my own person again. And still, how I'd ache to be back. A totally new and different kind of emotional pickle.

One afternoon, I was sitting on the living room rug watching Peter frolicking on a patchwork baby blanket before me, kicking his newly found feet in the air. Baa was sitting on the stone hearth across the room, leaning over her legs, watching both of us. Without thinking, I asked if she would consider

Baa and Peter.

quitting her job to help me. Only after I heard it come out of my mouth did I know how much I wanted it.

"If you do that, Baa, I'll always take care of you. I can't do this without you. I'm afraid to leave him with anyone...and it hurts me."

"I know," she said.

"But it wouldn't hurt as badly if I could leave him with you. Please, Mother, will you help me?" I remember thinking how strange, almost embarrassing: I had actually called her "Mother."

Without hesitation and in a deeper tone than her usual light register, she replied, "Always, Sal. For as long as you need."

So, for me, and for the love of Peter, Baa quit drinking...ish. And moved back into the center of my life.

PART THREE

I yearn for my work, because it always helps me make sense of things. For never was a horror experienced without an angel stepping in from the opposite direction to witness it with me.

—Rainer Maria Rilke, letter
to Marianne Mitford

He allowed himself to be swayed by his conviction that human beings are not born once and for all on the day their mothers give birth to them, but that life obliges them over and over again to give birth to themselves.

—Gabriel García Márquez,
Love in the Time of Cholera

13

Transition

THREE MONTHS AFTER wrapping the third and final season of *The Flying Nun*, I was a thin, determined twenty-three-year-old woman with an eight-month-old son. I owned a house in Bel Air, supported a husband in college, wore a Joan of Arc haircut, and had changed so radically it's hard to look back and see myself as the same person.

For sure, my restless generation was pushing me to rethink everything I had always accepted as "the way things are." Betty Friedan's book *The Feminine Mystique* had begun to trickle into my awareness. And I eventually heard the challenges from Germaine Greer in *The Female Eunuch*, inviting women to own their bodies, to examine that mysterious part of themselves by holding a mirror between their legs, to taste their menstrual blood and, most important, to be outraged. But because I could never make myself crack open the books, it felt like a conversation I could hear from down the hall, like I was eavesdropping and never actually in the room.

Much of the change in me had to do with my constant

participation at the Actors Studio and the secure place it gave me to experiment with myself. No longer an observer, I had been accepted as a member after doing a scene with Madeleine from *A Taste of Honey* by Shelagh Delaney. Unfortunately, Mr. Strasberg had returned to New York for the winter and wasn't sitting in his familiar front-row chair for my audition. Instead I performed for a group of longstanding alumni, which included Bruce Dern—who was frequently the moderator in Lee's absence and for whose focus and support of me I will always be grateful. Ultimately, I was given a lifetime membership. I was in the club.

And then there was Peter: this tiny creature with huge brown eyes, who lit up when I walked into the room, who

With my new haircut and my growing son. Onward.

reached for me when he was afraid, and who was soothed and comforted by my presence. And in return, I was comforted by him. His existence in my life enabled me to shut the door on the outside world, to be home without feeling lonely. As I took care of him—my all-consuming responsibility—I felt as though I were in command, becoming the more capable, confident part of myself, putting sadness in the back seat and consciously steering away from feeling helpless or powerless, as though I had a choice of what road to travel. With both hands on the wheel, I headed directly toward what I wanted, and what I wanted was as clear as a full moon peeking over the dark horizon: to be an actor, to have the chance to explore where that took me, what places it would push me, lead me, teach me. If I was not given that opportunity, it had to be because I wasn't ready, that the power to change everything rested in me. Like my stepfather, the industry had decided that it knew who I was, threatening me with failure and the ability to cut off the lifeline I had to myself: acting. But if I could take care of Peter, I could take care of me. If I failed to get a role, let it be because I wasn't skilled enough or talented enough or because another actress's interpretation was better; I could fix that. What seemed a harder path to find was how to be given the opportunity to fail when my name never appeared on anyone's list, when I was systematically dismissed, when no one wanted it to be said that the Flying Nun had been cast in their film.

I Never Promised You a Rose Garden is the story of a mentally ill young woman trapped in a make-believe world created as a defense against her frightening childhood, and when I read the book in March of 1970, I desperately wanted a

chance to play the lead. So when I wasn't allowed the opportunity to audition, or even to enter the room for a meeting,
I took a monologue straight from the book and decided to
make my own screen test. Steve operated a rented camera;
Lou Antonio—my friend from the Actors Studio—was the
director; and another Studio member, Lane Bradbury—Lou's
very talented wife—was our crew. I then sent the footage to
Al Wasserman, the New York–based producer affiliated with
the project. And the letter I received on April 1, 1970—April
Fool's Day—I still have. Mr. Wasserman writes, "In doing the
test I can see you ran into the dilemma that is going to face us
during the filming (perhaps even more so, because of the short
duration of a test and the need for immediate impact), how to
avoid a sameness of performance in playing a character who
is 'stone-faced' during most of the story; and, on the other
hand, how to avoid indulging in emotional pyrotechnics that
are not rooted in the truth of the character or the moment.
Quite understandably, I think, you erred on the latter side.
The director and I screened the test several times in order to
make sure we were isolating performance from conception,
and we both agreed that you handled individual moments
and a range of emotions extremely well. However, as I'm sure
you know, we were already well advanced in our negotiations
for the part. Your test would have had to carry extraordinary
impact—and this, I'm afraid it did not do..."

I have to say—mostly because I'm a spiteful little twit—
that for whatever advanced negotiations they were deeply
into, the film was not actually produced until 1977, and the
name Al Wasserman does not appear anywhere on the credits.
So there!

This is not to say that I didn't still have some opportunities. Though the motion picture industry wanted nothing to do with me, television was still interested, offering me several TV films. In the early 1970s, original movies made to be viewed on television seemed like a brand-new concept, but they had probably been inspired by *Playhouse 90*, *Schlitz Playhouse*, and all the live shows of the fifties and early sixties, shows where my mother had spent much of her career.

My first—an ABC Movie of the Week airing in February 1971—was probably the best of the lot. With a title song sung by newcomer Linda Ronstadt, *Maybe I'll Come Home in the Spring* was directed by Joseph Sargent from a screenplay written by Bruce Feldman (though Steven Spielberg told me years later that he had written the original draft). It attempted to look at the runaways of my generation, the young people who needed to escape the confinement of their families by vanishing into the world of hippies, only to find that coming home again—if they ever did—was not easy. Obviously, this wasn't something I had experienced in my own life, but I did understand inarticulate, dysfunctional families and, saints be praised, I wasn't playing a nun.

Happily, Lane Bradbury—who had helped me with my homemade test—played my younger sister, and since she'd been a member of the Studio much longer than I, we could confide in each other about the work. Playing my troublesome mother was the beautiful Eleanor Parker, who was at the tail end of a wonderful career and to me, she was fascinating. Never in my short time as an actor had I worked with anyone so frantic for control. Every time a scene required us to hug—which for some reason happened a lot—she would automatically turn my face away from the camera, making sure the only things on display were her glowing, tear-rimmed eyes and the back of my head. But Lee had always said, "The best acting is no acting at all," and since the mother and daughter had a contentious relationship in the text and I didn't feel exactly bonded with Eleanor, I "used it." As I watched this actress—who had been extremely successful by anyone's definition—I realized that she was a cautionary tale for me, a blinking hazard sign. True, she came from a different era of acting, and that was part of it, but as I sat quietly in a corner, observing how she worked, I realized that I never wanted to get to the point where showing my face on camera at just the right angle was more important than the work itself. This work that I was just now trying to understand.

David Carradine, who played my hippie boyfriend, wore a pair of suede bell-bottom pants that laced in the front, which was fine except that the panel of fabric usually placed behind the laces—like the tongue of a shoe—was missing, and because David wore no underwear, it allowed pubic hair and a great deal of the penis nestled there to be on constant display. But since that seemed to be his only costume in the show, the novelty of that eventually dwindled, and the more hypnotic thing became the forgotten food piling up in his capped teeth. I didn't much like kissing him, but he was easy to work with and right for the role, so what's a little visible gum disease between fellow performers?

To round out the colorful cast was the actor who played my father, Jackie Cooper. Yes, the man who had been an important executive at the studio where I had spent my entire career—all five years—had left his job at Screen Gems, gone back into acting, and was now playing my father. I met him face-to-face as an actor, seeing him for the first time through different eyes. In reality, he was a kind, gentle man, not to mention a good actor with a storybook body of work.

Right before *Maybe I'll Come Home in the Spring* aired, and just after I'd wrapped another TV film—this one about a newly married young couple, aptly called *Marriage: Year One*—Cecil Smith wrote in his *Los Angeles Times* column: "It's doubtful any two films have caused more stir here, partly, I think, out of curiosity about what Sally Field is doing in them. Both are highly complex dramatic roles, demanding the sort of acting resources that Sally never demonstrated flying out of that convent in Puerto Rico." Mr. Smith went on to say, "Strange, that the production company of *Marriage: Year One*, Universal Studios, swarms with fine young contract players, highly skilled in drama like Carrie Snodgress, Katharine Ross, Belinda Montgomery, Tisha Sterling, Pam McMyler and yet Sally was brought in from the outside."

Well okay, fine. But in the *Hollywood Reporter*'s review of *Maybe I'll Come Home in the Spring*—which I've only now read, forty-seven years after it was originally printed—John Goff calls it ABC-TV's most intriguing Movie of the Week and says it ranks highest largely because of a radical departure in performing material by its star. "Field, with Sargent's almost delicate direction, shows that she can handle a serious role as well as light comedy. She simply needs more experience at it. With this as evidence she should have no trouble getting it." Ha.

Marriage: Year One and *Hitched*—another NBC movie I made that year—were both two hours of uninspired viewing, as was a third film called *Mongo's Back in Town*. And just in case you're wondering, I wasn't Mongo. I was his girlfriend, basically a generic supporting role to Joe Don Baker's lead. The only interesting thing about *Mongo's Back* was that the cast included young Martin Sheen, also in a generic supporting role, and Telly Savalas, whose character was not unlike the one he played two years later in his *Kojak* series.

After a year and a half, what little cachet I might have had coming off my back-to-back television series was slipping away. I could feel it in my bones. I was repeating the same pattern my mother and stepfather had before me, working but going nowhere. Soon I'd be relegated to a guest spot here and there, to being a supporting player on TV shows I didn't know or like, and then what? Game shows? That was a horrifying thought. How would I make a living?

And Steve was still no closer to entering the workplace. He had written and directed a very good short play presented at USC during an evening of student one-acts, and even though he was fired up and engaged during his first semester of a two-year MFA program, he never wrote another play, never wrote a screenplay or produced another project at USC. He talked about wanting to be a writer, to pursue writing as a career, but he didn't push it anywhere, never explored options, and relied on me to bring home the bacon... and the eggs.

Then Steve's number came up. The draft lottery had gone into play in 1969, at which time he'd received a student deferment, but when Peter was not quite two years old, Steve got his notice to report for a physical the following month. And that news presented the possibility of being sent to Vietnam. With Peter on my hip and my heart in my throat, I stood stone still in the living room while Steve read the order again and again. What could we do? There had never been a patriotic, "fight for your country" feeling connected with the war in Vietnam, and by 1971, only a year after protesting students were gunned down at Kent State, angry demonstrations were happening everywhere. Proudly marching off to potentially lose your life in Southeast Asia was not high on anyone's to-do list. (But as I write this, I'm flooded with great sadness and respect for the thousands and thousands of young men my age who did just that.)

There was always the chance that when called, you might be rejected from serving for legitimate reasons, even if perhaps those reasons had to be embellished just a little. Steve had been a juvenile delinquent, was arrested several times, and spent a year in a facility for troubled children: These issues were real. Therefore, he requested and received a letter from a psychologist he'd been seeing off and on since he was a teenager. The letter stated that Steven Craig Bloomfield was mentally unstable and unsuitable for the armed services. Though I knew Steve was complicated, I did hope that the doctor was doing him a favor and exaggerating.

Each morning we woke feeling a little more anxious than the day before, until suddenly, out of the blue, two weeks before the designated day, Steve decided he needed to find his father, whom he only vaguely remembered. He had never reached out to him, hardly ever mentioned him, but after somehow discovering the man was still living in Fargo, North Dakota, Steve turned into a young Telemachus and off he went, in search of his long-lost father.

He had been gone only a day or two when Princess called to tell me that Jocko wanted to meet my son. Not quite eighteen, my sister had been working in a clothes store in Sherman Oaks, living sometimes with Baa, sometimes with whatever boyfriend she had, and sometimes with me. At one point we even tried to turn my garage into an apartment for her, but no amount of scrubbing could change the fact that it was a raw-walled concrete slab with a washer and dryer in one corner and an electric door that opened erratically and without provocation.

I hadn't seen or talked to my stepfather in a very long time, not since he walked out of his marriage with my mother, and the thought of being in the same room with him again made my stomach flip over. But Princess sounded thrilled, excited to include the fact that Jocko wanted me to meet Autumn, the woman he had waltzed away with more than two years before, then married directly after divorcing my mother. And I mean directly—doubt the ink on the documents had dried.

I was not looking forward to any of it, and when I heard the putt-putt of Princess's old Volkswagen bug (a hand-me-down from Steve, who had since purchased a motorcycle) I felt deeply relieved, knowing that we would have an hour together before Jocko's expected arrival. As we paced around the living room, my sister recounted her time with the happy couple, having nothing but glowing words about her new stepmother and acting slightly giddy about the whole thing. So much so that when he finally swaggered through the front door, Princess was awash in pure, loving approval. With a Cheshire Cat grin, Jocko introduced me to his wife, while I held Peter tight on my hip like a child hugging her doll, comforted by his clinging.

In one little group, we slid from room to room while I gave

them a quick house tour, Jocko walking with his arm slung around Princess's neck the whole time. Then, awkwardly, he and Autumn (whose name is actually Patricia) sat down with a sigh on the green sofa, and suddenly I felt ill. Autumn looked so frantically eager, like a golden retriever waiting for her stick to be tossed. Pale blond and angular, with a greasy shine to her face, she sat on the edge of the cushion, inching closer to my adjacent chair, focusing on Peter, who would have nothing to do with her. The new Mrs. O'Mahoney oozed warmth, talking of how much she wanted me to meet my new brothers and sisters—her children. I clenched my jaw and nodded, adjusting Peter's bent leg on my lap. After what seemed like a lifetime, Autumn asked Princess to show her the view from outside, and reached her arms out to Peter, wiggling her pearlized fingernails in his face as if that would seduce him to reach for her. Thank the good sweet Lord, he did not. So, empty-handed, she turned and walked out the glass door toward the backyard with my sister leading the way, leaving me with Jocko.

What on earth did this man and I have to say to each other? In reality, one hell of a lot, but that would never happen. Maybe it would if I could meet him today, with the sturdy legs of my history holding me up, but not when I was twenty-four with my baby son on my lap. Jocko chatted on, telling me how they were going to Hawaii to live on a bird sanctuary, and then, as casually as if he were requesting a glass of water, he asked if he could borrow $5,000. I thought, *Crap, didn't I play this scene before?* But when I noticed that his hands were shaking, I quickly looked away, embarrassed for him, not wanting him to know that I had seen. His voice got louder as I left the room, guffawing at nothing while I sat down on my bed and filled out a check: Pay to the order of Jock O'Mahoney. When he and his new wife said their goodbyes, waving from their white station wagon as it pulled into the street, I held a drowsy Peter on the edge of my hip, closed the door to the entrance garden, then leaned into the bushes and vomited. I was pregnant again.

Steve and I stood in the kitchen the morning he was to appear for his draft physical, whispering to each other in the predawn darkness, making sure he had everything he needed. He was

Pregnant again as two-year-old Peter hangs on.

still exhausted and numb from his trip to North Dakota, still wondering if he should have found a way to tell his father that he was coming. The man had tried to act pleased, glad to finally meet his son, but during the few hours Steve was with him, he had felt an unmistakable "get lost" vibration. So that's what he did. He came home to his own son, played with our little boy, and didn't have much to say about the man who had turned his back on him again and forever. He couldn't erase him from his mind, so he did the next best thing: He legally dropped the name Bloomfield and became Steven Craig. No more, no less.

That morning I had packed him a few things to eat, including three of the brownies I'd made the night before. Just as Steve had requested, they were gooey, were filled with tiny bits of walnuts and a shitload of marijuana. He walked out the door with his birth certificate, the doctor's letter, and his brown paper bag.

There were no cell phones in those days, meaning I couldn't hear from him unless he went to a pay phone, and even though I never expected him to call, as the hours ticked by and morning turned into late afternoon, I desperately wanted to know what was happening. When he finally walked through the door, I was sitting on the living room floor next to a playpen stuffed with toys and a toddler who wanted out. Both Peter and I stood up as Steve—looking frighteningly pale, his eyes red and nearly swollen closed—sank slowly onto the foyer floor, put his head in his hands, and sobbed. Maybe it was the brownies he had eaten or the growing fear of being drafted or the bitter blow of his father's cold shoulder, or maybe it was being sent to military school when he was four, or spending a year in an institution where there was no one to relate to—or maybe it was everything bubbling up all at once. But when he'd handed the psychologist's letter to the sergeant at the desk, even before the examination began, Steve started to cry, violently. Eventually, someone had to walk him outside and sit with him on the front steps. Even then he couldn't stop crying, sobbing and sobbing, unable to speak for hour after hour. By the end of the day, he was officially stamped 4-F and allowed to go home.

I put him to bed, made him drink some water, pushed him to eat some soup, while I kept telling him he was home, he had a family who loved him, no one was going to send him away. He was safe, he was safe. And he went to sleep.

Steve's flirtation with drugs, which had begun with pot in the midsixties, was now becoming a slightly more serious relationship, and it bothered me. I remember lying underneath Peter's crib, listening to the rattle of the toddler's breathing and the rumble of Steve's friends milling about in the other rooms of the house. Some of the guests I knew, others I didn't, and all had been invited that night to drop acid, along with a mix of other drugs, I suspected. But since I was frightened of hallucinogenics, or any chemical that might trap me in my head, plus the fact that I was newly pregnant, I felt comfortable sleeping under my asthmatic two-year-old, listening to him breathe, feeling the butterfly-like movements of the new baby.

Two things made this pregnancy different from my first: I wasn't working all day, every day—although taking care of a toddler is its own kind of twenty-four-hour-a-day job. And Lamaze, or natural childbirth, had appeared on the scene, offering classes for expectant mothers and their partners to learn about the birthing process, along with techniques for handling the pain. I didn't want to be placed in a room alone and clueless again, so six weeks before my calculated due date, I gathered a notebook, a pillow, a stopwatch, and Steve, and off we went to learn about visualization, breathing, and relaxation, about listening to the body and letting go. Tools I've used all the rest of my life, though how much I used during the actual birth, I'm not really sure.

My teacher was the soon-to-be-famous Femmy DeLyser, who in 1982 joined Jane Fonda in her book and video *Pregnancy, Birth and Recovery*. The Dutch-born maternity nurse and childbirth expert was part of the newly formed Lamaze International and in 1972, when I met her, she had just started teaching night classes at the old Cedars of Lebanon Hospital on Fountain Avenue in the middle of Hollywood. She lovingly explained the three stages of labor and how to recognize each of them, the last being transition. Hitting that final stage of labor, she laughingly told us, we might start demanding that everyone back off or become overwhelmingly irritated with a "let's call the whole thing off" feeling.

Like the good student I never was, I practiced the breathing techniques every night. Knowing now that most contractions lasted only a minute, Steve would start the stopwatch, then call out the passing seconds, which allowed me to know how much longer I had, and at the same time he'd pinch my leg as hard as he could in an effort to provide pain for me to breathe through (though the pain of him gripping my thigh and that of my cervix yawning open are not on the same Richter scale). But with whatever pain level we did or didn't replicate, eventually we were a well-rehearsed team and ready to take the act on the road.

At three thirty in the morning on May 25, 1972—one week before the due date and shortly after I'd been stabbed awake by a bright, unmistakable feeling—I stood in my mostly darkened bedroom before the full-length mirror with my nightgown held up. As the first contractions began, I could see the miraculous movement of the baby inside, shifting down toward his new life. Femmy had told us that Lamaze was still rather controversial in most American hospitals, that the staff might not easily cooperate, much less participate, so it was best that we wait at home, away from the hospital's rules, until signs of the second stage of labor had begun. She also coached us that once we were in the hospital we should repeat to everyone constantly, "I'm Lamaze. I'm Lamaze." I had it all in my head while I stood there, marveling at the process, feeling totally in control, not a single piece of me afraid—though I'd begun to notice that the contractions were intensifying.

Steve had gone to wake Baa, who'd been staying in the tiny guest room for just this reason, while I took my time dressing. I moved nonchalantly, making sure we had everything, including a collage I'd made of fabrics and ribbons, pictures of Peter, and a poem Steve had written to me when we were kids, the focal point that Femmy instructed us to have. I could smell coffee brewing in the kitchen as Baa stood in the doorway with a nervous smile, and when I finally started to walk out the front door, I felt the next contraction beginning to build. My disciplined, rhythmic panting abruptly stopped. I slid to the floor as if I'd been shoved and immediately got angry at Steve, saying, "I don't want to do this anymore."

When this monstrous wave of a contraction slowly began to pass, we looked at each other: I was in transition. How could that be? This was too quick; the house was a good forty minutes from the hospital. But forty minutes was not very long, surely I could do that. Our leisurely pace cranked into double time, but no sooner had I pulled my bulk into the car than I yelled out as if sighting Moby Dick rising to the surface, "...Here it comes!" Steve started both the car and the stopwatch, keeping track of the seconds and the winding road at the same time. "Ten seconds," he called. "Twenty...thirty..."

And at that, my breath suddenly caught, forcing me to grunt out a barely audible "I've got to push."

"No," Steve firmly shot back. "No. Blow...blow. Don't push."

While riding in a car that seemed to have Mr. Toad at the wheel—flying down Bel Air Road and onto Sunset Boulevard—I planted my feet on the windshield and rose up out of the seat like some levitating demon, all the time forcing air out of my already airless lungs. If the contractions ever diminished I was not aware. It seemed they came faster and faster, tumbling over each other, while the intensity sent me climbing higher and higher on the windshield. I remembered Femmy saying, "If ever it becomes impossible to keep yourself from pushing, allow your body to push just the tiniest bit with each release of the forced breath. Don't worry if you poop in your pants, who cares, you're having a baby and you're allowed to break all the rules of polite society."

When we finally pulled into the hospital's emergency loading and unloading zone, I could feel the baby's head crowning. Lost in frantic confusion, not knowing whether to stay with me or get some help, Steve ran to my side of the car and opened the door. I sat there, finding it difficult to peel my feet off the windshield, feeling certain that standing up would mean giving birth in the parking lot, so I awkwardly rolled out of my seat, onto my hands and knees, then crawled, crablike, onto the hospital's clean linoleum hallway—clean compared to the asphalt driveway, at least. A wheelchair was rolled to my side by a bewildered nurse's aide trying hard to act as if this were standard behavior, and even though Steve explained our predicament, the young man—with a "take charge" attitude—asked if I would please sit in the chair, stating patiently, "It's regulation." All I could do was blow air out of my mouth, which by then sounded like I was giving him the raspberries—which I was. We rode up the elevator with Steve standing next to the young man, whose hands were on the wheelchair, while I stayed on the floor.

In the maternity ward, people took me a little more seriously. I was lifted onto a gurney—still on my hands and knees—while Steve was whisked off to fill out the frigging paperwork. Knowing I wouldn't be able to keep from having the baby, I shook my head no, refusing to lie down, while spitting out, "I'm Lamaze, I'm Lamaze."

The nurse at my side put her hand on my back, speaking to me slowly as if I didn't understand the English language. "You have to lie down so I can get your clothes off and put you in a gown."

"Cut them off," I shot back.

"Oh no, we can't cut your clothes off."

I wanted to say, *For fuck's sake, cut the piece-of-shit clothes off of me*, but by then I could only blow and words were not an option.

So, without lying down, I let her slip my clothes off, helping as much as I could, which meant not at all. She then placed a gown on one arm, but couldn't get my other arm to cooperate, so the garment was never fully on my body and slid around willy-nilly.

I finally agreed to lie down when a young intern came into the room saying he needed to examine me to determine if I was truly in labor—I swear to you. His name was Dr. Paul Crane and he would eventually become a prominent OB-GYN in Los Angeles, and I will never forget him. He leaned down to talk to me as I lay on my side. "You're about to have this baby, Sally, and your doctor's not here yet. Do you want to try to wait or would you trust me to deliver it?" He said this while they rolled me into the delivery room, then stood at the head of the table looking into my eyes, waiting for my answer.

I barely got out, "You do it. I trust you," before the nurse snapped an oxygen mask over my face, which I found impossible to tolerate, immediately pushing it off to the side (but at least this time I wasn't tied down). Dr. Crane—who years later admitted to me how brand-new he was—gave me a casual smile, then moved toward the end of the table with a forced sense of ease, tripping over the oxygen cord connected to the unused mask around my neck, which jerked my head up fast, then plopped it down with a thud, like a puppet on a string.

Miraculously, Steve dashed through the door, tying a mask on his distraught face, looking as undone as I did, and from this young doctor came the most beautiful words I'd ever heard anyone say: "With the next contraction, you go ahead, Sally. Hold your breath and push. Okay? And here we go." With one glorious, heavenly, orgasmic push, my beautiful, impatient, and joyfully alive son was born. Elijah.

Steve, Peter, Eli, and me. 1973.

14

Culpable

I DIDN'T LOVE riding on Steve's motorcycle, but he wanted to show me something. So, one afternoon when little Eli was down for a nap and Baa was reading Peter a book, I wrapped my arms around Steve's T-shirted torso and off we zoomed through the emerald community, turning onto Chantilly Road, then up a steep driveway. At the top, branching off to the right, was the private entrance to a barely visible house. To the left was a large lot with only the remnants of a brick fireplace standing in the shadowy outline of a house that had probably burned down during the disastrous 1961 Bel Air fire. The site was spectacularly beautiful, lined with tall eucalyptus trees, which had either escaped the blaze or grown in the nearly twelve years since the house last stood.

I can't say I didn't know what Steve had on his mind. And even though it made absolutely no sense financially, the thought of having a home in this dream of a spot was jump-up-and-down exciting. Truth was, we had two children and lived in a rather small house, so having a larger place was not a bad idea. But I wasn't working regularly, and Steve had no career at all, so building a fantasy home at that particular moment couldn't have been a completely good idea either. Yet that's what Steve wanted to do: build a house. He was like a kid in a toy store, determined to get what he wanted. And no matter how many reasons I gave as to why we couldn't and shouldn't, he'd come back with reasons why we absolutely could and should: He would build half of it himself, be part of the construction crew, devote his life to it, stressing the point that he knew all about our finances and was positive it was a good investment. I wouldn't have known a good investment from a hole in the ground, plus I remained frightened of anything financial and therefore had no idea how much money we actually had. Part of me wanted to feel as if Steve knew what he was doing, that he could handle this part of our lives while I concerned myself with taking care of the kids and making a living. Which meant building a career, not a house.

Perhaps this was the beginning of the end for our relationship and if we had just stayed in our little place with the mountain view, the marriage would have survived. But we sold it in order to buy the lot on Chantilly Road, and when Peter was three and Eli not quite six months, we moved into a ramshackle rented house on Topanga Beach, where we would live while the home was being built. And in spite of the fact that the beach house seemed to be made of cardboard, it had a large wooden deck directly on the sand and was a mind-boggling place, as long as you were looking out toward the ocean. Inside, everything was tattered and falling apart, including my marriage.

The Chantilly construction moved forward, though I still don't know how. Maybe I was just overwhelmed with the lives of two little boys, but I don't remember seeing any architectural drawings or participating in the hiring of people, and I rarely visited the site. If it hadn't been for the large round rocks collected from all over and stacked in piles to be taken to the lot, I would have forgotten we were building anything.

As if he were on a treasure hunt, Steve would wander up and down the beach looking for the half-hidden dappled gray boulders, some huge and all of them smooth from sand and water. He would then find a way to drag or roll them back to our place, usually with little Eli tucked in a backpack the whole time. Unlike how he was with his first son—leaving most of the daily care to me—Steve kept Eli by his side as he worked around the rented house. It was as if Eli, who looked so much like his father, belonged to Steve, whereas Peter, who looked so much like his mother, was mine.

As for me, the few jobs I was being offered were either uninteresting or ridiculous, and the need for money, accompanied by the fear of everything being taken away, haunted me like a recurring dream. Steve and I both laughed at the half-hour pilot I was offered called *The Galloping Gour-miss*—a takeoff on a popular daytime cooking show, *The Galloping Gourmet*. Then the laughter faded, and he raised his eyebrows with a shrug of *maybe it's not so bad*. When I immediately passed on the project, I could feel his impatience, hinting that perhaps I was too picky. But sweet Jesus in heaven, can you imagine going from *The Flying Nun* to *The Galloping Gour-miss*? I could feel the nails being hammered into the coffin of my career. It's one thing to quietly learn your craft, unnoticed until that breakthrough moment, but I'd already used up my "on-the-job training" pass, and my fear of losing the house that didn't even exist was nothing compared to my fear that acting would be taken away.

I had to reinvent myself, to go away and not be seen until I had the right role and was skilled enough to play it. I accepted whatever jobs I thought wouldn't attract too much notice, like hosting the ridiculous Miss Teen USA pageant, a few TV guest spots, and even some game shows. But each notch down was physically painful, as if a chunk of my body was being lopped off. Next, I'd be doing a personal appearance at Jocko's bird sanctuary in Hawaii. How could I listen to the part of me that felt most alive when I was onstage or in front of a camera, take care of it, allow it to grow—and still be the sole financial support for my family? All while fulfilling Steve's dream of building a house?

Unconsciously, I felt I had to make a choice between these two loves of my life. I began to move away from the comfort of my childhood sweetheart and chose my love of acting. That's the love affair I focused on.

After I performed a scene from Jean Anouilh's *Antigone* at the Actors Studio one night, Lee cautioned me to take care of the emotional part of my brain, to guard that it didn't close up. He advised that I learn techniques for allowing expression without aiming directly for a specific emotional response, usually leading to a predictable performance. He then suggested I speak with him during the break, which of course made my heart lurch.

From the very beginning, people at the Studio considered me to be a teacher's pet, and even though that perception continued to grow with good reason, it didn't keep me from feeling intimidated of Lee. I could see how he treated actors he felt frustrated with, those who perhaps needed a kick in the pants to help them hear what he was saying, or ones who simply rubbed him the wrong way, and I was always relieved to *not* be one of them. And it was true, Lee did seem to keep his eye on me. Not obviously, but I could feel it. Often, he would say something to the class, then nod at me to make sure I'd understood.

"Get into therapy," he told everyone one night after commenting on a scene with only a few preoccupied sentences. "If you're blocked as a person, you'll be blocked as an actor. You have to know how to use yourself. You are your own instrument of expression and you have to keep it finely tuned." He used musicians as examples, like Vladimir Horowitz with his piano or Yehudi Menuhin with his violin, how they knew every inch of their equipment, were constantly practicing exercises to keep themselves and their instruments aligned. Actors should connect with themselves in the same way, he said, adding that they needed to know their physicality and habitual behavior, their history and emotional landscape, to own the information that would allow them to interpret a character through their individual uniqueness. "The pianist plays all the same notes," he'd say, "yet it's the way he plays... that something only he can add... his particular awareness of what he's doing." The great jazz saxophonist Charlie Parker once said, "Music is your own experience, your thoughts, your wisdom. If you don't live it, it won't come out of your horn." But you have to know what you have lived.

That night, as people milled around, stretching their legs and preparing for the next scene, Lee quietly told me to consider joining his master class series at the Lee Strasberg Theatre Institute, which he and his wife, Anna, had opened in 1969 not far from the Studio. Attending the institute cost money that I didn't want to spend, but it would mean working more intensely with Lee, three times a week. I immediately signed up and started classes the following week.

The four-hour daytime sessions were much as I imagined a college class would be and very different from the Actors Studio. Lee always began with a lecture of sorts, telling stories about acting and stories about life—which were ultimately about acting. Eventually he'd announce the specific exercise to be taught and call six or seven students to the stage, where everyone sat in a loose semicircle of folding chairs. First came relaxation—as important as anything else we ever did in class—and Lee would slowly move from person to person, picking up an arm to shake it, testing the shoulders, pulling the jaw open and closed, hunting for rigidity anywhere, telling us that a mouth held tight or shoulders tensed, even hands that are unconsciously clenched, can block impulses. After he replaced all the body parts where he'd found them, we'd begin the work of the day.

During the first week, we looked at ourselves in nonexistent mirrors, or sat in a windowless room feeling the touch of sunlight, or held imaginary cups of coffee, felt the weight in our hands, inhaled the aroma, tasted the bitter warmth—all sensory exercises that are about much more than the five senses.

On one particular day—after a month of classes—Lee chose me along with six others to work onstage, then announced that he wanted to guide us through the room exercise, an exercise that he said was underused and an effective back door into subconscious emotions. After we all had properly relaxed and each had moved to a separate spot on the stage, we sat down, waiting to have the task explained. "Pick a place in your life, at least seven years in the past, which stands out in your mind," he told us. "It could be your bedroom or your father's study, a location from your life." He advised us to pick something important enough to be remembered but not to worry about reproducing whatever emotions we might connect to the memory. He gave us a moment to think and when ready, we were to close our eyes and not just re-create the location in our brains, but put ourselves in it. "Do you see paint on the walls or is there wallpaper? What's on the floor?" he asked us. "Where is the light coming from? What do you hear? What do you smell?"

Sitting with legs crossed, eyes closed, I searched for a place to start until, without intending to, I began to see the carpet on the stairs leading to my stepfather's bedroom. As if I were turning a viewfinder, details slowly began to appear: the stains on the edges of the rug, the flat off-white walls, the worn banister on one side of the staircase, the dirt on the scuffed baseboards, the window on the first landing where I could see the tree, hear its leaves rustling like the sound of rushing water. Then came Lee's voice, softly urging us to investigate, to touch what we see in our mind's eye. I put my fingers in the worn carpet, felt the slightly sticky wool, and instantly I could smell dust and summer and bacon frying.

I feel the sun streaming in, glaring off the wall, stinging my face as I begin to walk up, my bare feet sinking into the carpet. I stop in the sun on the first landing, turn to see the next four stairs and the door. I'm wearing white shorts with a red-and-white checked blouse, and as I stand with my hand on the knob, feeling powerful, I undo the first button of my blouse and knock. I have not been called. I'm moving into his room because I want to go. I want to feel I'm important. He's surprised, then his smile glides into a knowing smirk, as if he sees where I am heading before I do. He sits on the edge of his bed, watches me, bemused. How could he know what I didn't? Was this my Achilles' heel he would threaten to reveal and destroy me with two years later? Was I not a victim, but a participant? I haltingly tell him that my skin is feeling dry and he chuckles as he slathers his meaty hands with the lotion that waits next to the bed, then rolls the goo over my bare legs, smearing his hand up under my shorts while I stand before him.

I'd become an expert at not feeling anything in that room, and though I still felt the familiar distant burn of humiliation, this time I felt something else. And suddenly, with a jolt, I was yanked back to the stage I was sitting on and it hit me for the first time—the deep shame and horror of my own desires, desires I couldn't feel when I was fourteen. Only at that moment, twelve years later, in an acting exercise with Lee Strasberg, did I realize what I had been asking for.

The exercise continued for a bit longer but the memory instantly cut off there. As hard as I tried then, and forever after, I can't see how I left the upstairs bedroom that day. I truly don't believe it went any further, however that moment in my life—though never consciously registered—had been so powerful that I instantly stopped talking to Jocko for almost two years, barely responding when he talked to me. And I had never known precisely what had caused the abrupt halt to our relationship, what had flipped the switch in me from needing his approval to despising him. From that day on, and for the rest of my life, I shut him out. But I had shut out a part of myself as well, the madwoman. Had sent her away to live in the attic of my brain, disconnected from the rest of me.

After we'd been wandering around in our heads for nearly two hours, Lee carefully called to each of us, whispering our names one at a time. Like waking a child from sleep, he said, "Sally, come back to class. Come back now and look at us."

I tried to squint, to open my eyes enough to see my folded legs and nothing else.

"Look at us, Sally. Can you do that?"

I couldn't.

"Look at us," he said.

"I can't," I whispered.

"Yes, you can," he gently reassured. "We're here with you."

I didn't want to look at anyone because I didn't want anyone to see me. When I opened my eyes, I looked only at Lee and cried for the little girl I once had been.

I've tried to piece together my childhood and early career most of my adult life, relentlessly going over the memories, occasionally telling some of the stories to a captivated few, and I realize I've become my own lore, halfway falling in love with the drama of it all. But when I try to look at my early years of motherhood, my relationship with Steve, and what it became, I run out of lore. Maybe it's easier to remember myself as a powerless victim and not the perpetrator, not a player in the mindless damage game. I've never wanted to see the reality: that I was a young woman who began to have violent rages, who needed to find her sexuality in other men, and who hurt Steve. And more than anything, I don't want to acknowledge how often I placed my children into the arms of my mother and walked away, only to feel jealous of her relationship with them when I returned.

My mother, my sister, and I had lived a life of musical chairs, never staying in one place very long before the music would start up again, and off we'd go. The only stationary structure in our lives was Joy's house, and even though I was now paying my mother a small salary to help me with the kids, that's where Baa went to live, along with Princess, who tried to convert another garage into a room for herself—this time Joy's spider-ridden, car-less barnlike thing.

Visiting only occasionally, my brother stayed removed from most of the family chaos, first in Berkeley, where he received his PhD in physics, then in Long Island, New York, where he lived for several years to do postdoctoral research at the Brookhaven National Lab. But in 1973 he moved back to Pasadena along with his wife, Jimmie, and their son, Jason, who was only a few months younger than Eli. Rick would be working at Caltech with the brilliant physicist Richard Feynman, which ultimately became an important working relationship and a powerful friendship.

Maybe the lure of having Ricky and his young family living so close was part of the reason why my mother moved back into her childhood home, though it couldn't have been easy for her. Over the years, my brother had become impatient and emotionally distant with our mother, like he was holding back from her any real affection. And though his disregard was palpable, she never asked for more or turned away, but always stood with her eager face toward him, waiting to be forgiven for things they never talked about. Joy once confessed to Jimmie that she could hear my mother crying every night—a tiny piece of information that Jimmie only recently told me, and the thought of that stays in my head. Baa must have felt injured in whatever direction she turned: Her husband had left for a younger woman; she was living with her mother, who criticized her constantly; and while her son was distractedly disrespectful, her oldest daughter was resentfully dependent.

And yet, on a moment's notice she'd drop everything to drive to the Topanga Beach house and wrangle two young boys for the day. Then, when I'd drag myself home from some dumb game show, I'd walk through the door and turn into someone I didn't want to be. Steve most often was nowhere in sight, while my mother led a little band of playtime junkies on a rampage through the house, looking for their next imagination fix. Blankets would be strewn across every piece of furniture, deck chairs pulled into the living room, and pillows piled into every woolen cave, leaving the house looking as if it had been ransacked. Never mind that she had taken good care of my children, that they had been entertained and creatively stimulated. All I could see was the fact that the toys—which I'd carefully organized into buckets and bins—were scattered everywhere, as if from a deliberate need to undo everything I'd done.

But the thing that turned me from Jekyll into Hyde was the sound of Baa's high-pitched voice playing Bob or Joe or Martha and having a conversation with Peter's character or

Eli's—and he, at that point, was pretty much preverbal. Most of the words were undecipherable, except for my mother's piercing "walky, walky, walky," which meant that whatever stuffed animal or Weeble Wobble she held in her hand was hopping around their make-believe world. The walky-walky game, as I called it. I wasn't sure whether I wanted to be included in their game—which I never was—or was glad to be free from it. Not knowing what I wanted from anyone, including myself, I'd begin to clean up the kitchen, slamming pans around as I fixed dinner, torn between my gratitude for her devotion and my frustration with her presence. Eventually I'd have some sort of dinner ready and with an irritated ring to my voice, I'd call them to the table, only to hear Peter emphatically yell, "Mom, go away. We're playing."

Unvoiced resentment brewed into quiet rage, keeping itself hidden until suddenly that's all I was: mindless red rage, unable to control impulses I didn't want to have. One evening, Steve and I were sitting outside in the midst of an argument, and I remember crying and wailing, going round and round in emotional circles because I either didn't know what was at the bottom of it, or didn't want to admit it. Steve, in a last-ditch effort to break through, got on his knees in front of me and said, "Hit me. Will that make you feel better? Then hit me." He kept saying it while refusing to let me move away. Suddenly I felt as if I were in someone else's body, a body whose clenched fist hit him again and again, mashing a club of a hand into his face until his nose began gushing blood. Only then did I stop. Wrapping my arms around him, fearfully clinging as if we had faced some terrible dragon together. Me. Steve never hit me. Not ever in his life.

*   *   *

In early 1973, a production of *A Streetcar Named Desire*, starring Jon Voight and Faye Dunaway, was being mounted at the Ahmanson Theatre in downtown Los Angeles and I wanted to be in it. I knew that sending them my picture was a good idea, but I still didn't have any eight-by-ten glossies, and the only publicity photos I had were either with my hair in pigtails or a cornette on my head. Instead I mailed them a family photo showing me looking worn and motherly, talking to Peter as I discreetly breast-fed his little brother…thinking maybe it made me look older. I had worked on three scenes, knew them, owned them, and was being given the rare opportunity to audition—albeit not with Mr. Voight or Ms. Dunaway. Arriving a half hour early, I walked around the courtyard of the Ahmanson Theatre trying to calm myself, and when that didn't work, I stretched out on a stone bench directly across from the artists' entrance. The day was hot and the stone felt cool as I looked up at the sky, breathing in deeply and out very slowly, like I was in the first stages of labor. "You have a right to be here, you're good at what you do, you have a right to be here," I chanted over and over, while flapping my trembling hands in the air to release any visible tension. But I couldn't quiet my heart, which pounded with such force that it made my thin cotton dress bounce around rhythmically.

I could say the reason I didn't get this part was because of my size, that I'm too small, that I didn't fit with the rest of the cast, or that though I was twenty-six years old at the time—the right age for Stella—I've always had a childlike, girly quality, and I didn't know how to leave it behind. All of that is true. But the real reason I was crossed off the list was because

I didn't know how to audition. By the time I walked onto the stage, a huge magical dark theater—empty except for the producers and the director who would judge me—I was overwhelmed by it all, overwhelmed with longing, disconnected from myself and the work and from any chance of finding my version of Stanley Kowalski's pregnant wife. I don't remember hearing my voice reverberate through the lofty space, don't remember playing any of the scenes I'd worked on. Maybe I never made it that far.

What I do remember is the bumper-to-bumper traffic, and the afternoon sun smacking me in the face as I drove away from downtown Los Angeles, feeling powerless to move my life or even my car forward. Finally, I walked into a house turned upside down, as usual, while Steve lounged on the deck smoking a joint, strumming his guitar, and watching the sun go down. From Peter's room, I could hear the dreaded "walky, walky, walky," and as I tried to sit down on the floor with them, Peter snapped, "No, Mom, no. We're playing. Go away." I then trudged to the kitchen, hoping to find something to scrub, which, of course, there was never a shortage of.

When I'd cleared enough space to get dinner going, Baa wandered in saying she had to go, and without turning I tossed out a quick "Great, see ya," not wanting to meet her eyes. She watched me from the door for a moment, then moved to put her hand on my back and her glass in the sink, asking, "Are you okay?" I could feel the dance between us—the one, two, cha-cha-cha as she stood there waiting for my lead. Part of me wanted to cry, to tell her how desperately I wanted her to stay, to hear her talk to me from under the closet door. But instead, I denied her any glimpse of my longing, ignored her question, and punched at her with my irritated words. "Well, thanks. That's *one* glass you brought to the sink."

After dinner had been made and eaten, after the kids had splashed in the bath and crawled into jammies, bedtime thankfully arrived. All I wanted was to throw myself down the dark hole of sleep, to be unable to feel for a while, but ten-month-old Eli was not going to cooperate. He kept crying, screaming to be picked up, to be rescued from his crib, demanding that the day continue. And after the fifth or fiftieth trip into his room, after patting his back and tiptoeing out thinking I was free to drift away, after waiting for Steve to stop reading whatever volume of Sandburg's *Lincoln* he was on, the banshee woman—who stood constantly in my shadow— marched into Eli's room, grabbed my baby, thundered back, and threw him onto the bed next to his distracted father. It wasn't a great distance, but it had been done recklessly, with the same fury-fueled impulse that had possessed Jocko when he flung me across the backyard into the swimming pool. And even though he was only ten months old, Eli felt as humiliated and outraged as I had when I was twelve. Steve picked up the wailing baby, carried him back to his room, shut the door, and rocked him to sleep. I sat outside on the wooden deck, watching the waves tumble to the sand, hitting myself in the face over and over. All in all, not my best day.

One night, maybe a week later, after putting Eli in his crib and patting his back until he seemed to settle, I slipped out and stood at the door listening while he started to cry, as he usually did. Knowing I'd probably have to go back in a few minutes, I was moving toward my bedroom when abruptly, the crying stopped. Could he have fallen asleep that quickly? I remember standing in the doorway thinking, *Good, he's learning*. But within seconds, my instinct sent me back into the room. Eli seemed to be soundlessly locked in the midst of a deep wail, like he couldn't catch his breath, like he couldn't release the sob and breathe again. I immediately picked him up, hoping he would relax and exhale. But he didn't. I screamed for Steve and started pounding on my little boy, saying, "Breathe…breathe." His arms and legs began to vibrate while his body became rigid, then his back arched and his face turned from red to blue. And still he didn't breathe. Slowly his body began to melt, until his head flopped onto my chest and he took a breath. Holding him tight against my heart, I sank to the floor, crying as I rocked back and forth. Minutes later, he opened his eyes with a look of vagueness, not really focusing on anything, and even without words, I could tell he was disoriented. I kept repeating to him that he was okay, that I knew what it was like when you couldn't remember where you'd put your arms and legs, that I knew how frightening it was and that it was over.

But it wasn't over; it was the beginning of what the doctors thought were petit mal seizures, although they were never witnessed by any medical personnel because I wouldn't let Eli go through the tests. I knew that the procedure of being held down while various pieces of equipment were attached would frighten him, and being frightened made him angry. The seizures only occurred when Eli got angry. From then on, whenever anything happened, I knew I had to get to him fast. If he fell down when learning to walk, if his brother took something he wanted, if I heard him start to cry for any reason, I'd run to pick him up, to soothe him before his anger became bigger than he was. And if I missed that tiny window of opportunity, then his body would send him into a helpless fit, until eventually he'd pass out and I'd rock my little son, trying to soothe him back into consciousness. And it wasn't just me; Baa and especially Steve were always on the alert. But the amazing thing is, at about two years of age, when Eli could say words like *shit* and *fuck*—words that Steve and I gleefully taught him—when he could use language to get angry and not his body, he stopped having seizures. Something that, in my heart, I had known would happen. But even now, I'm convinced that his episodes were my fault. Eli had to deal with a very angry mother any way he could, and if you can't beat 'em, join 'em.

We'd been living in the Topanga house for about a year when one morning I found a bewildered messenger standing unannounced in the middle of my disheveled living room, having wandered in off the beach and through the sliding glass door that stood open. In his hand, he held a manila envelope addressed to me with the Screen Gems logo pasted on. It contained a thirty-five-page screenplay, the pilot for a new series written by Bernard Slade, the same man who had written the pilot for *The Flying Nun*—and years later, would write the play *Same Time, Next Year*. As soon as it arrived, the phone started ringing and a stiff, unfamiliar voice announced it was John Mitchell's office calling for Sally Field. John H. Mitchell was the president of Screen Gems, a position he'd held for the entire time I'd been employed there, though I don't remember ever meeting him. Nor can I remember what exactly he said that day, but I presume he told me that Screen Gems wanted me back. Then came a call from Bob Claver, who had produced the *Gidget* pilot, and who had been my reading partner and support system through that summer of auditions in 1964. He would be producing this pilot as well, and if the network picked it up, he'd be there for every episode of *The Girl with Something Extra*, which, like the *Nun*, had been written for me. Last, and totally least, came a call from my agent to let me know that I'd been offered another series.

I remember standing at the stove a day or so later, holding Eli on my hip and stirring a pan of Campbell's tomato soup, while Peter sat on the floor dancing tiny plastic animals on the linoleum before him. It was just like the memory I had of my mother holding me perched to one side, my brother playing behind us, while she memorized Chekhov and cooked supper for her children. Now I stood, lost in thought, caught between what I wanted to do and what I felt I had to do to support my family. The script was funny—in a glib sitcom sort of way—and we needed money, plus I wanted to work. But I did *not* want to do another sitcom. I felt I'd be losing something, giving up, caving in. I couldn't think. I couldn't stand back and logically weigh all the pros and cons because every time I tried, fear would rise up and block any other points of view I might have.

Steve appeared in the doorway wearing shorts and a tattered T-shirt, wet from the ocean as if he'd jumped in on an impulse. I wanted him to say that I was worth more, to say, *We'll be okay, hold out awhile longer.* But he didn't. He watched for a moment, then, with a matter-of-fact "happens all the time" attitude, said that Bob Claver had offered him an associate producer position if I agreed to do the show. I felt immediately betrayed and angry and began to pound the wooden spoon into the hot soup.

"I don't want to do it," I flared back.

"But we could work together," he said, trying to convince me, and after a moment of silence he added, "You have to earn some money, Sal. I really think you should do it. And I'd get to work too."

When he left to take a shower, I watched the tomato soup boil up and over the edges of the pan, looking exactly like I felt. Was I being asked to walk away from what I'd been working toward, so that Steve could find a career for himself? Was I to give up on myself, swallow my longing, so that he could dabble in this new arena? Is that how I saw this moment, why I felt so angry? Or did I see Steve as Jocko, like a mole in my organization, appearing to be on my side but actually in cahoots with the enemy? Sometimes when I was caught in an argument with Steve, I'd be so overwhelmed with rage I couldn't find any other parts of myself. I'd lose sight of love and trust, then literally have to start packing my suitcase, blind to anything other than my need to run. Usually the fury dissipated before I had emptied the closet.

I think there was always a part of me waiting for a reason to walk out the door, to be safely alone and hear nothing but my own heartbeat . . . to put myself back into that little pine house next to the big sycamore on Libbit Avenue.

When the pilot was shot in February of '73, Steve worked in the production office, but by the time the series sold, with a schedule to go into production in July, he was no longer an associate producer—whether he quit or I was callous enough to tell the studio I didn't want him there, I don't remember.

He decided to focus on the completion of the house. We gave up the place on Topanga Beach to rent a house in Toluca Lake, only blocks from Columbia Ranch, where I'd be filming, allowing me to be closer to the kids. Steve didn't live there with us.

Cecil Smith's column in the *Los Angeles Times* on Wednesday, April 4, 1973, displayed the headline NBC DISCLOSES NEW FALL LINEUP. It goes on to say,

> Most drastic shake-up of the prime-time schedule NBC has had in several years. Nine new shows, four new half-hour comedies, two dramatic series and two anthologies. *The Girl with Something Extra* with Sally Field as a young housewife with such highly developed ESP powers that she can read the mind of her husband John Davidson (well at least she doesn't fly).

The Girl with Something Extra, which proved to have nothing extra, ran for only twenty-two episodes. Thank you, God.

15

Hungry

I READ THE script while sitting on the bed in the unfinished Chantilly house, propped up against a pile of pillows. It was late afternoon, and Peter sat on the floor near me, using the newly completed fireplace hearth—a two-foot-high, lumpy surface made from Steve's collected boulders—as his artist's desk. With paper and colored pencils scattered around, my five-year-old son quietly concentrated on the colorful creatures he called "weirdies," drawing them, then giving each an original "weirdie" name. From somewhere downstairs I could hear work going on—hammers and saws, lumber slamming onto an unfinished floor—and above it all rang out Eli's persistent not-quite-three-year-old voice: "Dad…Dad…Dad… Dad…look…look…Dad. DAD!" Every now and then I'd hear Steve's distracted reply.

For all the months that I'd worked on *The Girl with Something Extra*, even after the show was canceled, Steve had been camping in the lot while the house was being built, working alongside the contractor and his crew, taking ownership of it as the walls went up. And now, because I was no longer filming a series and hadn't worked since then, and because no money was coming in but a great deal was going out, the boys and I had moved into the not-yet-finished house too. Which meant that Steve and I were both living under the same newly shingled roof. Although not together.

And that's where I was, holding those pages, propped up against the recently painted pale yellow wall, directly across from the fireplace and Peter's artistry. I was sitting with my knees bent, feet planted on the bed, which was the same king-size mattress and box springs I'd carted around with me to five different houses in the past six years. My butt was snugly lodged into the permanent dent on my side, the side I'd always slept on no matter what house it was in. The slightly larger dent on the opposite side of the bed had held several different bodies over the last two years since Steve and I had unofficially separated, but more times than not, it stayed empty and haunted. The nights when Peter had an asthma attack and was struggling to breathe, he'd sleep nestled close to my side, never rolling toward his father's phantom imprint. And I would spend those nights wondering if I should take the little boy to the hospital. I'm sure I should have, countless times. But I never did.

I don't look back on this time of my life with pride, don't see it as a shining example of thoughtful parenting. I can't recall a single moment when I stopped to worry about how my actions would affect my sons, didn't wonder if I should consult a therapist to learn the best way to help them adjust to their parents' living apart. I simply told Steve I didn't want to be with him anymore, because that's all I knew to be true. But

Little Eli on the Chantilly construction site.

when he was gone, I missed him terribly, even if I was seeing someone else—and I was always seeing someone else, as if I were making up for lost time. I'd long for Steve to come back, to be comforted with his familiarity, and when he was back, I'd want him gone again.

In reality, it wasn't Steve that I didn't want to be with, it was me. I didn't want to be the person I became when I was with him, didn't want to lean on him because he expected me to, because he wanted me to, because he felt better when I did—or even because I felt better when I did. It seemed as though we were trapped in our childhood, like Dorian Gray's portrait. We got older but our relationship never changed.

It had been almost two years since I'd worked. Almost two years since I'd met with my business manager as he sat holding a slim file of declining bank statements and nonexistent pension plans, looking dumbfounded when I told him of my intention to turn down any television projects that came my way. Almost two years since he strongly advised me to accept the first offer I got, adding that, even if I was lucky enough to be cast in a film—which was unlikely—actresses got paid very little. It had been almost two years since I met with my agent, who flatly stated that only models were working in films, and no offense, but I wasn't pretty enough, insisting that situation comedy was the place for me, a place where I had a real foothold. It had been almost two years since I'd fired them both.

During those unemployed years, I'd tried to shake myself up, to push myself out of my own nest, to get stronger any way I could. Everything from doing six weeks of summer stock in Ohio to studying musical theater with a man named David Craig, who taught actors how to mount a song technically, not to be in front of it or behind it, but to ride it. And though he couldn't give me the vocal chops I longed for, the skills a singing teacher might have provided, David taught me how to build a structure to lean on, like a tree where I could hang all my Actors Studio ornaments. Most important of all, he taught me, and countless other lucky actors, the art of the audition.

Those years were spent in David Craig's joyful classes—where I'd sit in a roomful of other terrified actors, taking chances, flinging myself into the tightly structured, poetic world of songs, learning when to breathe and in what meter—then running off to Lee Strasberg's intense sessions, filled with exercises that were often emotional but abstract, many times performing scenes when the process felt intangible and undefined, when I couldn't figure out how to use whatever tools we were being given. Until one day something changed.

I'd been asked by a fellow student in Lee's class to partner with her in a scene from a two-character play entitled *The White Whore and the Bit Player*. In it, two actresses portray two different aspects of the same character, and my scene partner—a beautiful blonde I didn't know very well and whose name I swear I can't remember—was to play the Marilyn Monroe–ish, whore side of the woman, whereas I was to play the nun. For obvious reasons, I didn't especially care for this scene and probably should have turned it down from the get-go. But Lee expected us to participate in whatever work our classmates wanted to tackle, whether we wanted to tackle it or not. Because of that, I agreed to do it. In all honesty, I didn't devote much thought to the performance, which meant my work was lazy—mistake number one. And because I'd been working with Lee off and on for many years, I'd developed a slight swagger, confident of my secure place with him—mistake number two. When I stepped on the stage that day, thinking I could fake my way through it, my work was a deadly mix of uninterested and uninteresting.

After the scene, Lee spoke to my partner with patient, careful attention, then clicked the back of his throat a few times, looked laser-like into my eyes, and said, "Yes?" as though I were a stranger who'd come to his house uninvited.

I knew the drill, therefore I threw out the standard "I was working on a moment I once had with my father." And in reality, I had—very obliquely—been visualizing an episode with Dick for my preparation.

Lee paused, and—making sure the whole class could

hear—said, "When are you going to stop this shit?" I was stunned. I'd been caught and the rug I'd been so smugly standing on was being pulled out from under me. "I don't believe your father was enough. I don't think that moment with your father affected you very much." He pronounced this with such finality, as if he had just said, *NEXT.* I was being dismissed. Without taking a moment to gather my wits (wherever they were), I started stuttering, explaining, defending myself, while Lee shook his head, preparing to move on.

Suddenly, I jumped to my feet as if yanked by a bungee cord hooked in my brain, and began shouting through a gag of emotion, "Who the fuck do you think you are to tell me what I'm feeling? Who the fuck do you think you are?" Almost unable to breathe, I kept repeating the same sentences over and over.

Lee never backed off or demanded that I contain myself. Instead he rose to his feet, becoming red in the face while he worked hard to be heard over my raging, hiccupping barrage of protest. "Listen to me, Sally," he yelled. "You keep saying you want to be better, but you keep dancing around. I don't see anything important going on in you." Again and again he said the same thing while all the time I continued to spew, "Who the fuck do you think you are? You don't know what's going on inside of me..."

No one ever talked to Lee like that. And from the edges of my awareness I could feel every other actor in the room scrunch down in their chairs, suddenly looking at their feet or placing their hands over their faces, while Lee and I dueled with overlapping monologues. Finally, feeling embarrassed and foolish, I crumpled cross-legged onto the stage, like a puppet whose strings had snapped, my head hanging limp from my neck as I tried to sop up the river of snot pouring from my nose with the sleeves of my sweater. The whole room was silent; no one moved as I stared into my folded legs, seeing nothing but loss. Lee stepped to the edge of the stage, reaching out for the boards as if to hold himself up (this couldn't have been easy for him either), and when steady he said, "You keep saying you want to be better, that you come here day after day because you want to know how to be a better actor. But Sally, listen. Where you want to be is where you are right now. And it has cost you a lot. You have tried to hold it all in. You must always be where you are right now."

And what the holy fuck did that mean? He dismissed the class and I quickly gathered my things, without once looking at Lee. I would never again meet his eyes in a classroom situation.

Unable to understand what he'd said, I drove home in a blind blur, feeling betrayed and defensive and, most important, outraged. Furious for every moment in my life that I'd felt dismissed, discounted, or defined by someone else.

Did I take my wounded dignity to the music and laughter of David Craig's class? Did I whine that I'd become the victim of the famous Strasberg buzz saw? Probably. But it was soon after that, in April of 1975, that I received the script that I was now sitting on the bed reading.

It wasn't well written, and if telling an understandable story with believable, realistic characters was what I was looking for, then *Stay Hungry* wasn't it. But none of that mattered. By the grace of God—and a casting woman named Dianne Crittenden—I had been included on the very long list of potential actresses to play opposite the always-dazzling

Jeff Bridges, who was already a star. Even with the new and improved representation, my name had never been included on anyone's list, so when Bob Rafelson's office called requesting a meeting, asking if they could send me the script, I was as shocked as my agent, whose first reaction had been to ask if they had the right Sally Field—or so I was told.

Oddly enough, Rafelson had been one of the creator/producers of *The Monkees* television series, though we'd never met roaming around the Screen Gems lot. Bob went on to direct *The King of Marvin Gardens* and *Five Easy Pieces*, both well-regarded films with a liberal peppering of Actors Studio faces, Jack Nicholson's being one of them. I didn't know it at the time, but my work at the Studio over the years had started some chatter, at least among the Studio members, and that chatter had filtered down to Dianne, which was one reason my name had been put on the list. The second reason was the fact that Ms. Crittenden happened to be good friends with Zohra Lampert, the wonderful actress cast as my best friend on the thankfully short-lived *The Girl with Something Extra*. Zohra and I had been together for all those months, both of us struggling to make the show better, times that usually ended in a tussle between me and my bouffant-haired co-star, John Davidson—who once accused me of having Helen Reddy up my ass. Lovely Zohra, whom I hadn't seen since we wrapped, reportedly told Dianne that though I was well known, I was totally undiscovered. So my name went on her list.

I really couldn't tell what the script was about, but I knew my interpretation couldn't be unclear and vague, even if the screenplay was. The character of Mary Tate Farnsworth was

southern, and appeared to be uneducated, economically challenged, and physically inclined—a champion water-skier
(sweet Jesus, another water sport). She was also sexual, with
an open, easy, "no big deal" kind of sensuality, an ingredient
that I didn't own, or not on the surface at least. These were the
specifics I had to work with.

David Craig always said that most directors, or whoever was
sitting in the casting chair, rarely looked for the best actor to
play the part, but instead waited for the actual character to walk
through the door. Only when an actor has created a vast and
diverse enough body of work, with enough recognition attached,
will they be given the opportunity to play a character unlike the
very person that they appear to be. And even then, it's rare.

With that in mind, I knew my task. I had to *be* Mary Tate
Farnsworth, not Sally Field reading for the role. They had to
think that the work I had done in *The Flying Nun* and *Gidget*
must have been one hell of an acting job, because in reality, I
was exactly like Mary Tate with her "come here and fuck me"
attitude. I had to undo what they thought they knew of me,
had to prepare for the audition knowing that it would begin
the minute I walked into Dianne Crittenden's office. And that's
what I did. Wearing a pair of threadbare hip-hugger jeans and
a red crop top, I nonchalantly sauntered into Dianne's small
room, stopping briefly to shake hands and flash her a quick
smile. Hard to miss were the stacks of head shots scattered
across her desk, photos of actresses with their résumés attached
on the back, reminding me yet again that I didn't have any
eight-by-ten glossies to hand out. But for God's sake, I never
went on any auditions, so what was the point?

I flopped into one of the two chairs against the opposite

wall, slouching down until my butt almost hung off the seat, then began mindlessly snapping and unsnapping the top of my jeans. As I waited, fiddling with my pants, Dianne went in and out several times to inquire about the delay, always smiling at me with a little nod of acknowledgment. When she left the room for the fourth or fifth time, I knew that things were not running smoothly and I began to suspect that Dianne had put my name on the list without telling anyone else. Then, from the other room, the mumbled blur of a conversation got louder and more emphatic than it had been since I'd arrived, which by now was almost an hour before. I could hear a man—whom I assumed to be Rafelson—spewing aggravation, punctuating the end of a sentence with what I thought was my name. And when I realized that they were definitely talking about me, my pounding heart slowed. Using my newly acquired acting skills, I allowed my anger to fuel and not overwhelm me. I had a job to do and if I'd been a gun, I would have been locked and loaded.

When the door abruptly swung open and Bob Rafelson—wearing goofy-looking aviator-like glasses—stood in its frame, I didn't sit up. Like holding the reins of a bolting horse, I pulled back on the fury vibrating through me, remaining aloof as if I'd been waiting for a bus and this simply wasn't it. He invited me to follow him into his window-lined office, where I entered to shake hands with Charles Gaines, who had adapted the screenplay from his own novel and who would be my scene partner, playing the Jeff Bridges character. Dianne, who had insisted over much objection that I be allowed to audition, quietly slipped in behind us to sit on the sofa toward the back of the room.

I was directed to one of the two chairs across from Bob's desk, where he now sat with his feet over the empty top. It's not that Bob was rude, or cruel. He wasn't. He was only distracted and perfunctory, like he was going through the motions as quickly as possible, which meant—thankfully—there was not much chatter before he nodded to begin. With script in hand, I said my first line of dialogue looking directly at Charles, who was sitting in the chair next to me. When he dribbled out a flat response, his eyes never leaving the page, I realized he was either the world's worst actor or he didn't give a shit... or both. I waited, without saying anything, staring right at Charles, who never looked up at me. With deliberate calmness, I held my script in the air, let it drop to the ground, then moved to the writer, who became completely befuddled as I tossed his screenplay to the side and straddled him. Now I had his full attention and with a titillated smirk he stuttered, "I don't know the words." Slowly lowering myself onto his lap, I replied, "Yes you do. If not, fake it." The scene continued, but it was not the scene they'd heard twenty times before. Nor was the second one they asked me to read. And when I sensed they had run out of material, I grabbed my script, looked Rafelson in his now smug-less face, thanked him, then left the room and the building.

The following week, I answered the phone one afternoon, barely hearing it through the grind of the cement mixer outside and the bickering little boys inside. It was Jolene, Rafelson's secretary, or assistant in today's world. After she gave me a quick greeting and asked me to "hold on for Bob," I steadied myself, lowered my energy, and waited. He laughed when he came on the line, saying, "Well, we've now read every actress in this town and I can't believe that you were the best. It must be because you've had more experience auditioning than anyone else." I paused before telling him I'd not read for anyone since 1964. He went on to inform me that they'd honed it down to five girls, saying that none of the other actresses had read as well, but they all had the look he wanted: long legs and long hair. My hair had grown out several times over the years, but then I'd cut it off again, so no. My hair was not long and my legs were never going to be long, no matter what I did.

But even with my shortcomings, I had my first callback since I began in the business eleven years earlier, and when I sat in Dianne's cubicle this time, I waited only a few minutes before being summoned into Bob's glass office. Charles was now sitting with Dianne on the back sofa and Jeff Bridges was sitting in the chair across from Bob. Wonderfully alive, totally available Jeff, tall and quick to laugh, focused and fearless—I adored him the minute our eyes connected. I can't translate into words what it was like, that time with Jeff. Instantly we met in a hypnotic out-of-body world, a place where there is no space between impulse and action, no guard gate at the crossings between strangers and intimates. It felt as if we were breathing through the same air hose.

I don't know how many scenes we worked on. Actually, "played with" might be a better way to describe it, because that's what it felt like—the two of us, toying with each other, curious and experimental in an easy sensual way, a place I could never find in my real life. Or was this my real life? Was I there for twenty minutes or four hours? I don't know. But eventually I was driving home, feeling I'd done the work I set out to do.

Two days later, Rafelson called, perplexed. He was having a hard time owning the idea that he'd be hiring the Flying Nun

Jeff and me in a scene with wonderful Helena Kallianiotes.

(what a surprise) and it was driving him crazy. Plus he was leaving the next morning for Birmingham, Alabama, to scout locations for the film. He asked if I would come to his house that evening for one more meeting, and even though an alert went off in my head, I tucked it away with all the other pieces of me that didn't belong to M. T. Farnsworth.

Around this time, another recurring dream kept haunting me. This one stays with me through the years and even though it no longer visits me in the night, I can't leave the images behind. Much of the dream would change, but there was always a staircase and I was always at the bottom of it, looking up, paralyzed with fear. It's dark and I can see the curtains at the top billowing in and out, sheer and ghostlike, a breathing thing waiting at the top of the stairs. I'm standing there, surrounded by little children, all grabbing my shirt, clinging to my legs, while my arms are around them, gathering them to me, protecting them. But I don't turn and run. I don't look for a way out. I know I must go up the stairs to survive and, more important, for the children to survive. There's no other choice. And as I take the first step, from somewhere deep in my body comes a voice, guttural and primal: "I will not be conquered. I will not be conquered." With every ounce of life, I roar, "I will not be conquered."

And there I was, at the bottom of the dimly lit staircase after the housekeeper had invited me in. Bob stood barefoot in the doorway of his bedroom, his shirt open and hanging over his jeans, or was it a baggy gray T-shirt? I don't remember. He thanked his housekeeper, told her he'd see her tomorrow, then greeted me with "Hey, Sal, come on up."

To prepare a character, Lee taught me that you have to understand their history, their emotional ingredients, their physicality. You have to know their lives completely up to the moment you walk onstage, but when you do, you forget it all and just be. No matter what happens, if the other actors drop dead or the set falls down, you *are* that character. And so I was. Did I sit on an armchair somewhere in the room? Or did I throw myself freely onto the bed as M.T. would have? Did Bob offer me something to drink? Was he smoking a joint and did I take a hit? I'm not sure. But, as if it happened ten minutes ago, I remember Bob sitting on the bed, leaning against the headboard, while I sit before him on my folded legs with my feet hanging off the bed in midair, like some part of me didn't want to join in. I began to relax as I heard acceptance in his voice, as if the audition was over and I was in the film. In the midst of casually talking about the work, he told me to take my top off so he could see my breasts, saying since there was a nude scene in the film, he needed to figure out how to shoot me. Ignoring the sharp jab of emotion that shot through me, I removed my shirt as casually as he had made the request, then sat for his approval with my eyes closed—the only clue that those fingernails were clawing my insides. And when he asked me to go to the closet and use whatever scarves and shirts I could find to play dress-up, I did that too. I was a grown-up version of the child wrapped in plastic dry-cleaning bags, performing while an older man, whose approval I needed, watched. After I put the things back in the closet and my clothes back on my body, Bob walked with me to his bedroom door. "Okay, Sal, the job is yours. But only after I see how you kiss. I can't hire anyone who doesn't kiss good enough." So I kissed him. It must have been good enough.

When I left his house and climbed into the safety of my dark car, my hands were shaking. What was I feeling? Excited and slightly flattered? Bob had responded to me. I had won. Is that not what I had wanted? I thought about the fact that I was in the film, that I was going to be working with Jeff, that I'd beaten down the door. But a quiet part of me felt afraid, tarnished, shamed, and without a voice to scream, *Who the fuck do you think you are?* I couldn't consciously see it then, and not for a long time after. I had won the role, yes. But I had lost something important, something I was also fighting for: my dignity.

I packed my bags and kissed my kids goodbye, Baa constantly reassuring me that they'd be fine, reminding me that Steve would be there too, overseeing the completion of the house.

Then, feeling like I was leaving half of me behind, I flew to Birmingham, Alabama, where I lived for seven weeks in a squat, crumbling motel along with the other actors, a smattering of crew, plus the director and his brilliant wife, the production designer on the film (and that was the first I'd heard that Bob had a wife, brilliant or otherwise).

In 1966, when I spent the summer in Oregon filming *The Way West,* I was so young and unfocused, it had felt as though I'd been sent away to the wrong summer camp and half the time I couldn't figure out why I was there. But on *Stay Hungry,* I learned that filming on location is like being sent to the front lines of a foreign war; strangers immediately become friends, daily routines and patterns emerge, and everyone is speaking a new and instantly learned language: the movie. It's what you eat, sleep, and breathe for however long the film is in

As Mary Tate Farnsworth.

production—or as long as you, as an actor, are involved with it. I have almost always found it to be both exciting—that single-minded focus—and stupefyingly lonely. I wanted to be with my children and yet I wanted to be an actor. No matter what, one part of me was always going to be aching.

It helped to remind myself why I was there, to focus intensely on the work, and during *Stay Hungry* that meant being Mary Tate Farnsworth 24/7. Even without the drugs that were floating around in 1975, I felt wired, simmering with anxiety as I constantly hung on to the M.T. parts of myself, shoving every other aspect away. Hovering close to a character, whether in front of the camera or not, is a process I've learned to love over the years. But because I'd worked so hard to convince everyone—most especially Rafelson—that this nymphet and I were two peas in a pod, and because he constantly picked at me, hating my mouth, wanting me to hold it up in a semismile, to pout—just be sexier—it made staying in character feel less like an artistic choice and more like something I had to do to keep the job.

And my body was a constant worry. Mary Tate worked in a gym and the bodybuilders were her family. Presumably she'd slept with one of those family members, a character played by newcomer Arnold Schwarzenegger—who at that point was only a bodybuilder without a hint of what lay ahead. I'm not sure if Arnold was there the day that Bob stopped the whole company—the writer, the crew, the actors, the extras, everyone who was within earshot—to take a vote as to whether they thought I was sexy or not. I stood propped against the full-length mirror of the moldy-smelling weight room, my leotard-clad body starving-to-death thin, and looked around at everyone's slightly distracted faces. Being in the midst of the crew was always where I felt safest, and I didn't need to spend much time with this specific hardworking gang to know that I already knew them. With a shrug or a wink, they unanimously voted that I was grade-A material, whether they actually thought I was or not. I tried to laugh, to go along with everything, to be all easy-breezy. So when Bob—who was staying in the large suite directly above my tiny nonsuite—showed up at my door late one night, I had no problem letting him into my room and my body. Easy-breezy.

I can't blame Rafelson—well, yes I can. When I look at it through today's eyes and my now seventy-one years, I'd like to bash him over the head. But I wasn't anyone's victim. I was a twenty-eight-year-old grown-up, and in '75 it seemed like acceptable behavior on his part. We're all locked into the drumbeat of our history, but eventually you have to drown out that tune with your own voice. I couldn't hear my voice. I couldn't tell the difference between what was the work and what was real life. I felt powerful and important if I could please Bob—and yet I was being humiliated in the light of day by the same man who was happily devouring me behind closed doors at night. The only thing that Bob Rafelson didn't do was tell me to point my toes.

Where was the rest of me, the pieces that were capable of taking care of a child, of standing up for myself, that didn't care whether I pleased him or not? Nowhere I could find. I was participating in a secret relationship that in many ways filled me with shame and rage, a relationship that if discovered would be hurtful to Bob's wife, whom I liked and respected and who was only a staircase away—just as my mother had been only a staircase away in my childhood. None of that ever entered my mind.

16

Sybil

TIME IS A funny thing. My brother tried to explain it to me once. Why it moves so fast now when it used to move so painfully slow. It has to do with the percentage of your life that each day represents. When you've lived 25,915 days, one twenty-four-hour span is a very small part of the whole picture. But when you've only got 10,220 days under your belt, each day is a bigger portion of that existence.

After *Stay Hungry* had wrapped, when I was finally home getting up in the morning with the kids, fixing breakfast, doing all the things I had longed to be doing when I was away from them, every hour moved so slowly I wanted to chew my arm off. And while I can remember that aching impatience to move forward with my life, and I know where I ultimately ended up, I can't quite put together how I got there. Fortunately, tucked away in several old suitcases, I have over forty years of mental maps: dozens of spiral notebooks, leather-bound journals, and cute little diaries that I endlessly scribbled in. Starting in 1974, I threw up on page after page—well, not literally. I kept my book with me always, traveled with it, hiding with it in a bathroom sometimes to vomit my feelings using pen or pencil or even crayon. I think I always had a fantasy that those barely legible pages would someday read like the journals of Patti Smith or Anaïs Nin or Virginia Woolf. But I regret to tell you, and myself, that they do not. Even so, I'm glad to have them.

I open the book marked '75 and stop on April 17, where I wrote, *"Waiting, waiting, waiting."* Then: *"If I don't get the part in* Stay Hungry, *I'll find a way to move on, beginning with a banana split."* Turning the page, I find written in enormous letters, *"I GOT IT!"* Then on July 16, I wrote about being back home again after we wrapped, glad to be with Peter and Eli but worried about money. And that entry reminds me that my salary on the film was so small I had to beg production to pay my phone bill before I could check out of the motel. In August of that year, I describe how I stood in the unemployment line, determined to get my check while politely signing autographs the whole time. But seven months later, by March of '76, my whole world had changed: The finished but barely lived-in Chantilly house had sold, Steve and I were in the process of getting a divorce, and a young man named Coulter was in my life. How the hell did that happen so fast?

A few months after production was finished and postproduction began, Rafelson called to invite me to an early screening of the film in Aspen, where he lived. And with some reluctance, I agreed to go. Waiting for me at the airport when I arrived was a man wearing scuffed boots and a sweat-stained cowboy hat, looking more like the resident of a cattle ranch than a ski resort. He was two years younger than me, a foot taller, and at that moment, Coulter Adams was one heck of a lot savvier. He had lived in Nepal teaching English, spent his life skiing and camping, living by hook or by crook, then a year earlier he had begun working as Bob's assistant/right-hand man/ sometimes house sitter/sometimes playmate.

I remember how nervous I was when Coulter took me to Bob's Aspen house, nerves I never experienced when auditioning. Even though I'd been anxious during the filming, it hadn't been like this. Now I was trembling, felt shy and awkward. Without Mary Tate to define me, I didn't know who I was. And when Bob finally walked in, expecting to find the same girl he'd known me to be, I then felt trapped and couldn't imagine what I was doing there. I kept trying to hide the panic building in me, to buck up and swallow my tears while I calmly told Bob—who thought I'd lost my mind— that I needed to go home. Eventually, in a state of total confusion, I agreed to stay long enough to see a rough cut of the film. After the screening, when Bob stayed to talk with his editor, it was Captain Fun, as Coulter was called, who walked me around town, then took me dancing, showing me his Aspen hangouts. It was a rare moment of feeling young and footloose, with people my age, some of whom had college degrees but weren't driven by the need to find their place in the world, who wanted to play before they had to hunker down. I'd never done anything but hunker down and had no idea how to play. Coulter was not Steve, not filled with vehement opinions that would wipe out my own, and he was not Bob. I didn't need Coulter's approval; he needed mine. If this was fun, then I liked it and I liked him. By March, several months later, Coulter was in California with me and my sons.

*   *   *

Then someone flipped the switch and everything started happening at once. The release of *Stay Hungry* was fast approaching so I was needed to help promote the movie, which meant traveling to New York to do a few days of press. At that precise moment, the escrow on my house was closing, which meant I was once again MOVING! It meant I was truly walking away from Steve and the beautiful home he had built so that I could live in the inexpensive cracker box of a house I'd found outside of Malibu, in a community aptly named Point Dume. And it also meant that I would be living there with someone I barely knew, not bothering for a moment to think how bewildered my children must have been. Hell, I never stopped to think how bewildered I must have been.

In the midst of that total upheaval, I received a call from Dianne Crittenden, who, once again, wanted me to audition for a role against the wishes of everyone else involved. This time it was for a four-hour NBC miniseries produced by Lorimar, which would air over two consecutive nights: *Sybil*. Magnificently adapted by Stewart Stern from a book by Flora Rheta Schreiber, and based on a real case (though the accuracy has been debated), it's the story of a young woman with severe dissociative identity disorder, or multiple personality—and she supposedly had seventeen of them. At the heart of the story is the relationship between Sybil and Dr. Cornelia Wilbur, the psychiatrist who takes on the task of uniting the damaged girl with her fragmented selves.

This was it. The fact that it was a television project didn't matter. I had worked my whole life—lived my whole life—to play this role, and as I read the two-part screenplay, my hands shook. I knew her. She belonged to me. And though I never consciously saw how connected I was to Sybil, never saw myself as having similar psychological survival techniques, I knew my own childhood difficulties would fuel the work, knew this role was mine even if no one else in the room thought so.

All my energy was directed toward that meeting and not one ounce on the gloomy new house with its low ceilings and ever-present smell of fried food, which no amount of candle burning could eliminate. The entire house remained crammed with stacks of unlabeled boxes, making it difficult to move around the small rooms and impossible to find anything. I uncovered the toys, thank God, and a few kitchen supplies. But I was missing a big box of my old clothes, and that's what I needed. My task, this time, would be to convince everyone that I was a real-life version of this damaged young woman. And though I had several different personalities of hers to choose from, I knew I had to go into this meeting as the passive, shell persona of Sybil herself: baggy colorless clothes, no makeup, neat but uncoiffed hair. My old ragamuffin look.

To make things worse, at this very moment my mother decided to get her real estate license and hoped to work her way into the lucrative world of open houses and sales pitches. I was barely listening when she chatted on about passing the exam, telling me that she'd met with a few established brokers to possibly begin working with them. Maybe I didn't listen because I couldn't imagine her actually doing any of it, couldn't see her wearing a red blazer and selling anything to anyone. I had always worried that she needed to be independent of me and constantly felt that I needed to be independent of her. But every time we had tried to move away from each other, every time I'd tried to hire someone to help me, Baa would step forward saying, "Sal, I'm the only one you can really trust." And every time she tried to build a life of her own, I'd get scared and call for her. When one moved forward, the other moved back, then we'd reverse; back and forth the dance continued. Which left her without a job and me—at this exact moment—with no dependable help.

On the day of that first meeting for *Sybil*, I walked Peter to his new school, leaving him sitting uncomfortably in the first-grade classroom, then returned home to get dressed in some drab clothes with Eli close on my heels, desperately complaining that he didn't want to be left with our new housekeeper, that he only wanted his dad. In the midst of my trying to convince him of this woman's good qualities, the phone rang. It was my new employee, the very housekeeper we were debating about, who was already late and now, because of car trouble or something, couldn't make it at all. I had no time left and had to get out the door soon or I'd be late too. I ended up pleading with Coulter to look after Eli, but since I wasn't sure how long I'd be gone, and Coulter wasn't sure what to do with the disgruntled three-year-old, I broke down and called Steve, beseeching him to drive over. He was happy to do that but it had to be on his own timetable. By the time I got on the road for that hour-long drive over Malibu Canyon to Warner Bros. in Burbank, frantically trying not to be late, I felt like I was losing my mind. Fortunately, I was going to be reading for the role of a young woman who was mentally ill.

Dianne looked slightly concerned as she stood to happily greet the girl she'd last seen wearing next to nothing, the girl who had always been boisterous and flirtatious but who was now dour and reticent. Without looking in her face, I gave a guarded hello, then retreated to the back of the room as though total exhaustion were one step away. I sat, staring down at my hands, until I was finally called into the large generic office and introduced to four people waiting there. It took every ounce of concentration I had to contain the part of me that wanted to entertain them, to become the Gidget girl, energetic and joyful. That part of me automatically took control when I felt shy, had been doing that my whole life, and I could feel myself reining her in, pulling her back, permitting the shy part of me to remain visible.

I never completely focused on anyone in the room, but Stewart Stern's generous "open to anything" gaze was palpable, and I felt it even without looking at him. Two of the producers were present: Peter Dunne, who stood quietly watching from the back, and a short-haired, no-nonsense Jackie Babbin, who sat with her forearms resting on her knees, as though not wanting to miss a single one of my softly spoken words. Sitting in the most prominent chair was the director, Anthony Page, who seemed the least interested, hovering on the edge of dismissive, allowing the others to attempt a polite conversation. I could barely speak, but this time, my inability to talk was controlled by me, it was my choice. Awkward discomfort seeped out of me like a gas until everyone in the space felt uncomfortable and small talk fizzled out. With Stewart reading the Dr. Wilbur role, there came a nod for me to begin, and as I did I felt the room shift. I got lost in Sybil's mind, and they watched me disappear.

Through April and into the beginning of May, every time I returned to read, I'd end up dragging myself out of the office, but leaving behind a roomful of stunned, totally confused observers. How on earth could Sally Field, the girl who had been the Flying Nun, be the best choice to play this challenging role? The director didn't want me. I'd heard that he wanted Vanessa Redgrave, and who wouldn't? But Stewart saw the Sybil in me, as did Jackie. I was called in for a final, down-to-the-wire audition, a screen test of sorts, and this time I'd be working with the actor set to play Dr. Wilbur: Joanne Woodward.

In the midst of this, *Stay Hungry* opened to mixed reviews, and I worried that somehow it would affect the decision to hire me for this NBC miniseries. Even though I was told that the notices were generally kind to Jeff and me, I honestly never read any of them. But, as is my habit, I kept several. I still don't want to read them, but I'll close my eyes and pick one. *Variety,* April 23, 1976.

> Bob Rafelson returns to the screen with *Stay Hungry,* featuring an excellent Jeff Bridges as a spoiled but affable rich young Alabama boy who slums his way to maturity through relationships with street-smart characters. Among them is Sally Field, who has now and forever shed her cutesy TV series image...As a lower-class and likeable sexpot, Field is superb.

Okay, fine. I'll take it. Don't ask me to read any others.

As the weeks moved on, days that were filled with auditions and moving boxes and unreliable childcare, with a new house, a new man, plus an ongoing divorce, I slowly became an emotional jack-in-the-box. I'd enfold myself in Coulter's lap to be soothed, until suddenly I'd become exasperated, resenting him for leaning on me financially when I seemed to have no trouble leaning on him emotionally, literally hiding in him like a child frightened of the thunder. My sexuality was free to roam with Coulter, but without warning, that part of me would vanish and I'd want to squash him like a bug. I never knew what all-consuming emotion would define me from one moment to the next. Each one was intensely felt, until it wasn't felt at all, until it was totally wiped off the chalkboard and another was written in its place, in capital letters.

In one of my journals I found three folded onionskin pages, frantically typed without much punctuation and dated April 1976:

I just had a fit. The kind I used to have. Flashes of red and yellow, pressure in the backs of my eyes, my body rigid. It builds and builds while my outside stays calm. The only release is when I hit myself hard. Slap myself in the face again and again. At first I'm afraid it will hurt, then when I feel the sting I lose seconds, they flash by me in a color, a fury where I hit myself again and again. My eyes look puffy not from being hit but from the pressure behind them. Peter is screaming at Eli from down the hall. Eli. Eli. Eli, get off the phone. Eli is screaming and crying. I want to talk to my dad. I hold my voice in and carefully tell Eli to get on the other phone and then he can talk to his Dad. I don't know the number. I don't know the number. You don't have to know the number just get on the other phone. Peter won't let me get on the phone. Peter let him get on the phone. Dad's not on the phone. Just my friend, David. I want to talk to my dad. I want to talk to my dad. I hit myself in the face mostly on my eye. I want to talk to my dad. I hit myself in the thigh with my fist, three four five times. My wrist hurts. I stand straight, wipe my red puffed face, walk in a blur to the kitchen. Eli, just a baby, only three, stands there tears in his eyes. What is it E. . . . what is it? I take the phone from him and hear Peter talking to David. Little six-year-old talk. I try to sound sane. Who is this? David. Peter is your dad on the phone? No, I told Eli, it's not Dad, just David. Oh sorry. I hang up the phone and face my baby. He's not on the phone right now. Lijah, he's not there. He will call you when he gets to his house and I will take you to see him. Okay? I speak very calmly very plainly. I punch each word a little too hard, enunciate a little too correctly. I sound like a very bad actor in the fifth grade. As I walk out the door, fleeing to safety, I remember my baby. You're a good boy Lijah. I can't give him any more of me. His little dirty face watches as I rush away to finish my tantrum.

I remember now how I used to call Eli Lijah—until he told me to stop—and how I longed to talk to his dad too. But I also remember how angry I was at Steve. How he had fueled my fear of being penniless by spending money I was sure I didn't have, how I was so afraid of losing everything, the way it had happened in my childhood, that I sold the house without knowing if I actually needed to or not. More than that, I was furious with Steve for allowing me to hurt him. I walked outside that day, through the sliding bedroom door and around the edge of the house. Standing in an unfamiliar, shabby backyard, I put my arms around my body, whispering, "*I'm sorry, Sally. I'm so sorry.*" Then went back to get Eli, who was playing with Peter and didn't want me to come near. Who could blame him?

*   *   *

Unlike the screen test I'd done for *Gidget*—on a soundstage with a crew and all their equipment—the three scenes I was told to prepare for *Sybil* were to be videotaped in the same office where the meetings took place, using a small camera. For the first time, I was glad that my drive took so long because by the time I got there, I was ready. And from the moment we looked at one another, even before our how-do-you-dos, the relationship between the reluctant patient and the watchful doctor was in place. Joanne Woodward, with her intense gray-blue eyes, met Sybil, and I met Dr. Wilbur. We needed nothing else from each other. There was no polite chitchat, no conversation outside of the story we were telling. I can't remember who was in the room, although I do recall someone taking the video camera off its sticks to follow me around at one point. But the memory I hold most dear is the pure, generous connection I instantly felt from this beautiful, sturdy actor. She was sitting very still in a low upholstered chair most of the time, but during the last scene—which was long and emotional—I jumped to my feet, then scurried under a conference table. Joanne walked to where I had vanished and peeked under, trying to coax Sybil—me—out from hiding. As she returned to her chair, I—Sybil—slowly crawled to sit on the floor by her feet. Not looking at the script, she leaned forward over her lap, her voice kind but unsentimental as she hovered over this emotional girl at her knee. Through the chains of Sybil's childhood, I felt the need to touch the doctor, but knew that Sybil couldn't touch anyone, was afraid of being touched herself, so I grabbed the sleeve of Joanne's thick navy-blue sweater, held it as if it were a precious stuffed animal, then wiped my gushing nose on it. She didn't flinch—only tentatively, and with great tenderness, put her hand on the top of my head. I later heard that Joanne told the production: *If Sally is not cast as Sybil, then I won't be your Dr. Wilbur.* I was cast as Sybil.

I didn't feel excited when I got the "congratulations, you got the job" call. Everything in me went still, quieted by the thought of what lay ahead. I didn't doubt myself, but I couldn't congratulate myself either. I was going into battle, this time on the front lines.

As Sybil.

*   *   *

The schedule was to rehearse for two weeks on a stage at Warner's, then spend two weeks in New York, shooting the exteri-
ors, and a remaining five weeks in the sets built on the studio
lot. I needed my mother. I couldn't leave the kids for the two
weeks' filming in New York without her help. I couldn't do any
of it without her. She had moved out of Joy's house, was rent-
ing a tiny apartment at the beach, and was still trying to beat
down the real estate door. But when I called her, she, without hesitation, packed her suitcase. From then on, that suitcase
would be kept in the back of her car, packed and ready to go
at a moment's notice if I needed her. She even hovered nearby
when Steve had the kids, days that always made Eli happy and
Peter achingly homesick—though for what home I don't know.

Before traveling to New York to start filming, we rehearsed
the four-hour miniseries on an empty soundstage. With white
tape on the cement floor to indicate doors and room size, we'd
block out as many scenes as possible, then at the end of each
day, Mr. Page wanted us to run it all, full out. The process
felt more like we were rehearsing to open on Broadway, rather
than preparing a project to be filmed one scene at a time. And
while I appreciated the information it gave the actors as to
the evolution of the story, my instincts also told me to guard
against leaving the performance on the rehearsal room floor,
as they say. Very different from the discipline of creating and
repeating a performance night after night onstage, I understood the magical immediacy of working in front of a camera,
understood that the camera just needs to see it once, instant
and alive, sometimes only the blink of an eye, or a flash of a
thought that can never be repeated.

Because of that, I'd ask Anthony if I might simply touch on the emotions and not ask myself to land the performance day after day. That would not do. He needed to see all that I had to give, constantly doubting my ability and disapproving—many times vociferously—of my choices. He didn't like the physicality I was bringing to Peggy—the nine-year-old piece of Sybil who held all her anger. He would say he didn't believe her, that she was farcical and looked like an old lady golfer (which she actually did). I didn't know what to do. Rehearsal time needs to be free from the obligation of being a finished product, and I needed to flop around, to try this and that, to find things I didn't know I was looking for, to let my brain lead me toward behavior I couldn't have planned. I learned to rehearse at home with Peter and Eli walking in and out, away from his scrutiny and judgment.

To me the most complicated aspect of Sybil's condition wasn't her many personalities, because those personalities, in themselves, were very clear and uncomplicated, each with a different age and separate emotion. To me what seemed most essential was the moment when one self left off and another picked up—the transition. I was given several grainy video-taped therapy sessions conducted with diagnosed multiple personality patients, the same tapes that Joanne had studied when researching her 1957 award-winning role in *The Three Faces of Eve*. In one tape, the patient looks as though she's try-ing to pass a kidney stone before evolving into a personality that doesn't seem very different from her original one. And in another, the subject reacts so violently when transitioning, grimacing and contorting in such a way that it was laughable, looking very much like a case of bad acting—which was not something I wanted to emulate. In my mind, there had to be a moment when no one existed in the body at all. As if literally no one was home and the body was quiet, waiting for the arrival of its next occupant. But my vision, my interpretation, wasn't something I could reveal or explore during rehearsals for fear that Anthony would blow his negative directorial whistle and freeze me in my search. I felt protective of some tender part of myself that would not be safe under his gaze.

If anyone other than Joanne knew how dysfunctional the rehearsal time had been, or of Anthony's dissatisfaction and my frustration, I was unaware of it. And when I saw Stewart standing in the back of the stage at the end of the third day, then caught glimpses of Jackie lurking in the shadows by the end of that week, I wasn't sure if it was a good thing, or if the director's disappointment in me was spreading. But rehearsals continued, and on the last day, Anthony called in all the executives, producers, and anyone else he could find, to watch a full run-through. He wanted me, Joanne, and Brad Davis (a wonderful actor who played Sybil's friend) to run the whole thing, all four hours, at performance level. Joanne met my eyes, knowing full well what an irrational, unreasonable demand this was—not to mention potentially destructive. She knew that I was trying to tiptoe around the perimeters of whatever performance I had to give, and as we huddled together on the rehearsal sofa, she took my hand. "Do the best you can," she told me softly. "But don't throw it away, Sally. We all see what's happening. Trust us and yourself." So we stumbled through that agonizingly long run-through, then flew to New York the next day and began shooting.

A character—any character—can be played effectively

more than one way. But however Anthony Page wanted Sybil to be played made no sense to me, and nothing I did seemed to make any sense to him. I was exhausted, but not from the work, from refusing to give up what I saw so clearly in my head and to bend myself into some indefinable shape in order to satisfy the director's sensibilities. And at the end of the third day, when I was weaving my way through the crew—who were busy wrapping up—the assistant director asked that I follow him down a hallway of the abandoned hospital where we'd been filming.

Joanne's dressing room had once been someone's office but now had a piece of cardboard taped to the door with *Dr. Wilbur* scribbled on it, and after knocking once, the AD opened it to reveal a small group of conspirators. Handing me a cup of chamomile tea, Joanne told me sternly to drink it, then moved to the back, sitting next to Stewart on a window ledge. Jackie stood with her arms crossed, legs set wide as if she were about to coach a softball team, and for one horrible moment I thought I was being fired. She then moved to the door, locked it, and beckoned me to join them at the back of the room. As we crowded in with our heads together, it felt like the scene from *Dial M for Murder* when the true killer is about to be revealed. Jackie spoke in a stage whisper, looking straight at me: "Anthony Page will be gone as of tomorrow. We will shut down for one day, and Friday we'll shoot without an official director. It's not a tough day, just a lot of establishing shots. Then on Monday, you'll have a new director. He's flying in tomorrow, will come to the set on Friday so you can meet. And off you'll go. How's that?" I was flat-out stunned. She went on to say that Anthony had not been the right director, that he wasn't comfortable around emotion and really didn't believe in therapy in the first place. Then matter-of-factly she added, "He got in the way of your performance." I couldn't speak. There had been moments in my life when someone believed in me enough to extend a hand: Madeleine Sherwood, Lee Strasberg, and now these three people. Joanne Woodward, Stewart Stern, and Jackie Babbin.

In all fairness, Mr. Page was and is a wonderful director of British television and both British and American film, and he has always been an important stage director. The following year he directed the film *I Never Promised You a Rose Garden*, though I don't know if he had been connected to the project when I sent my ill-fated homemade test. Maybe the problem between us had all to do with me. Probably. That's show biz.

That Friday the whole set was vibrating, everyone pitching in to complete the day's work under the unusual circumstance of being director-less. Then, like the first sighting of land after a rough voyage, Dan Petrie's sweet round face appeared after lunch. He made no grand entrance, only stood on the edge of the crew with his hands in his pockets, looking like a passerby who'd just stopped to watch the film company on the streets of New York. I don't know what he'd been told about the director's dismissal or about me. He couldn't have seen enough film to have any opinion about the performances because there wasn't much film to see, and he hadn't been present during any of our rehearsal period. So when Dan started directing the project, bright and early Monday morning, he must have been working on blind faith. We would run the first scene of the day for him, a scene that we had already rehearsed in L.A. but that he'd be seeing for the first time. It was his reaction that I began to trust and rely upon. Through the remainder of the New York work and back on to the Warner's lot in Burbank everything was changed.

In the clearest part of my memory, I see myself standing in the hospital set on a soundstage after we'd been shooting in L.A. for about two weeks. That day had been spent filming, in order, the four scenes that occur when Dr. Wilbur and Sybil first meet. In each of the scenes, Sybil disassociates into a blackout, then awakens at the top of the following scene in another room, doing something totally different. When she becomes aware that the doctor has not only been watching but also having a conversation with her during those blackouts, the terror of having her mental illness discovered is momentarily outweighed by her need to survive. And for the first time in her life, Sybil tells someone. Each scene took place on a different set, with the passage of time indicated by a change in the lighting and the progressive chipping away of Sybil's defenses. It had been a very long day, at the end of two grueling weeks, and as we started to set up the last and most difficult scene, I felt slammed with fatigue. Even though Sybil herself couldn't cry—had blocked herself from feeling any emotion at all—to play her at this critical turning point in her life, I had to be filled with an avalanche of terror and sadness and yet desperately fighting to keep any emotion from emerging.

I was preparing on the set, standing in the corner with my eyes closed while the crew worked around me. Without opening my eyes, I heard Joanne quietly moving into her position so filming could begin and suddenly I couldn't think anymore. I bent forward, putting my hands on my knees as though I'd just finished a race. Immediately, Dan appeared at my side, gently telling me that several more setups would be needed to complete the scene, that it had already been a long, hard week and if I wanted him to pull the plug, we could finish on Monday. I just stood there, trembling as if I were cold, and yet I was sweating. I wanted to say, *Yes, please let me go home,* but I started to cry instead. And in my head, I heard Lee Strasberg's last words to me. *Where you want to be is where you are right now.* All of a sudden, I knew what he'd meant. That you can't dance on the edge, whether emotionally or otherwise; that you had to drown in the character until it was without thought. No longer acting. That to be excellent at anything, it must cost you something. Without looking at him I said, "No, Dan, this is where I need to be."

I don't believe I accomplished it throughout *Sybil*, but it was the first time I had a glimpse of what it meant to be inside a character. Exhaustion now came from the work, a glorious adrenaline-filled climb to catch some part of myself that I didn't know I knew.

Tucked in a calendar with some of her other memorabilia, I recently found a letter that I had written to my mother throughout the filming of *Sybil*. I had written it as part of my preparation, a kind of emotional razor blade to scrape myself raw. In the letter, I tell her how important she is to me, how I am doing what I'm doing because of her, how the only reason she isn't doing the work that I am is because she didn't have the mother that I do. And at the end of the letter I write simply, *Please come get me Baa, please come get me.* I remember writing it, remember writing those words before I stepped into the last shot of the day, knowing that Coulter was coming to pick me up because I was too tired to drive home. And yet I wrote that plea to my mother without understanding why.

I had lived inside of Sybil, felt her longing to know who she was, to know the parts that had protected her and the parts that she was afraid to meet. Did I start to know my own selves as I became more capable of calling on them in my acting? When I walked off the stage, away from the work, did I lose the ability to hear them freely, forget they were even there, becoming a version of Sybil's shell? I don't know.

At the end of the shoot I wrote another letter. This one was to Lee Strasberg. *I know now what you meant. I'll never forget. Ever. Thank you.*

Years later at an Actors Studio celebration with Lee.

17

The Bandit

ONE ROASTING-HOT DAY shortly after *Sybil* had wrapped, I decided the only way to make my stale, airless new house livable was to remove the sun-bleached fiberglass awning that stood over the minuscule back patio. Coulter was in Montana helping his friend shoot second-unit photography on Terry Malick's *Days of Heaven*, meaning he wasn't around to talk me out of it, or frustrate me by not offering to help. It was Princess who stood by my side, looking up at this stupid sheet of reinforced plastic, nodding her head in total agreement. It had to go.

After finding it impossible to live in Joy's garage, Princess had moved out and married her boyfriend, a small-time rock-and-roller. But when she discovered, a few months later, that he'd been sleeping with a checkout girl from Hughes Market, she ended the relationship and was now scrambling for a place to live again. My sister had worked in a clothes store and a bar, tried to become a model, an actor, then a real estate salesperson—studying to get her license at the same trade school in Sherman Oaks as Baa. But no matter what was going on in her life, whenever there was a birthday or a holiday, or a task to accomplish—like demolishing the multi-colored awning—then there she was.

I'm not really sure why we thought that this bit of aggression was the answer to everything but for whatever reason, we were fully committed. And while Baa played with the kids (both of the boys looking as ragged as the yard), Princess and I climbed to the roof, tools in hand, and began yanking the impossible-to-move awning. Let me just say this: My sister and I could have opened a business together—the Sisters Fix-it. Nothing was too big or too disgusting: dead rats, bugs, walls that needed demolishing or rebuilding, you name it. But this frigging awning almost killed us. We were crisp from the sun, our hands were torn to shreds, and I, for one, was sore all over—mostly from lying on the asphalt tile roof and laughing. God knows what kind of carcinogens were being sucked into our lungs as we spent the day hoisting and tugging, planning and figuring, being what we had always been. Sisters.

When the day finally slanted toward evening and the awning hung straight down, only half-removed, we collapsed onto the small stretch of crabgrass which was generously referred to as the lawn, both of us spread-eagle, looking up at the sky. I felt defeated by the hopeless mess that was now my backyard, disheartened by the greasy-smelling structure I was living in, until Baa sat down at my side. Looking at the day's work she said, "Just sell the damn place and chalk it up to 'Oops, I made a mistake.' Go find someplace else to live." It was like being given a get-out-of-jail-free card. Even before I had finished unpacking, I could simply sell it. How about that? I wasn't trapped. I hadn't been looking in the right direction, that's all. There were no bars on the other side of the jail cell.

And as if deciding to sell my house had flipped the switch again, the moment Princess and Baa—using their new real estate expertise—put my now mostly awning-less house back on the market, everything began to spin. My newest and most supportive agent, Susan Smith, called with a "guess what?" tone to her voice, saying that I'd been *offered* a film. No auditions necessary.

The offer came from Universal Studios and director Hal Needham, who had been one of the primary stuntmen on *The Way West* when I was nineteen, doubling for Kirk Douglas. Since then Hal had moved from performing the stunts to choreographing stunts, to directing the second-unit photography on several movies with big action sequences, to now directing his first film, which he was offering to me. But before he sent me the script to either accept or decline, the star of the film—a newly minted sex symbol—wanted to give me a call, presumably to explain what was *not* on the pages I was about to read. And though Susan thought the screenplay was an undecipherable piece of poop, she felt that starring opposite the man who was on his way to becoming one of the most popular actors in America made it worth considering.

How can I write this? I walk around and around but can't make myself sit down and start. Can I find some truth in the shreds of my memory, or the gibberish in my journals, in the letters I wrote and never sent, or the letters he wrote and I kept? Can I paste it all together and make any sense out of it? And how can I dish out these thoughts, this reassessment of a time that was so private and confusing, when in my mind's eye, all I can see is the press circling around, like sharks smelling blood? I want to protect him from that, from their ongoing titillation with him, protect him from me. But I can't. I'll write it. Maybe I'll leave it. Maybe I won't. Problem is, even if I delete it from the page I can't delete it from my mind, my history, or my heart. If I write it down maybe I'll understand it, finally.

August 26, 1976

I'm on an airplane on my way to Atlanta for five weeks. I'm to do a picture with B. Reynolds called Smokey and the Bandit. The script stinks but when I talked to Burt he told me we would "improv" our way through it. I can't figure out why he wants me. I don't seem like his kind of leading lady. He said he hadn't seen Stay Hungry but always liked me in Gidget. What?? And that's why he wants me to sit opposite him in a car for five weeks? I feel guilty about leaving the kids, of course. I hope they'll come to see me. Coulter is still in Montana. Everything always happens at once. I just sold the house. Was it for enough money? I don't know. I guess if you make a mistake it's not the end of the world.

August 27

I arrived in Atlanta yesterday thinking he would be here to meet me. Wrong. He doesn't arrive until today. He called this afternoon, 'Hello, Burt Reynolds movie star here. What are you doing for dinner tonight?' I tried to spar with him on the phone to cover my nerves. God, Field, get a hold of yourself. This was the conversation.

'Pick you up at 8:00, or someone will. I won't be able to come to your room to get you.'

'Why?'

'It's hard for me to walk through that lobby.'

Oh, of course, I thought. How stupid of me.

'You drive by the hotel at 8:00 with the car door open and I'll dive in.'

Nothing but crickets on his end, which didn't matter because I couldn't hear anyway, my hand was shaking so badly the phone was never fully on my ear, always beside it or under it, pressed too hard, too soft. I tried to keep it still by holding my elbow with the other hand. Maybe his hand was shaking too. I doubt it.

'My bodyguard will come get you.'

A bodyguard? Ugg, he just called again. He's going to be late. Swell.

'I'm a gentleman, thought I'd call my date.'

'Is this an actual date?'

'Yes!'

'Are you gonna bring me a corsage the color of my dress?'
And there was nothing.

Now I wait... tick-tock, tick-tock. I wonder how many actual dates I have been on in my life? Not many.

August 28

Then the curtain went up. I walked through the dreaded lobby with the bodyguard, Pete... something or other, out the hotel entrance into the parking lot. I was standing on the top

step. Where was he? There, leaning in a car window talking to
the people inside, part of our group. I had imagined we would
be alone. He seemed much smaller than I had thought, maybe
'cause I was standing on three stairs. He's handsome but dif-
ferent. Wearing my black velvet pants and orange—slightly
see-through—blouse I stamped my feet in a wide "come and
get me" stance. He sauntered over, grabbed me. He must have
felt my heart. I could no longer be responsible for it.

He was incredibly charming, adored at the time for being
who he was: a funny, self-deprecating good ol' boy. A normal
guy on a big ride and getting one hell of a kick out of it. But
he was also a man engulfed by a massive wave of seemingly
instant notoriety, a sex symbol, and when this tsunami of the
collective unconscious slammed into him, he couldn't breathe.
He also couldn't talk about it, couldn't articulate how it made
him feel both empowered and terrified. He had been brought
up by his very southern, well-meaning parents to act like a
man, and he spent his life trying to prove to his father that he
was a man worth loving. He once told me that when he was a
senior in high school, the varsity football team—of which he
was a proud member—won the state championship. It was a
hard-fought, emotional win, and when Burt—or Buddy, as
he was called—stood on the field with his victorious team, he
started to cry. That inflamed Big Burt, his father, who thundered onto the field to slap his son upside the head. Buddy
needed to act like a man, a real man.

And now that man had become the heart's desire of all the
people who wanted a dream figure, the quintessential definition of masculine pulchritude to emulate or fantasize about.

But the human inside that dream figure was just a good-looking, ordinary person, frantically trying to fulfill everyone's expectations and always waiting for the Big Burts of the world to smack the daylights out of him if he failed. He tried to hide everything about himself that he saw as being imperfect, to camouflage himself, which meant that he got locked into the stressful trap of faking it. In my own way, I knew what that kind of public pressure felt like, but my solution had always been to isolate myself, or to hide behind my children or in the Actors Studio, or just to put my head in the sand. But Burt seemed to wallow in it, both loving the focus and spinning from its assault. By the time we met, the weight of his stardom had become a way for Burt to control everyone around him, and from the moment I walked through the door, it was a way to control me. We were a perfect match of flaws.

It was instantaneous and intense. Blindly I fell into a rut that had long ago formed in my road, a preprogrammed behavior as if in some past life I had pledged a soul-binding commitment to this man. On our second date we were no longer with a group of his friends but had dinner in his suite—at a more expensive hotel than mine—and except for Norman, his wardrobe man, who constantly walked in and out of the connecting rooms, we were alone. Burt started to fill me in about his life, the kind of thing you do when you want someone to know who you are. And as I started to tell my side, little bits of me, I began to get subtle—or not-so-subtle—hints that he didn't want to know. That he wanted me to be who he thought I was, and not who I truly was. Immediately, I started clamping down on myself, stuttering when I admitted I'd been living with someone, as if confessing a transgression.

On the set with Burt.

Seeming caught off guard, he paused, then said that he was unaware, not discouraged but disappointed. And whether he meant it that way or not, I interpreted his disappointment as disapproval, and felt embarrassed. Without hesitation, I threw sweet Coulter under the bus, telling Burt that I hadn't been happy with my live-in entanglement for some time, as if the situation had been thrust upon me against my will.

Gently, Burt began to housebreak me, teaching me what was allowed and what was not. If I wanted to tell him what I'd accomplished or talk about my children, or Lord knows, disagree with him about anything, he'd listen glassy-eyed for a moment, maybe offer a distracted comment or two before turning away. Then with a grimace of pain, he'd bend from the waist as he pushed his fingers into his rib cage, quietly belching over and over while gasping for air. Whatever I had wanted to say would be halted by the urgency of his odd attack and the wordless accusation that I was somehow the cause of it. I felt as though I'd been smacked with an invisible newspaper. Automatically, I began to sift my thoughts through a mental sieve, checking for hunks of information or feelings, even words that might trigger another bout, and then preemptively, I'd discard them. I eliminated talking about my struggle with work and money, about Lee and the Studio, about my children and how I ached for them. He disapproved of my prolific use of swear words—something I dearly loved (and still do)—so I eliminated them too. I knew early on never to mention the men who had been in my life, and later became terrified of running into somebody I might have known, whether sexually or not. Burt would pinch my face in his hand, demanding I tell him who the guy was and what kind of relationship I'd had with him. No matter who it was, if I knew him well or only barely, I'd lie with my heart racing as though I'd been caught at the dinner table with pink lips. Feeling that I should, I shared with him only the sunny parts of my childhood and eliminated the darker ones. I eliminated most of me, becoming a familiar, shadowy version of myself, locked behind my eyes, unable to speak.

Three days after our first dinner alone, Burt and I were flying down the back roads of Georgia in that black Trans Am, aided and abetted by Hal Needham and his tribe of stunt folks. I always had an immediate affinity with the crew, any crew, but because I'd grown up with Jocko, a legendary stunt hero, all the stunt guys—and the one stuntwoman—treated me like their little sister, a member of the family. Hal, who not only was Burt's longtime friend but had been living in his poolhouse for the past twelve years, was incredibly skilled with action: how to plan it, how to perform it, and where to put the camera to capture it, while all the time making sure that the stunt people stayed safe as they accomplished their mind-boggling feats. What's more, Hal never pretended to be something that he wasn't: an actor's director.

Every morning, at the traveling circus of a base camp, Hal would carefully oversee the camera being mounted on the hood of the car, and after he discussed with Burt whose coverage to do first, another camera would be mounted facing the passenger window, or driver's, depending. Then with a mirror, a powder puff, and a honking goodbye, off we'd go, Burt and I. Which meant that Hal and the camera operator would frequently be left behind. Having only a vague idea of who the Bandit character was or why on earth I was sitting next to him—never mind my character, because I had none—I'd turn on the cameras, clap my hands to emulate the slate, then Burt and I would play the scene with an occasional line of scripted dialogue slipping in along the way. When we'd run out of ideas, Burt would announce into the walkie, "Got it. Heading back." And whether shooting or returning to base camp, he'd always drive forty thousand miles an hour while peering through the maze of camera equipment clamped and tied and bolted to the car.

The company moved around erratically, in such remote

locations most of the time that the civilians never knew where we were until we were packing up to leave. But every now and then, word got out and a huge crowd of rambunctious fans would appear out of nowhere. When they caught sight of that cowboy hat perched atop the Bandit's recognizable saunter, all hell broke loose. As Burt grabbed my hand, Pete and Tom (his makeup man) would quickly move into position, flanking us while we made a beeline for the safety of his camper. Tom and Pete—blockers to Burt's quarterback—ran interference, pushing the opposing team back long enough for Burt to pop the door open and scoot in, followed closely by his linemen, who would then slam the tin door behind them—frequently leaving me standing on the outside with the clamoring others. Never sure what to do, I just stood there with my head down, hoping all the frantic admirers would think I was one of them (maybe I was one of them) until slowly I'd slink off, maneuvering a path to my own, but rarely used, motor home. And in the air-conditioned quiet, I'd sit alone, flooded with longing for my children and my life. Eventually Burt would realize I was not in his RV—which sometimes took a while—and Pete would be sent to get me.

In the evenings, when we were away from the set and back in the hotel, Burt's mysterious and painful episodes seemed to be escalating. Regularly, a doctor would appear with bag in hand, and after a quick check of the patient's vitals, he'd proceed to give Burt a shot (containing God knows what) directly in his chest. This could not have been a good thing, and I couldn't understand why everyone around him acted so nonchalant while the man was either writhing in pain, panicked that his heart was about to stop, or was having needles jammed into his thoracic cavity. As the others backed away, quietly leaving the room and shutting the door, I stood there, bewildered that his suffering was being treated so cavalierly by his own team. Little by little, I began to step up, doing anything I could think of: giving him a paper bag to breathe into, wrapping hot towels around his feet, on his face, his hands, assuring him that this was an old and trusted remedy. For what, I didn't know. The only time he liked me sounding knowledgeable was when it came to his health, and on that particular subject, I didn't have a clue. I soothed him with dedicated calmness as though he were Peter with asthma or Eli with epilepsy, as if I'd known him my entire adult life, not six or seven days.

Even then, at the very beginning, a sliver of me jabbed, urging me to back out of the room with his guys. I can see it written in my journal, a line here or there, questioning why I was doing this. Why didn't I run? But those words are disregarded when I write a rebuttal, caught in an argument between me and myself. I'd emphatically state that I had feelings for him, that he had no one but me, that I was concerned about his illness, focusing on my need to heal something unknown—nursing a wound that clearly was not located in him, but in me.

Burt's condition was nothing new. It had been going on for a while, and though everyone in his inner circle believed—with a shrug—that the episodes were related to stress or anxiety (serious conditions in themselves), I resisted accepting that as an answer because how could you know for sure? Whatever it was, the pain was real to him. As a result, during the day, when we were riding in that car—whether he was in the driver's seat or I was—part of my attention was on his health, or his heart. Oh, let's face it, on him. It was my job to dispense the only method he had of

Burt and Hal deciding what to shoot.

dealing with the agony, and whenever he'd signal with a nod of his head or a raise of his eyebrow, I'd hand him a Valium, then another and another, offset by an occasional Percodan or two. Good Christ almighty, he was zooming the car down narrow roads, barely able to see around the forest of equipment, and spouting reams of dialogue while I fed him barbiturates hand over fist. Clearly, I didn't have my wits about me.

Halfway through the shoot I turned into Crusader Rabbit, emphatically insisting that Burt's health be taken seriously. He needed to know what was causing the pain, whether it was his heart or stress or some unknown condition, because only then could he accurately deal with it. Mind you, I was the girl who could barely call the operator for information—back when there was such a thing. Now I took charge, researching where to go for an examination and when in the schedule the other racing vehicles—either the one containing Jackie Gleason and Mike Henry, or the truck driven by Jerry Reed and the drooling dog—were to be photographed. During that tiny window of time, the occupants of the Trans Am, Burt and I, flew to the Miami Heart Institute with Pete the bodyguard in tow. All very hush-hush—we were to stay the night, then in the morning, under a general anesthetic, a thin tube would be inserted into Burt's heart to check the coronary arteries and overall functioning of the vital organ. Not a risk-free procedure, but barring any complications, and if no immediate problems were discovered, then he'd be released that day. I was part guardian, part mother, and part spouse, spending the night in his room, sleeping on a chair-like futon in the corner. Early the next day, he bravely kissed me goodbye, saying with a twinkle, "Well, we've made it this far." (Meaning the relationship, not the procedure.) And as they wheeled him away, I stood in the door to his room, tears actually "welling" in my eyes as though I were in a scene from *Dark Victory*.

I'm not sure if Burt was relieved to hear that he had a strong, healthy heart or if he would rather have heard something dire. Certainly, he wanted to feel that he had the right to be in pain, whether from blockage in a major organ or from signals sent from his brain. It's still pain. I tried to reassure him that he didn't need to have heart disease to die, that stress could kill him just as dead as any ol' thrombosis—which he found oddly soothing. But when I told him that the doctor recommended he get into therapy of some kind, that he needed to learn methods to deal with his stress and anxiety, Burt balked, saying that talking to a shrink was self-delusional poppycock. After that I dropped the subject. We went back to work, back to camera mounts, to dusty roads, to driving with the pedal to the metal, and to pharmaceuticals. Did my children ever visit? No. Did I break Coulter's heart by telling him I'd met someone else? Yes. Did it make any sense at all—then or now? That's what I'm trying to figure out.

After the film wrapped, my life bounced back into the familiar routines: being with my kids, my mother, my sister, and finding somewhere else to live. But no matter what I was doing, no matter how important or pressing things in my own life were, I'd instantly drop everything whenever Burt called from his home in Florida—as regularly irregular as those calls might have been.

Burt always told me that he'd been born in Waycross, Georgia, and whether that's true or not, I do know that he grew up in the Sunshine State and over the years, he had accumulated enough land to build an unpretentious, no-frills ranch for his family. The house he'd made for his parents was a simple one-story home, with an easy arrangement of well-worn furniture scattered atop the indoor/outdoor carpeting, which ran throughout, including the kitchen. To the side of this concrete block house was an awning-covered path connected to a smaller but identical version of the main structure, the only difference being that the smaller one had red-flocked wallpaper and black shag carpeting. And it was here that he had gone to recuperate after we parted in Georgia.

I think Burt always considered this rudimentary compound in West Palm Beach his real home, though he'd also owned a place in the Hollywood Hills—a kind of bachelor's pad with a backyard guesthouse where Hal Needham had been living. Right before filming had begun on *Smokey*, Burt had sold that Hollywood home and purchased a hacienda-style gated estate in exclusive Holmby Hills—a beautiful, perfect place with high-vaulted ceilings, polished dark wood, and terra-cotta tile floors, a house that stayed cool in the blazing summer and was almost unheatable during the mild winters (something I loved about the house and he didn't). When Burt finally returned to L.A. that fall, his new piece of real estate was undergoing the massive renovation he'd requested, so he decided to live in the guesthouse located behind his new four-car garage. This one-bedroom cabana had already been completely redone and decorated up the wazoo with a lavish Moroccan theme—no flocked wallpaper but lots of shag, this time off-white, not black.

In that late October of '76, just as I was packing up to move into a rather decrepit though charming house I'd purchased in Studio City, just as my whole life was about to vanish into Burt's needs again, I was asked to go on a publicity tour for *Sybil*. I hadn't seen the miniseries, other than the few grainy clips I'd watched projected on a screen while looping (rerecording pieces of dialogue to fix sound problems). And because I'd felt popped on the nose whenever I'd talked about *Sybil* with Burt, I had tucked the whole experience out of sight, hidden it in the back of my mind, until eventually I quit thinking about it altogether. But then I got to San Francisco and Minneapolis, Chicago, New York, and Dallas, and I remembered that part of me, that vital part that I had worked so hard to own. I remembered my work.

Five days later, when I returned home, it was not only my

thirtieth birthday but also the night of the four-hour industry screening. I'd been planning to go with Princess and Baa, but much to my surprise, Burt insisted on escorting me. By the time we arrived at the screening, it was already full and I couldn't find my family, didn't know where their seats were located. Scanning the packed theater for their faces, I held Burt's hand as we were guided to our reserved seats in the back row. It was then that I realized I was to sit on the slightly worn velvet chair situated between Mr. Reynolds and Joanne Woodward's husband, Paul Newman...whom I had never met. The second I laid eyes on Paul, I blurted out, "Where's Joanne?" hardly acknowledging his existence and barely listening while he explained that his wife would not be joining us, due to the fact that she couldn't stand looking at herself on-screen. Sitting between two matinee idols in a crowded, airless theater, feeling that my head or my heart would explode, I realized that Joanne had the right idea.

By the time the screening was over, my face was on fire and my teeth were chattering, as though a case of malaria had set in. If there was a reaction from the audience, I was too overwhelmed to hear it, and the only thing I wanted was to know where my family was sitting. I longed to see Baa's face, to meet her eyes, to feel proud of myself because she was proud of me. Only then would I know if I had accomplished anything. I wanted to talk to her in the car all the way home, to have a bowl of soup in bed and watch *A Charlie Brown Thanksgiving* with Peter and Eli. But I disregarded that voice, simply shut it out. Where was the part of me that could look at the situation and realize that I felt more alone with Burt than with my children? That I felt trapped not because of him but because

I couldn't hear myself? I had found someone to love, to pour my heart into, someone I felt frightened of, and I was seeking to be loved the only way I knew how: by disappearing.

I went to Burt's place and without discussing what we'd just seen on the screen for three and a half hours, he gave me two Percodan for my throbbing head. It wasn't that he was mean. In a way, I felt he was trying to take care of me for the first time. But when I said that I'd rather have an aspirin, I recognized the sound of his irritated impatience, the "how dare you doubt my know-how" tone, recognized it without registering the recognition. It was a "do it now, go!" command, so I took the pills and immediately felt sick. All night my heart raced, either from the drugs or from the day or both. I lay next to Burt, perfectly still, staring at the ceiling.

18

Treading Water

EXCEPT FOR THE tasty little bits that Jackie Babbin shoved under my nose, I didn't read the reviews when *Sybil* aired at the end of November. But true to form, I've kept many of them.

> *Variety*: "Sybil" boasts an extraordinary performance by title character Sally Field that is as moving as anything ever seen on TV...It is further evidence, following her 'Stay Hungry' film performance, that she is now one of the finest young actresses in the U.S.... The impact is devastating.

> Cecil Smith, *Los Angeles Times*: The bravura role here is Sally Field's—and wonderfully does she play it... Sally's ability to shift from one of these [personalities] to another in an instant, sometimes to find them tumbling over each other, is little short of astonishing.

The Hollywood Reporter: But it's Field who dominates the screen, switching from personality to personality like a sparrow hopping from branch to branch in a maple. And it is this tour-de-force performance which allows the viewer to see how nearly normal Sybil really is. After all, we all have our own multiple personalities that we fling up at a moment's notice. The only difference being that we are in control: Sybil is not.

The response in the country was enormous and impossible for me to wrap my brain around. The reaction wasn't simply because of the quality of the work—which I still can't properly evaluate—but because it was the first time that child abuse had been tastefully, but graphically, explored in any film, much less on television, where millions and millions of viewers were watching. Some of those viewers—to one degree or another—saw their own lives. It opened a national dialogue. People stopped me in the market, or on the streets. Once, a man jumped out of his car after braking at a red light, then ran to me as I stood slack-jawed on the sidewalk, just to shake my hand. They didn't want an autograph or a photo or to take anything from me. They wanted to give me something: their appreciation. I got letters, not only from fans but from doctors, psychiatrists, and social workers and from the people who were struggling to pull their fragmented selves together, to heal.

I felt that reaction and was undeniably strengthened by it. But I didn't talk about it at all when I was with Burt, and I was always with him or preparing to be. What would have happened if I'd allowed all of me to enter the relationship? Perhaps Burt would have been different as well. I don't know.

But as I got quieter, he got louder, becoming short-tempered and impatient, constantly snapping at me as if I'd piddled on the floor. I didn't live with him in his Holmby Hills back-yard cottage, but long before he hired his wonderful British "manservant" Harry, I took care of him, doing all the cooking and cleaning, guarding his health as he began *Semi-Tough*, his next film. Every day was spent trying to make his temporary spot comfortable, buying things for him, fulfilling his every wish before he could even wish it, prepared to give him every-thing I had. Need some oxygen? Here, take mine.

But I wasn't a child playing in my little pinewood house, and at some point I had to speak up, I had to tell him that every-thing I was feeding him, every comfort I was providing, was coming out of my own empty wallet. Why couldn't I just tell him that I was flat broke and that if he wanted those towels or vitamins or toothpaste, for God's sake, then I needed the cash to go get them? I hemmed and hawed, rehearsed the words in my head over and over, delayed saying anything whenever he was feeling an attack coming on. One day I finally blurted it out. For a moment, I thought he hadn't heard, then he matter-of-factly replied, "My business manager gives me only a thousand dollars a week. If I give you two hundred, that'll leave me with almost nothing." I took it once and felt ashamed.

Still, woven through everything were so many good moments, real and lasting things. When that revolution-ary device, the VHS player, first came on the market in the late seventies, the big black box immediately appeared in the Holmby Hills house. Long before there was a channel called Turner Classic Movies, or a Blockbuster—which didn't open until 1985—Burt gave me the movies. Movies I'd never seen, no matter how often I'd stayed home from school to watch *Ben Hunter's Movie Matinee* on TV. He gave me *Red River* and *The Searchers*. Sat with me as I watched *Now, Voyager* and *Kings Row* and *The Treasure of the Sierra Madre*, all the time chattering with excitement about a moment coming up, or explaining the backstory on an actor, details that added to the impact of what I was watching. Together we'd watch grainy bootlegged copies of *Mr. Skeffington* and *Rear Window* and *The Letter*. We loved something together, which made us love each other.

There were also times when he'd shove the big clunky cassette into the machine, then leave me sitting there while he went off to do God knows what, wandering in to check on me periodically, as though I were a child being distracted in an effort to keep me from the grown-up conversations. And perhaps those mostly black-and-white stories did distract me, allowing me to forget for a moment the painful fact that Peter and Eli weren't there, and they were rarely there. I kept thinking if I brought them into the relationship slowly, we might transition into becoming a family. But Burt was uncomfortable having them around and they were uncomfortable being around. They'd lean on me, pulling my shirt with a flat "when are we going home?" look on their faces. Burt's few attempts to charm or seduce them always flopped like a juicy fart at a family reunion. Bless their little hearts, they were not impressed with anything he did, not even the go-karts he gave them for Christmas. Peter at seven and Eli, just four, would have nothing to do with him, and couldn't be bought or bribed out of it. They were the guards at their mother's gate, and to have me he'd have to go over them—not easily done. Torn in two, I'd fix dinner for my boys, put them to bed, give them a quick back rub, then pack up the dinner I had prepared for Burt. Making sure my mother had his phone number, I'd then drive to Holmby Hills and serve dinner to the man in my life. The next morning, I'd get up in the wee hours, drive home, fix breakfast for the kids, and take them to school.

I can still see my mother standing at the kitchen sink holding a cup of hot coffee in one hand and her robe closed with the other. She'd watch me, saying nothing as I slammed through

Me and my boys. Can't believe we had a cat. Peter was allergic.

the back door in a race to beat the morning. She'd say nothing in the evening as she watched me pack up the car, not hindering but not helping while I covered the flank steak with tinfoil to keep the marinade from spilling on the drive back to Burt's. And when I was overwhelmed with guilt, with an anxiety I couldn't identify, when I would turn to her and bow my head, muttering the only thing I could say, "Thank you, thank you," she said nothing. But as I see myself now, leaning toward her, was there a part of me that wanted something other than her wordless support? Did I want something from her she could not give because she was as blinded as I was?

She had never warmed to any of the few friends I'd had in my life, never responded with anything other than quiet scrutiny or out-and-out disapproval, saying, "I have to tell you this for your own good." She had loved Steve the child, but she had felt certain that I shouldn't marry him when he became a man, and though always pleasant to him, she had barely tolerated Coulter. But when I introduced her to Burt, I watched my mother turn into the young woman she once was, her eyes sparkling with a look that I remembered. And my grandmother put her rumpled hankie over her mouth, just as she'd done when she first met Jocko.

Perhaps Joy was automatically charmed by this kind of man, but when the press started reporting about Burt's adventures with other women, it was my grandmother who made sure I knew about it, sometimes calling early in the morning to report what the *National Enquirer* had printed, describing the included photos. If I avoided talking to her on the phone, then she'd mail them to me, thick envelopes filled with carefully underlined articles, stories that always included my

A rare hug from Joy at a 1977 family gathering.

name. Not one missed her attention or, ultimately, mine. At first I was annoyed and aggravated, then I just tried to ignore her. With Burt, I held my head up, too proud to say anything. I'd think, *What the hell, I've been on countless fan magazine covers with stories linking me to people I've never met. I didn't just fall off that godforsaken turnip truck.* But part of me knew it was all true. I felt duped and a fool.

I never mentioned it and neither did he, but those were usually the times when Burt would toss gifts at me, some of them very expensive things that felt as though they were meant for someone else. Once he gave me a yellow Corvette, reminiscent of the long-ago blue Ferrari and equally ridiculous. Why give me a small sports car with virtually no back seat? I'd never expressed any interest in cars and had two young children, plus I was frequently expected to chauffeur Burt's Great Dane, Bruiser, around with me during the day because the dog got lonely. Can you picture what the four of us looked like in that car?

Though *Sybil* had aired to great acclaim, *Smokey* had not been released yet and the industry didn't know what to make of me. To everyone's amazement I had somehow become a strong actor, but if *Sybil* was any example, then I was definitely not pretty enough to be leading lady material. Not only that, but to play across from most of the leading men at that time, I appeared too young, and certainly not sexy enough—whatever sexy is. How long could I wait for the right project? I couldn't let myself sink back into a sitcom, but I had to earn a living. I had to find a way to tread water, to keep afloat until I could catch another project, a place where I could do the work I now knew how to do.

My next film was not that. The script wasn't very good and while I worried that I wasn't moving forward, I didn't think I'd be going backward either. Plus, sometimes you have to do the best you can with what you've got, and that was *Heroes*. So when Burt was on location in Texas filming *Semi-Tough*, I agreed to do a film co-starring Henry Winkler, fresh from his Fonzie success.

Because of my work in *Stay Hungry* and then *Sybil*, coupled with the fact that I was now starring opposite the very popular Mr. Winkler and dating America's current heartthrob, I was informed that a new magazine wanted to do a cover story on me. It seemed like something I should do, like an important part of my transformation. But how would I tell Burt and how would he react to the fact that I'd agreed to do an interview with *People* magazine? I worried and stewed, let days go by, phone call after phone call, not wanting to face his wrath, and when I look at the childish angst written in my journal, I wonder what on earth the fuss was all about. On my part. On his. I know that he always worried about the press, felt that they were out to get him, to uncover something that would be hurtful or destructive. And there had been times, on other films, when potentially disastrous stories had been printed, so maybe he was feeling the scars from that. Maybe he was afraid that I'd inadvertently say something that the journalist could twist, or perhaps he didn't want to be linked with me any more than he already was. Or maybe it was because he didn't want the focus, any focus, on me.

I wouldn't rely on my memory to accurately recall his reaction, but in this case, I wrote it down. "Why?" he asked. "What about me? Aren't you concerned about me? How could you do that? You just want your face on the cover of some damn magazine. Why didn't you ask before you agreed to do it? I'm disappointed in you." Burt didn't call me a smart-ass like Jocko did, but even without that, I felt fifteen again. It was our first real fight, and the tiniest thimbleful of my anger seeped out, telling him that I thought it was my job to help promote the film, that I'd been on lots of covers and didn't give a "darn" (I wasn't allowed to swear) about being on another one...which wasn't completely honest. The following day, I profusely apologized, and he accepted.

I did the *People* cover story dated April 25, 1977, and only now have I read the three snide pages, beginning with the title "The Flying Nun Grows Up: Sally Field Makes a Movie with The Fonz and Has a Fling with Burt. When Sally Field Wanted to Kick the Habit, Burt and Henry Were Waiting." Maybe I should have listened to Burt.

Out of nowhere, and not long after both of our films had wrapped, Burt became possessed with the idea of directing William Inge's *Bus Stop*, with the role that Marilyn Monroe had famously played in the movie to be performed by me. I was flattered at first, but when I realized that the play was to take place in a run-down, tin-roofed theater in Jupiter, Florida, on precisely the same date that *Smokey and the Bandit* was going to open, I thought perhaps it wasn't the best time for either of us to be doing regional theater. He was outraged. How could I do this to him? I had agreed to do it. I couldn't pull out now. Plus, he had asked my mother to play Grace, the waitress in the bus stop café, a lovely role. It was either incredibly generous or a way to ensure that I truly couldn't walk away from the production. And even though, in the back of my mind, I suspected that Burt had some ulterior motive behind this remote production, I didn't walk away but flung myself at it, conjuring up some version of Cherie, the sexy small-time chanteuse, while all the time squelching the piece of me that kept saying I needed to be somewhere else, availing myself of the energy that was finally coming my way.

Before the play even opened, Burt—who was the director—departed to promote our film, while I stayed behind, performing in a theater containing about seventy-five seats. It was located so close to the railroad tracks we had to incorporate the passing train into each performance—which meant the entire cast turned toward the upstage window as if

Baa and I in Jupiter, Florida, where we were performing in Bus Stop.

watching the thunderous thing roll past. But when a Florida rainstorm would unleash itself onto the old tin roof, vibrating the tiny box of a theater with pounding noise, we had to move onto the apron of the stage and scream dialogue directly at the audience. The hardest thing was to keep from laughing, and in that we weren't always successful.

In retrospect, I realize what a wonderful time that actually was. Since the show ran early in the summer, Peter and Eli were out of school and could come with us. As soon as Burt was gone, the kids chose their spots. Peter wanted to stay in the small wharf-like actors' commune with Baa and Princess, who had joined us, but every night Eli was mine. After the curtain went down—even though there was no curtain—he would nestle next to me in Burt's old MG while I maneuvered the pitch-black half-hour drive back to the beach condo, the newest Reynolds acquisition. Throughout every performance Peter would sit backstage, memorizing all the dialogue as he listened to it float through the wings, while Eli waited impatiently to have his mother all to himself.

Early in '77, it was announced that the Emmys would be canceled that year due to an ongoing dispute between the New York and Hollywood chapters of the National Academy of Television Arts & Sciences. A new ceremony, the Television Critics Circle Awards, was formed to take its place and *Sybil* was nominated for five awards: best miniseries, best direction, best screenplay, and two nominations for best actress in a leading role: Joanne and me. But the Television Critics Circle Awards were clearly not the Emmys, and as the date for the ceremony approached everyone seemed to question what the hell they actually were. Even so, my agent wanted me to go, Jackie and Stewart wanted me to go—especially since Joanne had refused to attend any awards ceremony, ever. Burt thought the whole thing seemed rather bogus, not to mention rinky-dink, but was willing to go if that's what I wanted. It was decided. I would go to the first Television Critics Circle Awards ceremony with Mr. Reynolds on my arm, or rather I would be on his.

In those days, an awards ceremony was not treated as if it were the American equivalent of a coronation, the way it is today. But coronation or not, I had no idea how to do any of it. The only awards show I had attended before that, I'd been bedecked in pink taffeta and launched into the audience, two things I wasn't anxious to do again. This time I purchased a spaghetti-strap dress from I. Magnin department store and sat on the floor of Burt's enormous bathroom on the day of the ceremony, shortening the floor-length hem while hot rollers cooled in my hair. When at last I slipped into my wine-colored jersey gown, Burt looked at me and with great authority announced that I was too pale. Immediately, he pulled out his personal stash of pancake makeup and rummaged around until he found the half-used cake of Max Factor's Dark Egyptian—the same stuff that had been slathered on me by an alcohol-smelling body makeup lady using a mildewed sponge in the wee hours of the morning during *Gidget*. Not only does it itch like crazy when it dries, it also rubs off on everything, and Dark Egyptian is not exactly a subtle shade. But when I think of that moment, standing nervously before a wall of mirrors as Burt carefully painted my exposed body, I realize that I'd take his Earl Scheib job over the finest hair and makeup artist anytime. True, I ended up looking like Sacagawea with very curly hair, but it was what he had to give. And it makes me smile.

That had been a remarkable year on network television. Both Alex Haley's profoundly important miniseries, *Roots*, and the made-for-television movie *Eleanor and Franklin: The White House Years*, which the wonderful Dan Petrie had also directed, were nominated for awards. Needless to say, *Sybil* didn't win a Television Critics Circle Award in any category. But it didn't matter. The whole evening I was so worried about Burt's health, about the frenzy we had caused at being seen together, and about the unmistakable smudge I was leaving on everyone, I didn't have much room left to feel disappointed.

Then, three months later, the Academy of Television Arts & Sciences reinstated its award season, and *Sybil* received the same nominations, which meant this time I was nominated for an Emmy. Unlike Joanne, I didn't have enough miles in the saddle yet to understand that winning an award is not the truest indication that your work is excellent. I longed to feel that I'd actually conquered something, something that perhaps only I could see, and deeply wanted to be included, to go to the Emmys as a nominee. But my gift card from Burt had already been used up, and when the ceremony rolled around, I was in Santa Barbara, where he was both directing and starring in *The End*, a film in which I'd been hired to play a small role. For the rest of the shoot, weeks and weeks, I'd stay in order to take care of Mr. Reynolds. As the evening of the ceremony approached, everyone started calling, pleading with me to break away for a few hours, insisting that the studio would send a car, wardrobe would find a dress, and Stewart would be waiting to accompany me. "Go if you want, but be prepared to lose again" were Burt's words, or maybe the only ones I heard. But what was I looking for? Permission? With only the slightest hint of disapproval from Burt, I felt ashamed of my desire to be accomplished, to be successful, to be recognized, embarrassed that I wanted to attend this award show, to feel that I was no longer a joke in the industry. And if, for a moment, I started to lean in the direction of accepting the studio's offer, he'd sit on the edge of the bed, gulping air, jabbing his fingers into his chest. I felt stuck in an old pattern: To be loved I had to stop being me. Matter of fact, I had to stop being anyone.

In my journals, I'd constantly write that I wanted to run

away, to escape from some hidden trap. But at the same time, I was bending myself into a pleasing shape, a soothing, compliant cup of warm elixir that Burt was then lured into drinking over and over, until he became addicted to the seemingly unconditional love I was offering. And perhaps in that way I was his trap. Once he was undeniably addicted, needing a fix of me, I'd be gone. He would never know what had hit him or how to get another supply. My anger was much more lethal than could easily be seen. Even by me.

I didn't go to the 1977 Emmy Awards show. And just to make this story even more reminiscent of "The Little Match Girl"—who used her last match for warmth before freezing to death in the frigid night—I ended up watching the show in the rented condo, sitting alone on a stiff living room sofa with the sound turned down so as not to disturb the man who perhaps didn't know, or maybe didn't care, how much it meant to me. And as I sat there—matchless in the snow—I heard my name announced.

I'd won the Emmy for *Sybil*.

19

Norma

HOOPER WAS MY third film with Burt, each role getting smaller and less interesting just as I was getting smaller and less interesting. But honestly, I hadn't been turning down other projects to play these cookie-cutter characters. Nothing else came my way and I couldn't even find a project to fight for. I was hanging on, grateful to be earning enough to exist.

Tuscaloosa, Alabama, was the location this time, though for what reason I don't know, because the Hal Needham–directed film had nothing to do with Alabama and all to do with the rollicking, action-packed life of stuntmen, a kind of homage to the dangers of stunt work. Not only was one of the main characters (played by Brian Keith) named Jocko, but my stepfather—who was now living with his wife in a small apartment in Sherman Oaks—was also given a small role, making the whole thing utterly surreal. And in the midst of this, of spending most of every day shopping for Burt's dinner, or running his errands, I received word that Marty Ritt wanted to meet with me. Considered to be one of the most important voices in the industry, Marty was responsible for films like *Hud*, *The Spy Who Came In from the Cold*, *The Great White Hope*, *The Front*, and *Sounder*. He had been a member of New York's Group Theatre—which eventually became the Actors Studio—and was a revered actor's director.

Since I was primarily there to take care of their star, the *Hooper* production didn't need me for a while. So without looking for Burt's approval, I agreed to fly home the following morning, informing Burt of my decision without hesitation. He nodded, saying Ritt was a great director, then tossed the subject aside only to pick it up later in the evening when he began coaching me on how to behave in the meeting, treating me as if I were a ten-year-old on my first excursion away from home. I listened to him talk, trying to see his focus as loving, but kept reminding myself that once I was out of his sight, I'd be free. He ended the lecture by criticizing me for running lickety-split back to L.A. without reading the script first or knowing exactly what the meeting was about.

But lickety-split I did run, with zero idea as to what the meeting was about. And not giving a rat's ass. Not only that, but since my meeting was set for three o'clock at 20th Century Fox and my flight didn't get in until twelve thirty, I wouldn't have time to read the screenplay that waited for me at home. Here comes the cavalry: My mother read it for me. She was standing at the front door when the car dropped me off, watching for my arrival as if we'd planned it that way, and as we hugged in a quick greeting she patted my back, saying, "I'll tell you about it as you get dressed. We can do this."

While I started yanking things from my closet, trying to decide what on earth to wear, she followed me around, slowly recounting the screenplay while enduring my frantic need for more character details, telling her I didn't care about her opinion of the story, or whether she would want to see the film, I needed details. Eventually, we both agreed that I couldn't fake a character I knew nothing about, and that I should go as a blank slate—which should have been easy after living in the shadowland for so long. I dressed all in beige with my long hair pulled back at the base of my neck.

Though I wasn't late, Marty was waiting for me with his office door wide open, saying nothing as he watched his secretary greet me in the waiting area before ushering me into the room where he stood. Wordlessly, Marty gestured to a straight-backed chair, then moved behind his desk, getting right to the point. "Have you read the script?"

"No," I replied flatly, though the thought flashed through my head to lie.

"It's very strong," he said, then sat quietly as if thinking. We didn't chat so he could determine if I was right for the role, there were no pages he wanted to hear me read, he merely sat in his polyester jumpsuit, wearing big, smudge-covered glasses, and watched me. And even though his focus never wavered, I didn't feel uncomfortable, there weren't awkward moments of being judged. He simply looked directly into my eyes, asking nothing of me but to be as unguarded as he was. When he finally spoke, he said, "You were quite good in *Sybil*...very good."

"Thank you," I answered, without a hint of humility.

He then asked me a question I'd never expected. "Are you serious about your work?"

Feeling how deeply I meant it, I answered, "Yes."

"The studio doesn't want you. You're not a name to them,

not a name they want. Several other actresses, who are names to them, were offered the film. I think they would have done a fine job, but for whatever reason, they all passed and things have a way of ultimately working out as they should. I want you to do it and if you want the role, I'll fight for you… and I'll win. Read the script, then let me know."

In my beige dress, with my beige flats planted squarely on the ground, I answered as calmly as I could, "Even before I read it, I know. I want this."

That night while sitting propped up in bed, Eli asleep on one side, Peter on the other, I read *Norma Rae*. I read it again on the airplane heading back to location the next morning, this time with my hands shaking as they had when I read *Sybil*. I wasn't anyone's vision of the uneducated, promiscuous southern mill worker who stumbles into becoming a hero. I wasn't even Marty's. But he had wanted to meet me, over the studio's objections, because he thought I could act. And as we sat together in his office, he saw something in me that I didn't know I was showing, that I couldn't have planned because I didn't know I had it within me to call on. Marty saw the place where Norma and I met, where we were the same. Two days later in the rented Tuscaloosa house, I answered the phone to hear Marty's voice: "Sally, the part is yours."

I wouldn't have asked Burt to read the screenplay, but he wanted to, acting as though he were doing me a favor. When he finished, he threw it across the room at me, saying it was a piece of shit, and in an outraged sneer accused me of simply wanting to play a whore. And wham, without thinking I found myself speaking up for Norma and ultimately for Sally, and the part of me that I valued most.

"First of all, she is *not* a whore. She's a wonderful, complicated character. And sure, I'd play a whore. Why not?"

"Well, no lady of mine is gonna play a whore."

"I'm an actor, Burt. I'm not a whore. I'm not Norma or
Sybil or Gidget or whomever I'm supposed to be playing. I'm
an actor."

"Oh…so now you're an actor. That's all that matters now,
right? Ha…You're letting your ambition get the better of you."

"My ambition *is* the better of me and you can't touch it." I
felt that I was inside my dream again, standing with my arms
around the children, protecting them from being destroyed by
something unseen at the top of the stairs. The children were
me, all of me, and the love I had for a craft that had allowed
me to hear them. *I will not be conquered.* With that, something shifted, and the debate inside my head that had started
the moment I met Burt ended.

Even in 1978, the unionization of southern textile mills faced
substantial opposition from management, who didn't exactly
want this film to be made. The story was based on Crystal Lee
Sutton, a heroic union organizer and advocate who in the early
1970s bravely stood up against the J. P. Stevens mills for the
mistreatment of their workers. But luckily, the Opelika Cotton
Mill, located in Opelika, Alabama, was a family-run, recently
organized plant that had been operating since 1901 and was
struggling against the larger, more lucrative companies. Which
meant it was the only working mill willing to give the production permission to shoot in and around their factory. Of course,
the large compensation check didn't hurt. So, with a welcome
letter from Governor George Wallace, the three-month location

for *Norma Rae* was set for Alabama—the state where my grand-mother was born and the place where my friendship with the man whose words I still hear in my head began.

Born in New York City in 1914, the son of Jewish immigrants, Marty attended Elon College in North Carolina, which forever imprinted on him the stark contrast between his Bronx child-hood and the Depression-era south. He then attended St. John's University but quickly gravitated to the theater, first as an actor, then as a director. Work was hard to find during those Depres-sion years, but he was able to get employment with Roosevelt's WPA Federal Theatre Project as a playwright. And though he always said he had never been a member of the Commu-nist Party, he was certainly influenced by the radical left and proudly called himself a true "lefty." In 1952, Marty was work-ing as an actor and director plus producing television programs when he was mentioned in an anti-communist newsletter called *Counterattack*, published by American Business Consultants, a group formed by three former FBI agents. Though he was never asked to testify, Marty refused to cooperate in any way with the House Un-American Activities Committee and was ultimately blacklisted by the entertainment industry when he was charged with donating money to Communist China. For five years, he supported himself, his wife, and several other blacklisted friends by teaching at the Actors Studio and handicapping horses. He understood the Norma Raes of the world. He was one.

Two weeks of rehearsal time, on location, is what Marty always insisted upon and I've never worked with a director who used that time more productively. Before moving out to the real locations, with a handful of scenes that he thought were essential to understanding both the characters and the relationships they had with each other, we spent three days in a conference room located in the same building as the production offices, a short drive from the mill. Three days of nothing but asking questions and exploring the text with pencil in hand, beginning on that first day with the inevitable read-through.

The majority of the cast were present, starting with instantly likeable, easy, and funny Ron Leibman, set to play Reuben—the Jewish New York union organizer. The brilliant Pat Hingle was to be Norma's father, Barbara Baxley her mother, and Gail Strickland was cast as her best friend. The only major character not there was Norma's husband, being played by Beau Bridges (Jeff's older brother), who was finishing another film and wouldn't be arriving until the second week of production. Just as everyone was settling around the table, Marty called me to the back of the room along with Gail, whom I had instantly bonded with. As the two of us stood in the corner wondering why we'd been summoned, Marty looked directly at Gail and said, "You know you too could have played Norma, you're a strong actor. But I gave this one to Sally. Your time will come." I was so struck by that. Not only was it a kind and generous thing to do, but it was also incredibly insightful. He didn't know either of us at that point, and he needed a believable friendship to be instantly created on-screen, one in which neither of us was more or less important than the other. He was helping us to pave that road. Plus, he understood actors, understood how much they want to be given the opportunity to do complicated, interesting work. I wanted it. Gail wanted it.

During that first week, I hardly looked at my new director. He was matter-of-fact and perfunctory, as though he didn't want to waste precious time being charming, so he wasn't. Even in the second week, I looked in his eyes only when he stood in front of me, quietly urging me to go further with what I was doing or suggesting I add a new ingredient, always speaking the kind of acting language I understood. And as I began to find and expand Norma, from the length of her stride, to the twang of her accent, to the heat-induced slowing of her rhythm, I felt Marty's trust in me expand, approving my choices, appreciating my skill. But Norma was mine, and though he never tried to manipulate or invade the character with some preconceived vision of his own, Marty knew how to take what I was presenting and hone it. He understood the use of activity and the power of stillness, how to complicate and simplify a performance at the same time. He warned actors to be aware of when they nodded their heads and said, "Yes" at the same time, underlining with their bodies what was coming out of their mouths. Marty called it "capitulating to the moment," one of the many Martyisms that I began to use constantly. "Aggressively illiterate" was another Martyism, this one having little to do with acting and a whole lot to do with the Republicans.

When we began to shoot, I could feel Marty's excitement at the prospect of challenging me, not like Jocko had done with his aluminum pole of humiliation, but with the sheer joy of watching me explore, of seeing me flat-out fling myself toward his suggestions, showing him that I could keep all those balls in the air while daring him to throw me another. It was as if we were playing a game of competing skills and my desire to

On the set working with Marty while fabulous Ron Leibman watches.

please him was not about diminishing myself, but about finding how far I could stretch my wings.

But sweetness and light Marty was not, often becoming a gruff curmudgeon, impatient with actors who were unable to change their performance or even a line reading to adapt to what he wanted, and downright sharp with an actor who was late or lazy or indulgent. If an actor or a crewmember—including the cinematographer—ever stopped or cut the scene themselves, he'd go apeshit. It didn't matter if you forgot your words or fell in a ditch or swallowed your tongue, you kept going. And never would he stand for anyone instructing the actors other than the director. If another actor casually commented on or tried to correct another's performance, watch out. The performances belonged to the director and the actor hired to play the role, period. Anyone wanting to make a comment had to go through Marty, and even then, it might not be welcomed. When I once heard his wife, Adele, quietly try to express an opinion, he replied with a wry grin, "Well, when you direct your film, I suggest you try that."

That's not to say that he didn't value everyone's specific participation. He never took a "film by" credit, saying that when he had written, photographed, edited, and acted in it, playing all the roles, then it would be a Marty Ritt film. Our husband and wife screenwriters, the brilliant Harriet (Hank) Frank Jr. and Irving Ravetch (who had also written *Hud*), were on the set every day, constantly conferring with Marty on the sidelines, and yet I never knew what their comments were—although as time went on, I was able to decipher a Ravetch note from a Ritt.

Strict as Marty sometimes seemed, his rules never felt like an invasion but a protection, a safe space created for the actors to explore. And in that space, he invited and encouraged any notion an actor could come up with. But at the same time, he was never unsure or wishy-washy. If he didn't like what an actor was doing, that actor sure as hell knew it. He was a no-nonsense man who wore a one-piece jumpsuit—often food-stained—and never adhered to anyone's book of etiquette. He bluntly said what was on his mind, didn't chit-chat, coddle, or patronize. If you came to him with a whining complaint he'd say, "I'll run you a benefit." Which basically meant, get on with it. He was direct and succinct, but always generous with his intelligence, his passion, his delicious sense of humor, and his wisdom. He said what he meant and meant what he said.

When we were about three weeks into our nine-week shoot, moving along so swiftly we tried to slow down for fear the studio wouldn't take us seriously, Marty knocked on the door of my motor home, opened it, and stepped inside without waiting to hear my response. I sat frozen on the sofa, my needlepoint in midair as he plopped down on the swivel chair across from me. Because he'd never been in my camper before, I worried that I'd done something wrong—which is no big surprise—but when he acted as though he'd just wandered in, like he had nothing else to do, I suddenly felt shy. What would I say to him? We'd been together socially several times when Adele had gatherings in their bungalow next to mine, small dinner parties that usually included other members of the cast and crew, and once it had been only the three of us. But Marty and I had never been alone together.

As he looked out the window, watching the smattering of crew weaving around the pine trees, he began talking about the spinning room and the dinosaur-like machines that several of us had learned to operate. He laughingly told me that one of the actors had to walk outside because the old wooden floor's swaying vibrations had made them seasick and asked me why I hadn't needed a break. After I told him I was too busy to think about it, and he refused to tell me which actor it was, we sat in an easy silence. Then he stood, looked at his watch, and with a "time to mosey back to the set" attitude, stepped down into the well of the door and grabbed hold of the handle. He paused for a moment, then turning to look at me said, "I want you to know, Sal . . . you're first-rate. Just wanted to tell you." With that he left the trailer, closing the door behind him. No amount of applause, praise, or accolades that I might receive in my lifetime will ever mean more to me than those few words from Marty Ritt.

Every day was filled with focus and challenge, with calling on skills I didn't know I owned because I'd never had the opportunity to use them. And in the evenings, I'd enter my rented condo, still exhilarated with accomplishment, only to feel how far away my children were, in more ways than one. When I'd make my nightly call, hoping that one or the other would deign to talk to me, would consent to a few mindless seconds of chatter, it was usually Peter taking the phone, not because he needed to hear my voice but because he knew I needed to hear his. Afterward, Baa would reassure me that they were fine, repeating over and over that they missed me but they were honestly just fine. And I'd cross another day off the calendar I'd hung on the wall, feeling torn and grateful for my mother's presence. But when they stayed with their father for a few days or a week, I'd lose all contact with them, which made me feel a whole lot of things, grateful not being one of them.

Steve was a devoted, caring father, but his life seemed even more chaotic than mine. He had found a way to acquire two tattered houses next to each other, then created his version of a freewheeling hippie compound in the middle of Sherman Oaks. Whenever the boys spent time with him they'd return looking like two starving refugees, their dirty arms and legs covered in fresh scrapes or poison ivy or mysterious bug bites, Peter looking hollow-eyed with his asthma in full swing. I'd hear Steve's anger coming out of the mouth of one son, see his attitude on another, letting me know that they thought ambition and careers were for fools, that their father lived in the real world and that mine, the superficial world of show business, was fake. And even though that rhetoric tapered off after a bath and a hot meal, I selfishly felt relieved knowing that when I was away, my children spent the majority of their time with their grandmother and not with their father.

But halfway through *Norma*'s shooting schedule, Baa was going to be traveling to Switzerland for three weeks with Ricky and Jimmie, who now had two children of their own. My brother was still working at Caltech with the Nobel Prize–winning theoretical physicist Richard Feynman. They had published several important physics papers together, and because of this, Ricky had been invited to CERN for six weeks. This physics facility for nuclear research would soon become the most important international scientific establishment in the world, home of the proton-colliding LHC (Large Hadron Collider), which is a massive underground ring, twenty-seven miles in diameter, between France and Switzerland. It was at CERN, on July 4, 2012, that my brother, along with hundreds of other scientists, announced the discovery of the Higgs boson, or the "God particle." But in the summer of 1978, Ricky was making his first trip there and had invited Baa to join him. That meant that I would lose the help of my mother. Once again, it was my sister who jumped to the rescue.

Princess agreed to bring the boys to me in Alabama for two weeks, then take them back to stay with their father for a week, until Baa's return. When I look back at that time, it makes me think that perhaps this was the beginning for my sister, the first step toward discovering the career in which she could truly excel. On film after film, as my movie career continued, Princess would join me, first as my sister, then my

*The two of us on a movie set in the early
eighties.*

assistant, and then, all on her own and with bone-wearying
hard work, becoming an assistant director. Accomplished
and well respected, over the next ten years she would create
the shooting schedules and run the sets on countless movies, big and small. Then in 1991, when her daughter, Maggie,
was born, she moved into episodic television, staying close to
home, always relying on Baa, just as I had, to take care of
her baby while she worked. But during that June, she was the
nanny, the boys' aunt, and my best friend.

One day, toward the end of their time with me, Peter and

I were sitting in the camper looking out the front window, watching everyone slowly returning to the set after their half-hour catered lunch under the pines. Princess was standing outside beside a tree, out of harm's way as the dangerous Eli rode his rented bike around in circles, dodging crewmembers, who were busy dodging him. With his knees tucked up under his chin, Peter sat adjusting and readjusting the big foam driver's seat, turning first one way, then the other, while asking me a nonstop stream of questions: Who is Norma Rae? Why does she work in a mill? What is a union? Always wanting to know the story and who I was in it. (No surprise he became a novelist and screenwriter.) I watched his antsy behavior from my seat on the passenger side, carefully answering everything he asked, until slowly Peter began to cry, deep inconsolable sobs. When I asked him why, what had made him so sad, he said, "It's Norma's life, just that, Mom. I feel so bad for her." But as I moved to sit on the floor next to him, patting his back, I had an inkling that it wasn't Norma who had affected him so sharply. The following day he would be traveling back to Los Angeles and Sherman Oaks, back to his father, and it was a sadness that we both felt. He had begged to stay with me, begged and begged like only an eight-year-old can. If his grandmother had been the one waiting for him, perhaps he wouldn't have felt so powerfully alone. Perhaps I wouldn't have felt as though I were bleeding internally, making a kind of *Sophie's Choice* decision. My work or my children. And as I look back, from so many years away, I want to scream at my thirty-one-year-old self. Could I not have kept Pete with me, a boy who only wanted to sit and memorize the dialogue, and let Princess take five-year-old Eli back to Steve? It would have

Eli and Peter on the set with me. The supportive local folks standing in the background were extras.

split my focus, but it would have eased his heart and mine. Can you not have a do-over? Ever?

The day before *Norma* wrapped, Burt arrived at our Opelika location, driving up to my condo in a Cadillac convertible and a cloud of red Alabama dust. For the first time, he was coming to *me*, visiting *my* set, where I was working and he was not. It was late afternoon after a day of filming, and when he stepped inside my location home he held me to his chest and I could feel his heart jumping around frantically, just as mine had done when we first met. Awkwardly, he presented me with a little white box tied with a red velvet ribbon, and it was hard not to notice that his hands were trembling. But when I opened it to find a diamond ring, not huge but not me, he didn't speak and

I didn't know what to say other than thank you, awkwardly. For the rest of the evening, something unsaid hung in the air, something that neither of us wanted to pluck out and examine.

We had only one scene to shoot on that last day and it's one of my favorite moments in the film. In it, Norma returns home late at night after Reuben has bailed her out of jail. With quiet purpose, she strides through her tiny house and, one by one, wakes her three children, then sits on the worn love seat with them tightly tucked around her. Unemotionally, she gives each of them a picture of their different fathers then tells them the men's names, who they were, and whether she had been married to them or not. She looks into the sleepy faces of her children and says, "This is who I am. I want you to know that."

Since it was a bright Alabama summer day and the sequence took place at night, large sheets of duvetyn (dense, feltlike black fabric) had been placed over the windows and doors, turning the shoe box of a house into a cave filled with movie lights— airless and stifling. The scene was shot simply, with the cinematographer, John Alonzo, following me handheld as I moved from room to room, collecting Norma's sleeping children, then into the front room to flatly explain their existence. And as I held my body in Norma's world, sweat rolling down my neck and between my breasts, I had the flicker of a thought: Burt was going to be arriving on set soon, maybe he was already waiting for me in my motor home. I could feel a tug on my mind, some part of me preparing to leave myself, leave what I wanted behind, to give over, to serve someone else's needs. This sliver of a moment is so clear in my mind. I felt Norma's strength, just as she was beginning to feel it herself. It was as if Norma gathered that fragile piece of me in her arms with the rest of her children, set me on the sofa, and said to me, *I want you to hear it from me. This is who I am*, without sentiment, apology, or appeasement.

While they were setting up the last shot, Marty and I stepped outside to get some air and as soon as my eyes adjusted to the light I saw Burt, laughing and talking with the crew. I walked toward him, looking like a greasy-faced, sweaty mess, and hugged him, my arms wrapped around his neck. Even I could smell the unmistakable field-hand odor radiating from my body. But when my condition registered on his face, his disapproval an instant smack, I immediately turned around and walked back into the airless cocoon, keeping Norma away from Burt's critical eye, leaving Marty to welcome him, shaking his hand. I was sitting on the floor in the corner, hovering over the performance, when Marty returned to the set, and after looking through the lens to check the shot, he sat on an apple box next to me, putting his hand on my shoulder. I looked at him from the corner of my eye without turning my head, and I could feel words through his steady tender grip. Words he didn't need to say.

As with Sybil, I never stood outside of Norma Rae to see how much of her story was, in reality, mine. On first read she'd seemed as foreign as if she'd stepped from a flying saucer, but when Norma is pushed against the wall, when everything in her is on the line, she springs onto a worn worktable with a sign over her head—the coffee table of my past. Her struggle to stand up, her fight for respect, was the same as mine, for my work and myself. Through each day of working side by side with Marty, as Norma's sense of dignity gradually emerged, I stood taller. As she unleashed her rage, I felt freed. When she found her voice, I heard mine. By standing in Norma's shoes, I felt my own feet. If I could play her, I could be me.

20

The End of the Beginning

In a small screening room at Fox studios, I sat next to Baa, an audience of two as we watched *Norma Rae* for the first time together. As with *Gidget* fifteen years earlier, I'd never visualized the film becoming a product to be put in the marketplace. It was all so secondary to the experience of doing the work, secondary to having Marty in my life. Even after the film had wrapped, that moment when everyone vows eternal friendship only to vanish from sight, Marty had never let me go. Months later he was still reaching out, asking me to join him for lunch at the studio where his office was located, or Adele would invite me to their home for an early dinner, telling me to arrive at 5:30, and if I didn't show up until 5:45, Marty, no doubt, would have started eating without me.

And as my mother and I sat in this tiny room with a huge screen, saying nothing when the film ended and the lights came up, I didn't know what to think. I waited for Baa to respond, for her unbridled enthusiasm, her avalanche of joyous support allowing me to be joyous too. But she looked as numb as I felt and as we wandered out of the building, she sounded only lukewarm, expressing concern about Marty's simplistic, documentary-style approach, saying, "I don't think he helped you very much. He doesn't even use any music."

I worried that she thought it had nothing glamorous to offer, probably because I worried *I* had nothing glamorous to offer. I'm sure she was frightened for me; I was totally on the line. But even now I can hear the swipe she was taking at Marty, knocking him for his direction, and I distinctly remember pulling away from her, from the importance I'd always given to what she thought. I can see in my mind the two of us driving home that day, so different from the drive home after my first performance at school. We had both traveled an unimaginable distance since then. This time it was my hands on the wheel, my eyes on the road, away from hers as she watched my face. Feeling damned with faint praise I said, "It's scary. It's just me."

"Yes," she said. "It is."

What flashed through my head was the fear that I wasn't enough to hold an audience for two hours. After a deep breath I exhaled. "Yikes. Bring on the dancing girls."

Norma Rae was the first film in which I was the star, and from the moment I was given the role my mother's reaction had seemed subdued. Did I feel that way then or is it just as I'm thinking of it now? She had so diligently stood by me, never complaining that she needed a life of her own, and when I'd dream of running off to live in New York or the mountains of Colorado or an apartment in Paris, she'd clasp her hands together with one smack, then hold them under her chin as if she were saying her prayers, "Oh…take me with you." And all this time I'd thought that I had been taking her with me, thought that what was happening to me was happening to her as well. But it was not happening to her. It was happening to me...alone. I had grown out of her sphere of influence because it had happened to me, every day of my career had happened to me. Not her. I had left her behind and it jarred us both.

Marty called a few days later to tell me that *Norma* had been accepted into the Cannes Film Festival, which would be held, of course, in France. Up to that point, the only people who had seen the film were the production team and a cluster of 20th Century Fox executives, which included Alan Ladd Jr. (Laddy), head of the studio. But now the festival's selection committee

Taking pictures of the paparazzi at Cannes. Beau and Marty thought I was nuts.

had clearly been added to that list. Plans were immediately put into motion; Laddy and his wife, along with several other executives, would be attending the festival. Marty and Adele were going, as were Hank and Irving (the Ravetches) and Beau Bridges (who is wonderful in the movie). They all agreed to fly to Paris, then down to the Côte d'Azur to stay in the historic Carlton Hotel for ten days. And they needed me.

The change in me over the last months, since *Norma* wrapped, had been gradual but unmistakable. And even though I couldn't completely sever the pull that Burt had on me, deeper, truer pieces of me had started to flare out, moments that were always met with Burt's shocked disapproval. *Who is this selfish, angry person? Where's that sweet girl you used to be?* That sweet girl I used to be had never existed, not singularly. And never would again. The dynamic between us had changed, because I had changed. He couldn't hold on to me and I wouldn't stand still. As I began pulling away, he tightened his grip, sometimes literally.

When I called to let him know I was planning to attend the festival, he asked in a huff what the hell I intended to do there. It was a waste of my time. But it was the South of France, I told him, and I'd never been there, hadn't traveled to Europe since my one disastrous trip after *Gidget* with the girl who'd been my stand-in. His tone then changed to one of deep disappointment, explaining that I'd be seeing places he wanted to show me, that I was spoiling it for him. When I couldn't be either bullied or seduced out of my decision, he lashed out: "You don't expect to win anything, do you?" And I truly didn't. Never even considered it. But I was going. And when I wouldn't change my mind, he slammed the phone down, cutting off any more conversation—if that's what it had been. For the eleven-hour 747 flight to Paris, I sat with Hank Ravetch, feeling wondrously free.

Why is it easier for me to write about the times in my life that felt humiliating or shameful? Is it because those are the things that haunt me? Do I hold on to those dark times as a badge of honor, are they my identity? The moments of triumph stay with me but speak so softly that they're hard to hear—and even harder to talk about.

I remember my tiny corner room on the eighth floor in the big Carlton Hotel, and how I had packed for the South of France not knowing that the South of France can be freezing in May, and how I would wrap myself in the twin-size satin duvet and stand in front of the armoire, sliding my few flimsy outfits back and forth, wishing something warm would miraculously appear. I remember how the phones rarely worked when I tried to call the kids, and how I never felt the pressure of Burt since we weren't speaking. And the French windows opening out onto the Croisette—the promenade along the beach below—and how I'd stand outside on the half-moon balcony, watching the carnival-like commotion, and later, the swarm of paparazzi taking pictures of me while I used my Instamatic camera to take pictures of them. I felt like Audrey Hepburn in *Roman Holiday*—seeing a whole new world after spending a lifetime locked behind the palace gates.

Before the new Palais des Festivals was built in 1983, films at the Cannes Film Festival premiered in an enormous theater, famously atop twenty-four majestic stone stairs. The interior of the theater looked like a movie set for *The Phantom of the Opera,* and those associated with the film were seated for the screening in a grand baroque balcony at the back of this Gothic space. I had never seen the film with an audience, much less with one of the notorious audiences at Cannes—didn't even know they were notorious until the night before, when Marty and Laddy tried to prepare me. Throughout the dinner they carefully explained that, unlike demure American audiences, this group could react vociferously if they didn't like what they saw. And if they weren't booing, then they were walking out in droves. I wasn't sure how anyone could be prepared for that.

By the time we were finally grouped together in the elaborate balcony I was almost catatonic with nerves, and when Marty, Beau, and I were separated from the others, then seated in the

Marty held my hand the whole time.

front row, my knees were literally knocking. This was the *Queen Mary* of theaters and being in the front row of the back balcony felt like we were on the edge of Mount Everest. Not only were my knees vibrating, but I was now flooded with vertigo and the fear that if I stood up too fast, I'd tumble over the edge onto the velvet seats below, dead before the lights even went down. But then they did go down, and the film flickered away.

Every scene felt torturously long, without a single entertaining moment, topped off with the achingly slow roll of the end credits, an endless list that went on and on while everyone in the packed opera house sat, making no noise at all. They didn't applaud, but hell, they didn't boo either. They were motionless in their seats. When the studio's logo finally scrolled by, there was a moment of darkness, and then, suddenly, bright spotlights flared onto the balcony, smack into our faces. And in one connected group, the people below rose to their feet, turned to us, and cheered. They stood applauding for ten minutes. Marty—who had been holding my hand because I was visibly trembling—gently slid away, moving to the side, extending his arm in my direction as he retreated. And I heard the surge that was meant only for me, the sound of that universal appreciation, recognition, and regard for my work. I started to cry.

I won the Palme d'Or for best actress and went on to win every award for best actress that existed in the United States that year. Including the Academy Award.

21

Me, My Mother, and Mary Todd

AFTER *NORMA RAE* I was considered to be an honest-to-God movie star. Although I was never besieged with offers the way I'd always dreamed it would be, every year one compelling screenplay would come my way and I'd be thrilled, not to mention relieved. But even after winning my second Academy Award in 1984 for *Places in the Heart*—a film I was proud to be a part of—I never saw myself as being an important, highly sought-after talent at the top of my game.

Slowly, very slowly, I became aware of a soft buzzing, a voice telling me to prepare myself because soon my hard-fought position would be gone. Even as I tried to evolve into each phase of my career, building a production company, developing and producing films—including *Murphy's Romance*, which my beloved friend Marty Ritt directed—this whispering voice kept repeating that before long I'd be facing the same mountain that I had just climbed, but without the strength to move anymore.

When I was thirty-eight, a rather flimsy project was presented to me, and while the film might have been dull, the producer was not. He was a tall, gentle man who enjoyed being around people, someone who made friendships less difficult for me. He was easy to like, good to have around, and since I wanted a family and needed to feel safe, I married him. That was Alan. Once again, I packed up my two sons, now twelve and fifteen, and we all moved, this time to a home in Brentwood.

Three years later, when Eli was preparing to get his driver's license and Peter was a freshman in college, I gave birth to my third son. At forty-one, I was the mother of a newborn again and it didn't hit me until Sam was five weeks; as a parent, I was starting all over—from the very bottom of the mountain.

I remember sitting in the baby's room wrapped in the arms of a huge stuffed bear that had been flung into the corner, feeling stunned. I was looking down at this tiny stranger's face nursing at my breast when suddenly I didn't want to do any of it anymore. It wasn't that I didn't adore this little boy whose eyes had instantly latched onto mine. It was that I didn't want to love him as deeply as I knew I would. Didn't want to care about my work or whether Peter was finding his way or Eli was driving safely. Didn't want to worry about money or my weight or what to cook for dinner. After spending my whole adult life struggling to find more, the only thing I wanted now was to put a *Closed* sign on my forehead and sit in this corner staring at the wall. Perhaps in that way Alan had been a perfect choice. Without meaning to, and through no fault of his own, he had allowed me to become a stationary, lifeless lump, unseen by him and unaware of myself.

For all ten years of our marriage we lived in that one place, the Brentwood house. But like a dog chewing on a hot spot, I was constantly fussing with it, irritated and uncomfortable.

Endlessly I'd move the furniture from room to room, then change all the carpets and the paint color, remodeling the whole thing more than once. Even after deciding that it wasn't the house causing my discomfort but the marriage, even after divorcing Alan with one unemotional blow, I remained stationary. Ultimately, I lived in the Brentwood house for almost nineteen years, telling myself it was better for Sam. But in reality, I didn't know where to move or how to find comfort.

Then in 2004—and for no apparent reason—the evil spell was broken. Instead of standing stock-still, I was flooded with my need to run away: to pack my bags, my boxes, my son, and disappear. I sold my lovely, perfectly situated Brentwood home for a perfectly disgusting five-bedroom house at the top of the Malibu mountains, a house as isolated and hard to reach as I was. But hell, I would have moved to a deserted island if it hadn't been for Sam. Now sixteen, with his two last years of high school to finish, he had become my connection with the world. I may not have wanted to love him, but I did, and just like it had always been with his brothers, I would have turned myself inside out for him. But unlike how it had been with his brothers, I'd lost the strength to leave him when I worked, simply couldn't do it anymore. So I carted him with me. Starting when he was not quite six months old, Sam was my location sidekick: in Louisiana for *Steel Magnolias*, in San Francisco for *Mrs. Doubtfire*, in South Carolina for *Forrest Gump*. He and Baa even traveled with me to Israel, where we stayed for three months to shoot *Not Without My Daughter*.

But after each film—some more successful than others—the feelings of accomplishment would quickly disappear, drizzling out through an invisible crack inside me, a crack

Trying to protect little Sammy's ears at a very loud wrap party with Olympia, Shirley, Dolly, and Julia. The stupendous women.

that seemed to be growing. Even when my movie career was securely chugging along, even before the first stall—dips that always occur—I began to feel defeated. It was like I was looking for it, waiting for it to happen, wanting to believe the same words about myself that I'd worked so hard to erase from people's minds long ago; that I was trivial, uninteresting, a lightweight. I believed it about myself whether anyone else did or not, and I was constantly looking for someone or something to make me change my mind...about me.

During a social gathering in 2005, Steven Spielberg took my arm, pulling me to the side, and as we stood in the corner he explained that he'd purchased the film rights to the wonderfully dense *Team of Rivals* by Doris Kearns Goodwin. He wasn't sure how long it would take to find the perfect writer, but once that screenplay was in his hand, he said emphatically, "I want you to play Mary Todd." To portray the much-maligned, mentally challenged Mrs. Lincoln in a film directed by one of the most creative filmmakers who has ever lived was an opportunity I felt with every cell in my body. Yet I remember faking an excitement I couldn't quite find, as if I'd already seen the movie of my life and knew the ending. When I walked away that day the droning voice inside my head warned, *Don't start wanting that. It will never happen!*

I don't know if I had accurately foreseen the future or if I became my own self-fulfilling prophecy, but throughout my fifties I felt crippled with grief because the love of my life was dying. Not a lover, or a husband. My work. I was forever saying to myself, *This is what you've got and who cares? Does it really matter? Do you need to be in prestigious films, in leading roles? Just find some work, somewhere, and if it happens to be a character in a story worth telling, fine. If not, suck it up and do it anyway.* And some-how, I did, earning enough to give all three of my children the education I had longed for my whole life. Then, when Sam was heading off for his freshman year at NYU, and Peter and Eli were launching their own careers and marriages, were becoming par-ents themselves, when I was turning sixty and felt like the sink-ing ship on which my whole family was standing, I agreed to do another television series, *Brothers and Sisters*, once again on ABC.

I'm not sure why I pushed Baa to live with me, don't know that I wanted her there any more than she wanted to be there. For months I had been telling her that it was time, that she would probably be living with me at one point so why not now? There had been little episodes, like the time she mistook superglue for eye drops, or when she showed up at my house hobbling on a swollen foot that was black and blue to the ankle, laugh-ing it off with a shrug and a flimsy explanation. Times when Princess and I would roll our eyes at each other, wondering if she'd been under the influence of alcohol or only accumulated years. And though she'd had a bout with breast cancer in her early seventies, she had long since been cancer-free and was a strong, independently capable eighty-three-year-old.

Besides that, my mother loved the small home I'd purchased for her ten years before, a prefab metal house in a gated com-munity nestled above Zuma Beach. But I would sometimes wonder why she even had the place, since it stood empty most of the time. All she needed was the hint of an invitation and there she'd be, in my driveway dragging the suitcase out of her car and into my house to stay with Sam, or eagerly standing at the back door waiting for Peter and his two little girls to arrive for a sleepover. And if she wasn't at my house, then she was at Princess's place in the Valley, looking after Maggie, my niece, who was a full-of-life teenager.

Maybe I thought Baa would put a dent in my loneliness. But that couldn't have been my reason for pulling and prodding her to live with me, or at least not the obvious one. I'd long to see her, to talk to her about the kids or life's little dramas, but eventually I'd feel that same ol' tug. I'd sense her eyes searching my face for something and I'd turn away, annoyed and uncomfortable. She must have been aware of the raw edge between us, but we never talked about it, and over the years it had grown, festering into a gnawing wound that I couldn't find or heal. Always I felt it was my fault, that I lacked patience, or was a control freak, or simply resented having to support her. Constantly juggling my fear of money with the cost of private schools and universities—undergrad and grad—and trying to be the safety net for my sons, while all the time looking after my mother's needs, was an anxiety-filled circus act. And jabbing at me was my conviction that I was a rotten, selfish person for feeling anything but gratitude toward her.

Even so, a year after I moved into my snake-infested, coyote-friendly retreat, and shortly after I began filming that fourth series, my mother reluctantly left her tiny place near the ocean, giving it over to Eli and his newly pregnant wife. With a clenched jaw she moved in, jamming everything she owned into one room and spreading out into the rest of the house—as though she actually lived there—only when my granddaughters would arrive. As soon as they stepped inside, before I could give them a hug, Baa would re-create that infuriating walky-walky world, a world that I could never join, and our old tug-of-war was back.

I began to dodge her, to wait in my bedroom upstairs so I could sneak, robber-like, into the kitchen as soon as I heard the pop of her bedroom door closing. And there was always the pop of doors closing, a door-slamming opera that echoed through the house from early morning till late at night. I never knew if it was a loss of hearing on her part, or a conversation meant for me to interpret. And if it was, then what was she saying?

June 25, 2007

Tonight. I was in the kitchen cooking dinner when Baa's report came in and after she hung up the phone we just stood there, staring at each other. It seems that Baa has several small growths?... tumors?... in various locations all over her body—remnants of the breast cancer she beat ten years ago, or so we thought. The doctor reassured her that there are count-less drug options available, treatments that they've had some success with, and advised her to start immediately. "Well," she said after a while, "it had to be something, sometime." Then laughed, saying she was just happy she wouldn't be slowly los-ing her mind. That was one disease she didn't want. "Okay, there you go," I said. "Thank God for small favors." I put a big glass of red wine in front of her and when she went to call Rick and Jimmie, I called Peter, then Eli, and finally Sam.

She knocked on my door around 9:00, said she wanted to be with me and that she was a little bit drunk, maybe. She was a lot drunk maybe. I told her to get into bed and we could watch TV, but instead we ordered books for her online. Everyone has to face death sometime, she said to me with a slur. I told her it was a good thing she was drunk.

Who wouldn't be? I've always been uncomfortable when she's messy drunk like that, but tonight I tried to let it go, to move past it, to let her be fragile. She's scared I guess and wanted to be with me. I'll remember that always. It's going to be hard to understand all that I feel about her. I'm going to lose her.

Once, when I was about twelve, I asked my mother, "How do you get a boy to like you?" She thought for a moment, then answered, "You listen to everything he says and laugh at all his jokes." Now I was sixty-three and she was eighty-seven, cancer-ridden and savaged by the unsuccessful chemo treatments, but whenever she'd hear me starting dinner, she'd mosey out of her room with a paperback mystery in hand, then patiently sit at the kitchen counter, listening to everything I said and laughing at all my jokes. We chatted sweetly, stiffly discussing the kids or their kids, or Princess and her daughter, anything to keep talking. But then we'd be struck with it. The quiet. If I looked at her, she'd look back down at her book, and when I turned to the sink, I could feel her eyes on my back. I'd clamp my mouth closed in a soundless scream, then turn back toward her, my face showing nothing as I pleasantly chopped and stirred and served—a do-si-do that went on and on. I felt helplessly locked into step, unable to shake it off and reach out to her.

On the rare mornings when I didn't have to get up before the sun, when I didn't face the hour-long, traffic-filled drive to and from Burbank, where the *Brothers and Sisters* sets were located, I'd wake to the slam of a door, followed by the nonstop barking of Baa's look-alike dog, the dog that peed every time I tried to be nice to it, the dog that went insane, running up and down beside the steamy, overheated pool while Baa swam her few laps. On those mornings, I'd sit in my bed, or on the floor of my room, unable to breathe. Baa, in the ongoing battle for her life, was downstairs swimming in the pool, while I was upstairs drowning in nothing, feeling panicked and futureless, as if I were the one who was dying. And when I felt like I was going down for the count, I finally reached out for help.

Dr. Dan Siegel quietly led me into his glass-filled office, then sat in a straight-backed chair, while I sat on the sofa across from him with my heart pounding. After a moment of stillness, he gently asked what had brought me there. Slowly, I started telling him about my life, dribbling it out until it became an emotional flood, as if I'd been storing everything up, waiting for this one moment. I relived memories, episodes, and events that had happened long ago, but which now felt fresh and scab-less.

One day, after we'd met a handful of times, Dan asked me in a casual tone if I could name all the different parts of myself. "Parts or fragments or aspects or personalities, whatever feels right to you," he continued.

"I call them pieces" was my reply. No one had seen me like that before, as being a divided person, and at the time I hadn't yet begun to see it clearly myself. But, as if it were a question I'd answered before, I immediately, without hesitation, named all the pieces of who I am. From incident to incident in my life, I could name the parts of me that had been most present, and if any others were involved. Little by little, memory by memory, I could see it, could feel the system of behavior, the cooperation and alienation between the members of my interior family. It was something that I had known instinctually but had never pulled into the front of my awareness and certainly never articulated. The powerful, elusive Madwoman who had always frightened me and the deeply sad Ragamuffin who had fueled much of my work but whom I despised and would banish from my mind, except when acting. Then there were the easy ones, the red rage of Fire, reliable Rock, and Airy, the entertainer. Dan urged me to talk to each of them, to visualize them in my brain like they were separate people and, as if I were playing a game of "Red Rover," to finally call each one over, to allow them to join the group, and me. It was a version of the very scene I had played in *Sybil*.

But this couldn't be the reason I felt so frantic, so panicked and frightened. I'd been like this all my life.

I tried not to think about the Lincoln project as the years passed. I didn't want to know how it was progressing because for every month it dragged on, for every year it was delayed, my loss of it was also delayed. With all my might I tried to not want it, as though the film were a hungry animal, and if it could smell my desire, it would eat me. Several scripts came and went, as did the writers, and the possibility of the film ever happening seemed to dwindle. Then it was announced that Tony Kushner, the Pulitzer Prize–winning playwright of *Angels in America*, had been hired to take a stab at it, and a year later, he delivered what I consider to be one of the finest screenplays ever written. Instantly, an elaborate table reading was assembled in the East Village's historic Cooper Union and I was invited to participate, along with an extraordinary group of New York actors, including Liam Neeson—who was to play Abraham Lincoln. The producers kept insisting that my attendance wasn't required, that the reading was "only" to give Steven and Tony a chance to hear the script out loud, and maybe that was true. But part of me, quieted for so long, refused to listen. That part knew very well that the reading would be more than that, no matter what they thought or said—as every reading is. Fortunately, during that week's schedule of *Brothers and Sisters*—then in its fourth season—I happened to have a few days off, meaning I didn't have to sell my soul to the devil to get to New York.

I could feel the battle going on inside me, one part repeating that this reading was dangerous, exposing me to an inevitable loss that I might not have the strength to get up from. While all the time another voice softly persisted, arguing that if this was truly my only moment as Mary *then by God, grab it fully*. And so I did. I worked to own as much of the text as I could in the forty-eight hours I had it, put on a blousy black dress, pulled my hair into a knot at the base of my neck, and without hedging my bet, launched myself toward Mary Lincoln. For two and some-odd hours all the voices in me came together, and I was lifted by the eloquence of the words, the skill of a huge tableful of actors, and the craft that had always been my lifeline. When I walked away on that glorious day, I knew that my work had been well regarded. But the further I got from the afternoon, the louder that frigging voice became, telling me that I'd better protect myself because the whole scenario had already been played out and I had failed.

When Liam dropped out of the film a few days later for personal reasons, I silently hoped that the whole project would fall apart and I wouldn't have to worry about it anymore. Then several months later, when it was announced that Daniel Day-Lewis had agreed to take on the role, I felt sure that this was it: my death knell. I was back to being a television actor, whereas Daniel was considered to be the finest actor in the world. I wanted to dig a hole and bury myself, to beat my mother to the grave so I didn't have to feel any of it. Including my mother's death.

During one of my sessions with Dr. Dan, he asked if he could show me the "Still Face Experiment," a short video made by Dr. Edward Tronick and his developmental psychology team. The film shows a nine- or ten-month-old baby sitting in a high chair, open-faced and gleefully fixed onto the eyes of her mother, seated before her. The baby is preverbal but clearly communicating back and forth, in a joyous conversation of love with her responsive, playful parent. The mother is then told to turn her head away for a moment, and when she turns back, it is with a blank, lifeless expression, no longer responding in any way. The baby is immediately affected, confused as to why her mother is not reacting, becoming anxious as she tries to reestablish the attachment, at first babbling, then reaching out, then screeching with alarm, until finally the baby turns away, trying to escape from the discomfort, and starts to cry. If no one comes, if the mother still does not hear her distress, she begins to chew on her own hand, hoping to soothe herself. Then, after a few minutes—which seems like an hour for both the viewer and, no doubt, the baby—the mother comes back to life and the connection is reestablished. The bad is gone and the good returns, and if done with loving support this process can help the baby build inner resilience. It is a powerful and moving study of a child's need to have an attentive parental connection and the hardwired reaction of that baby when the attachment is lost, even for a short time.

"But," I protested, "parents and caretakers have to look away periodically—they're human beings. And my mother was there, always caring for me, or making sure I was with someone who would, my grandmother and my brother. Baa was wonderful and loving," I kept declaring. "I'm here because I don't know how I'll live without her. Not to tear her down. She has been my life!" Dan listened while I repeatedly told him he had it all wrong, nodding his head with acceptance, until he sat quiet for a moment. Thinking.

"A child instinctually knows that it cannot survive alone," he told me a few days later, and I wanted to say, *No shit*. He continued, with a "be patient" look on his face, "But if their survival is dependent on someone who might be dangerous or deeply flawed, then the knowledge of that is too terrifying to accept, so the child creates a better scenario." Even though I was tapping one foot against the other, giving off the appearance of being bored to death, he began speaking now for the imaginary child. "'The problem can't be my mother's fault because I can't live without her, so it must be mine. My mother is already perfect, she has to be, and I am not. I can fix me. I can make myself better.'"

I stopped moving. And something popped out of my mouth before my brain had formed the words. Stunned by what I'd revealed, I sat with my mouth wide open, astounded and horrified. Had this never registered before, never penetrated my brain until that moment? When I got home, I pulled out my many journal-filled containers, and sitting on the floor, I went through the books until I found it—a day only five years earlier, one of the many days I'd spent packing to move out of the Brentwood house. I glanced at the journal to verify that it had indeed happened. I had written it down, for God's sake, but

I had never let the thought register in my mind. Even then, I hadn't wanted to know.

May 15, 2004

Mother told me the most amazing thing yesterday. I was packing, talking about…I don't know…feeling remote, slightly perturbed, the way I often do with my mother. Sometimes I can break through, can be with her, but mostly I stay remote, in a place where she can't reach me and she keeps trying. She finally caught my attention when she said something about always fighting with Jocko. I looked in her face and asked if she ever really fought with him. "Yes," she said. "If alcohol was involved." I laughed. She said she would let out all of her anger then, and it was mostly about me. I felt jabbed with a long hatpin. When I was a teenager and no longer speaking to him, he once accused me of being the reason his marriage was such a mess, but Baa had never told me that I was the cause for any of their fights. Had she? I wanted to be quiet, didn't want to talk at all, but as we sat in silence, without thinking I asked, "Why were you fighting about me?" "For what he did to you," she said simply. The world slammed to a stop. I stuttered something like, "But I didn't tell you, not really." And when she said, "He told me," I kept packing but felt dizzy. Calmly she continued, "He told me how he had suffered for what he'd done. He wanted my sympathy, for me to know how hard it had been on him. Of course, I was appalled and knew it was the end of us." I couldn't look at her. My hands were shaking. "If he admitted it, then why did you and

Princess treat me like I'd made it up? I tried to tell you both once. Remember? When I was doing the Nun?" "I know," she said. "I told Princess the truth and I tried to talk to you, I think…I tried. I don't know." At first, I felt a wave of relief and gratitude, that she had tried to help me…but…but. Something's wrong. I don't understand. I don't understand.

My cherished mother had known…something. What exactly that was, I didn't want to hear, because even at that time, when I was middle-aged, I couldn't bear the idea that she hadn't run to my side, that she hadn't come to get me. Even now as I write this, I remember the wave of fear that rolled through me. I had spent my life hanging on to the vision of her being a glowing treasure who loved me, that I was worth loving and protecting, and if I lost her, what would I have? Even as she was dying, I fought to keep that vision safe, but in doing so, I was losing myself. I was the one who had kept me safe. All of me, including the parts I found unlovable: They had protected me, had steered me outside of my fears, pushing me toward things I didn't feel capable of doing.

Suddenly something lit up. It was as if I'd been standing in a dark room, panicked and sightless, until I realized I was holding a lantern and all I needed to do was turn it on. Light filled my head and I saw the childhood illusion I'd fought so hard to live in. I had accepted the idea that I was broken in an effort to keep my mother whole, always battling with a part of myself that expected to be knocked out, the buzzing voice that had come out of nowhere and grown over the last years, telling me to duck even before life took a swing. *Lincoln* wasn't lost, not yet, not until it was actually taken away from me. I couldn't give up the battle before there was a battle to fight. And I couldn't let my mother leave her life without knowing what had so powerfully affected mine, without asking her the questions whose answers I'd never wanted to hear. I couldn't bury her while she was still alive, getting into the grave right with her.

Feeling as though I needed to gather all the necessary equipment, I closed my eyes and visualized that rock-solid piece of me, then picked up the phone and called Steven's office. After waiting a moment, I heard a click and then his friendly "Hey, Sal, I've really owed you a call." And like the first shots at Fort Sumter, I knew the war had begun. He went on to tell me how thrilled he was that D.D.L. had agreed to play Lincoln but—and here it was—unfortunately he no longer saw me as Mary, saying that he'd always imagined me playing opposite Liam and just couldn't see me with Daniel. With certainty I said, "I'm ten years older than Daniel and Mary was ten years younger than Lincoln. I know all of that. I'm older than Mary was at that time, but she was worn. They were both worn."

"But we're not going to be using prosthetics," he said. "And the lighting will be harsh."

"Daniel will be brilliant, with or without prosthetics, I have no doubt. And my Mary will *not* look older than his Mr. Lincoln, I guarantee you. Not in any kind of lighting."

But I also felt that some of Steven's reluctance had little to do with my chronological years and a lot to do with my many years in the public eye, whether in television or film, whether in worthwhile projects or not. That it was my accumulated persona he would rather not lug into his film, that he'd rather find a Mary who could meet the audience as a fresh, blank slate.

"Steven, I know who I am, know the baggage I come with, and if I thought there was another actor to bring Mary to you—her age, her physicality, her emotionality and volatility—then I'd throw up my hands and walk away. But I'm telling you right now, this is mine and if you disagree, then, with all due respect, you're wrong." And before he could fire another shot, I tossed out, "Test me, Steven. How about that?"

"But Daniel's not ready to do that. He's in Ireland just beginning his transformation," Steven explained.

"I'll do it without him. Let me have wardrobe and hair, the whole nine yards, and test me."

There was a moment of silence, then, "Okay, Sal. You got it."

Saturday, about two weeks later, looking vaguely like Mary Todd Lincoln, I stood on the floor of Amblin's screening room at Universal Studios, where Steven's offices are located. With Academy Award–winning cinematographer Janusz Kaminski operating a small video camera and Mr. Spielberg standing at his side, I delivered a two-page monologue from Tony Kushner's screenplay.

Maybe I couldn't wrap my mouth around the brilliant but difficult and newly learned dialogue, or maybe my concentration was strained because the actor I was working with was in reality a piece of tape stuck on the wall. Or perhaps I couldn't quiet my heart and get out of my own way. Maybe all of the above, but ultimately there's no excuse. As hard as I tried, I never lifted off the ground, only ran along the edges of the scene. You either take flight or you don't. And that day, I didn't. I knew it and Steven knew it.

When he called me at work a few days later, struggling to tell me how sorry he was, how he just didn't see it, how he had put it against old footage of Daniel and how it just wasn't going to work, I begged him not to feel bad, thanking him for his generosity and for giving me the chance. Turning off my phone, I sat down on my dressing room sofa, feeling as old and worn as it appeared to be. At least it was over, at least I didn't have to feel anything for a while, until the day the film was finally cast, until the day someone else would be playing Mary and it would not be me. Dragging through the rest of the day, I kept telling myself to be grateful for what I already had, to focus on the work right in front of me. No matter that it was the same dialogue I'd been saying for the last five years, it was work. *Brothers and Sisters* was good enough. I was earning a living. I was lucky.

The next morning, as I was about to step into the first shot of the day, my phone rang. It was Steven again. Eagerly, he said that he couldn't stop thinking about our conversation, couldn't get it out of his mind, that he'd spent the day walking around the studio lot and finally...that he'd talked to Daniel, who thought that the tape was quite moving. At that point, I actually squealed, then stuffed my fist in my mouth. I didn't know whether to be thrilled that Daniel had responded to the test or appalled that he'd seen it. "He wants to meet you," Steven said, and before I had time to figure out what to say, he suggested that since Daniel was in Ireland, we should meet in the middle, fly to New York for a drink or a cup of tea.

By then, if there was air in the room, I no longer needed it. I had quit breathing altogether. "Okay" was all I could say.

"Great, let's do it next week," he said, and hung up. I stood, with both arms out straight, leaning against the big dirty window that looked down at Disney Studios below, until the second AD banged on my door, calling me to the set.

The following week I waited to hear about the Big Apple

meeting and when it was to take place, hoping I could be released from filming. It wasn't until ten days later, as I was dashing up the stairs from my dressing room to the production office, that I received a call from Spielberg's assistant asking if I wanted to use the same hair and makeup people.

"For what?" I said. "A cup of tea?"

"Oh, no," Christy said. "I thought someone had told you. Daniel felt Steven really needed to see the two of you on film together, so he's agreed to come here. Hope that's okay."

Two weeks later, in the same rigged-up makeup room, I slowly became the vague version of Mary I'd been a short time before. I hadn't met Mr. Lewis, didn't even know where he was presumably going through the same readying routine as I was. The whole thing felt like a bride and groom sequestered out of each other's sight until the big moment. With my dress overflowing the golf cart, almost blocking the driver's view, I was once again taken across the Universal lot to Amblin, then guided to an office adjacent to the screening room's lobby, and in a regal-looking high-backed chair, I waited—the corset as well as my instincts dictating my posture.

A sliver of sunlight broke through the blinds, beaming itself onto my throne just as I heard a shuffle of movement coming from across the lobby. Motionless in the Vermeer-like shaft of light, I kept my eyes on my hands until I felt the energy approach, and when I could wait no longer, I turned to face the figure loping toward me. Wearing his black top hat, a coat with sleeves that were slightly too short, and a wry smirk on his face—which I returned, smirk for smirk—he positioned himself at my side. Only then did I stand, give him my hand, and say, "Mr. Lincoln." His face curled into a smile as he placed his lips on my hand, and just as Lincoln would have responded to his wife, he said, "Mother." Did I hear a barely audible gasp from the many people who had faded into the shadows? I don't know. But when I buried my face in his chest, whispering, "Thank you," and he put his face in my hair, replying, "My honor," I felt radioactive.

What followed was an hour-long improvisation of sorts, a blur in actuality. I'd done enough research to have a decent idea about the Lincoln-Todd relationship—as had D.D.L.—so we instantly became something. If not precisely the Lincolns themselves, then at least we were two actors unafraid to poke around in the right direction. When the filming was stopped and things were winding down, I thanked Steven and Daniel, and with Mary still clinging to me, I nodded to all the others, saying it was time for me to leave so they could talk

Mary Todd and her Mr. Lincoln.

amongst themselves. I then bundled my dress and my heart out of the room and back to the Malibu mountains.

No matter the outcome, I walked away from it all feeling awake and alive. An hour later, as I stepped through the door of my home, the phone began to ring. "We're both on the line, Sal," Steven said. "We want to ask you together. Will you be our Mary?" Then Daniel: "Yes, will you please?"

Sharing any of this unfolding adventure with my mother had seemed out of the question. I don't remember even mentioning the film to her until that Saturday after the two men had called, and then only because she had rushed out of her room, worried that a rattler had gotten me, since I was jumping around the kitchen, screeching like a stuck pig.

Yet when I relayed the events to her it was with unemotional brevity, containing all my excitement, never inviting her to relive it with me. And in that way: cutting off my nose to spite my face.

But at the same time, a force was building inside me, an urgency to face her, to finally jump off the platform, over the pool pole, and into the icy water. Baa had been determined to try every different treatment that the doctor suggested, some making her sicker than others, until now she looked like a baby bird, big-eyed and featherless. Seeing her made me want to find something she would eat, so I was constantly making things like tapioca pudding or peach cobbler or rice and beans, foods that might seem appealing.

One evening, not long after Mary had become mine—a Friday, I think—I'd been released from work early and decided to make Baa's favorite dinner: pot roast with egg noodles. I hadn't planned to talk about anything, didn't pick the time or gear myself up. It was just an ordinary night. And as she sat at her usual counter spot, I leaned against the sink a short distance away, watching her cut up the food on her plate into tiny pieces like she was about to feed it to a two-year-old. When I'd felt trapped as a child, caught in the heat of my stepfather's scorn, I would look for my mother's eyes, hoping to be saved. And now, so many years later, I looked for those eyes again, half-hidden in the loose folds of her shrunken face, and started to talk.

I began with Joy, asking her questions about my grandmother, the woman whom I had loved but who had always seemed rigidly straightlaced. "Joy could be funny, and even playful when she was young," Baa told me. I shook my head, sympathizing with how difficult it must have been for my mother to be raised by someone who herself had received so little parenting, who had spent her childhood in a loveless world of fear. We both smiled, recalling little things about my grandmother, then laughed when we remembered how she would grit her teeth at the hint of anything sexual, even a word. Aware of my own jabbing discomfort, I asked Baa about her sexuality, if she'd ever found it difficult—then watched her flinch, just as Joy would have, just as I was. She turned her head, looking out the window for a moment, then reluctantly told me that there had been a time, once in her life, when she had seen a psychiatrist to "work some things out." And oh, how I wish I had that moment back again or had more time, or could have been the me I am now. I never asked her about that. Never asked her how old she was when she'd seen that psychiatrist or what it was she had hoped to "work out." I wish I had.

But on that night, I was focused on where I needed to go and couldn't get sidetracked. "You told me once that Jocko had confessed to you, told you that something had happened with me, that he was seeking your forgiveness." (Her forgiveness, mind you, not mine.)

With a quick nod she said, "Yes."

"What did he tell you had happened?" Without taking her eyes off me, she took a deep breath, and with a slight stutter she recounted how he'd explained that it had been one terrible incident, that he'd been drunk, that he'd always felt awful and had suffered because of it. And when I calmly asked her again what exactly he'd told her, she braced herself, took a beat, then continued.

"He said he'd put his *thing* between your legs and..." She took another breath and gave me a gift, which cost her a lot. "And...and came."

I was slapped in the face with the truth. What he had done was real and it was unforgivable. And for years and years and years my mother had known, talking to my sister about it but never me. Only then did my heart begin to race, my insides vibrating as they always did whenever the memories came near.

Without looking away or hesitating I flatly told her what needed to be said. "It was not one moment of drunken indiscretion, Mother. It was my childhood. My whole childhood."

She sat back in her chair, horrified into silence for a long moment before defiantly crying out, "I don't believe you. I don't believe you!!!"

I waited, not angry or frightened, feeling only clarity. "Mom, why would I lie? Why would I do that right now, knowing what's happening in both our lives? Why would I do that?"

With her face trembling, her meal cut up before her, she searched my eyes until all the tension drained from her body and she knew it was true. "Why didn't you tell me? Why didn't you tell me? Why, why?" she kept repeating, over and over.

Very quietly I replied, "I was a child, Mother. I was a child and didn't know that it was any different than any other child's life. I was afraid. I don't know, Mother. I was a child."

I could see her wander around in her head, not knowing whether to eat or to remain as stunned and overwhelmed as she truly was. "Then he was a monster. You never told me what a monster he was. You should have told me."

"I don't know if he was a monster or just a wounded, flawed human like the rest of us. Well, yeah. Okay. Maybe a little worse than the rest of us." She silently nodded, hardly moving, her frail, defeated body sagging with shame and regret, and I felt engulfed by her pain, instantly wanting to take it away, to beg for her forgiveness. "I'm sorry to tell you about this right now when you're struggling. I'm so sorry. I've been alone in it and needed you to know."

My job had always been to protect her from everything—most especially from me—and my need to do that begged me to forget myself and to keep her unimpaired. When in reality it had been her job to protect me, not the other way around.

But that was then and this was now. "Mom, it's fine, really. Look at me. I thrived," I said, doing a clownish jig around the kitchen. "Come on, let it go for now. Don't let me ruin your night."

And after that understatement of all time, she agreed with a meek "Okay."

I put her dinner on a tray, then carried it to her room, demanding she let it go, telling her she needed to eat and then to sleep. "That's enough, Mom, let it go."

"Okay," she said with her eyes down. After closing the door slowly, I climbed the stairs to my room, feeling just as stunned and shamed as she did.

I don't know that I slept that night. I'm certain that she didn't. The next morning when the house stayed quiet, absent of its usual door slamming, I went to her room praying she was still alive. Gently knocking, I called to her, heard nothing, then tried again. Suddenly she threw the door open with a strength I didn't know she still possessed, then grabbed my arms as though she were about to scold me. In a strong, clear voice she said, "You are not alone in this anymore. It's mine too and I want to hear it all, every bit of it. You will never be alone in this again. I let you down and I'm so very sorry, Sally. This belongs to me too. I own it with you."

I couldn't move for a moment. Then awkwardly, I wrapped my arms around her emaciated body, clinging to this person who was now even smaller than me. The once-beautiful woman who had held me, soothed me, had encouraged and enabled me. The mother I'd spent my whole life looking for and who had ultimately given me everything she knew how to give. There we stood, not a mother and a daughter, but one whole person.

Feeling as drained as she must have, I said, "Later, Mom. We'll talk later. We'll sit outside under the oak tree and talk. But not now, okay?"

"Okay, Sal, my baby girl. We'll talk, for as long as it takes." We stood in the doorway of her room, looking into each other's eyes until slowly we started to laugh, wiping the tears from our faces in exactly the same way.

I promised her I would tell her everything. But I never did. I never brought it up again. I didn't need to.

Epilogue

THE SMALL TIN dressing room was the lower half of a two-banger—a long cargo-size container separated into two units, then placed on wheels to be trucked from location to location. And on Friday, November 4, 2011, while wearing Mary Todd's underwear—or at least a close facsimile—I stood in the middle of this overly heated little room trying not to move, knowing from experience that I could get three bars on my cell phone if I stayed in that one spot. It was four o'clock in the afternoon, the company had just broken for lunch, and even though it was three hours earlier in California, I hadn't waited till the end of my day to call, aware that by then, she'd be too tired to talk. I wasn't looking for a long conversation, only had a half-hour break, and wanted to hear my mother's voice and for her to hear mine. Baa always laughingly said she felt like the photo of the little kitten clinging to a bare branch: just hanging in there. But she'd promised she would continue to cling to that branch for the three months that I was to be in Richmond, Virginia, filming *Lincoln*. And every day, I called.

After *Brothers and Sisters* had wrapped, and during the months that I was preparing for *Lincoln*, Baa's health had been declining. Then, just as summer was beginning she made a final request—make that a demand. She wanted to live near the ocean again, and to have a place of her own. Princess and I both felt that our mother living alone at this point was a frightening notion, but Baa was determined. So with my sister's help she found a tiny apartment located directly on Carbon Beach, walking distance from the famous Malibu waves. One last time, we packed all her things, or at least I did, with Sam and Eli helping. When the tide was high enough to roll under the building, Peter and his two daughters, Isabel and Sophie, appeared, just in time to help us carry everything inside.

By late September, when I was departing for the Virginia location, Baa was in a serious uphill battle for tomorrow. Luckily, Princess had taken a leave of absence from *Shameless*, the television show where she'd been working as the production manager/producer, so she'd be able to visit daily—though my mother preferred to be left alone a good chunk of the time. Even the lovely hospice helpers had restricted hours and needed to keep their distance.

Baa had watched me gain Mary's weight, had read the script, talked to me about the scenes and the eloquence of the language while the whole time I had beseeched her to hang on, constantly telling her that if she died before I got back, I'd kill her. I'd hunt her spirit down and strangle her. "Go," she said with a laugh. "Go do what you do. I'm so proud of you and don't worry, I'll see you when you get back." I hugged her goodbye as she sat in her bed, turning to go quickly to hide my tears, and cheerfully called her daily, telling her about the filming, asking how she was doing, and always reminding her she must hang on. She had to, God damn it.

That day she sounded chipper and relatively strong, excited about the adjustable hospital bed I'd ordered to be delivered in the afternoon, gleefully saying she'd soon be sitting in front of the sliding glass balcony doors, looking at the panoramic ocean view and watching the sun go down. We were three-quarters of the way through filming, and as I stood there, having my normal conversation with her, without knowing why, I said, "Mom, if you can't hang on it's okay. I won't be mad." Maybe I'd heard someone say that in a movie once, or maybe I was hearing how difficult it was for her to breathe, like she was running behind, trying to catch up. I told her again that I wouldn't be mad, not knowing if I meant it or how she would take it.

"What?" she said. "Do you think I'm about to die?"

"No, no. I'm just saying that if it gets too hard . . . I'll understand. Really."

She laughed, saying, "I'm hanging on till you get back." Thinking I was changing the subject, I casually asked her who she wanted to come and get her, to take her away. It was the question I'd heard her ask my grandmother years ago as Joy lay in her hospital bed, not in this world and not quite in another.

"Do you want Joy to come?" I asked.

With a guffaw she said, "No . . . absolutely not. She'd be too critical."

"How about your father? You always wanted to see him again. How about your dad?"

Catching her breath, she said, "Yes, I would like to see him."

"Good," I said. "He'll be there." After a tiny pause, I continued, "Mom, try to haunt me, if you can. Just generally bother me all the time."

"You mean same ol', same ol'?" And we both laughed. "I will if I can." I heard her looking for a breath. "And Sally, I want you to know how important you have always been to me, always...and I'm so sorry I let you down."

My heart crumbled. "No, Mom, you have given me everything. And listen," I swallowed hard. "Please promise something. Promise you'll be the one to come and get me...Please, come and get me, Mom."

Whispering fiercely, she said, "I promise you, Sally. I'll come and get you."

That night she began to loosen her grip on the bare branch to which she had been so bravely clinging. Was it because I'd given her permission? Do you need the ones you love to let you go before you can leave?

Princess called me early the following morning, and when my sons raced to her side, Baa asked Eli, "Am I moving on?" He took his grandmother's hand and gently said, "I think so."

I stayed on the phone, listening, trying to understand how dire the situation truly was. She'd had other episodes, times when she seemed to be fading, but then she'd recover and keep on going. I paced up and down in my hotel room, talking to Princess, not knowing what to do. It was then that Eli—who has always given me strength when I feel weak—grabbed the phone, walked out to the small balcony of the apartment and said, "Mom, come home. Come now. Baa may snap out of it and live for months but *I* need you."

Peter picked me up at the airport at nine o'clock that night and by the time I stood next to her hospital bed overlooking the Pacific, her breathing was shallow and she was unresponsive. Rick and Jimmie, who'd been living in Florida for many years, were unable to leave and because I'd been unsure about Baa's condition when I was running to catch my flight out of Richmond, I told Sam to wait in New York until further notice. I wish I hadn't. The next day, after gasping one last ragged gulp of air, Baa passed away. I was standing on one side and my sister was on the other and we looked at each other, across the enormous distance of our mother's existence. After a moment I closed her eyes, kissed her face, laid my head on her body, and cried. It was my sixty-fifth birthday.

That very day, I flew back to Richmond, and a week later, I kissed my dying husband before being guided out of the room by hands I couldn't see, blinded by tears of grief and loss that were not for the long-gone Mr. Lincoln, who lay on the bed in the form of Daniel Day-Lewis. They were for my mother.

And as I look at this, all the words and memories, my life on these pages, as I spread these pieces out and fit them together, what picture do I see that I couldn't find before? My mother and me? How we fit together? I see her in my mind, when she was young with her straight black hair and long legs. When she was old, her bespeckled hands, now my hands. I don't know what the current theories on child-rearing or proper parenting might be; they always seem to be changing. What I do know is this: How you care for your child from the time they are born until they're eighteen is important, but who you are as a person and parent for as long as you live also counts, and counts one hell of a lot. My mother might have blinked when

I was a child—she made huge mistakes, without a doubt—but I cannot fool myself into thinking that I have been a perfect parent either...though my gaffes have been different. But I hope that I have learned from her, because on this writing road that I choose to hoe, what becomes most clear to me is that my mother never backed away. She never deflected or ducked or left my sight. I didn't need her to be perfect. I needed to know her, warts and all, so that then, perhaps, I could know myself. She struggled to give me that, unflinchingly. She was my devoted, perfectly imperfect mother. I loved her profoundly and I will miss her every day of my life. And I know, without a doubt, that when I close my eyes for good, she will come to get me.

Till then, Baa.

Acknowledgments

Throughout this seven-year writing journey I have had the help of hovering angels who supported, empowered, challenged, kicked me in the butt, and patiently listened to my rants and raves. Elizabeth Lesser, who quietly demanded in 2011 that I give the keynote address to a Women and Power conference at the Omega Institute, insisted that I had something to say. Her initial shove and constant care of my fledgling writer's wings has enabled them, and me. Dr. Daniel Siegel, whose influence is on every page, taught me to recognize the comfort of holding my own hand and I did a lot of that. Long before I knew where I was headed there were the encouraging words from Maia Danziger and her weekly Studio City writers group and, at the halfway point, Beth Rashbaum, who taught me important lessons with her smart, tough-love red pencil on some very young pages. While nearby and always at the ready has been my longtime publicist, my constant kvetch-catcher, Heidi Schaeffer, with her endless optimism and hard work; my steady assistant, Jennifer Rima, who adroitly learned the skill of acquiring clearances without a moment's hesitation; my eagle-eyed lawyer, Don Steele; my faithful friend, Tricia Brock, who was a patient listener and generous early reader; and my sister Princess, sister-in-law, Jimmie, and daughter-in-law Sasha, whose cheering voices still ring in my ears.

And then we come to Molly Friedrich, my literary agent, who wasn't sure we were a match until I wrote the first hundred pages, but who, forever after, became my goalposts and has always given me something hard to find: the truth. Lucy Carson, also my agent (as well as Molly's daughter), joined the team, and together they carefully led me in the search to find a proper home and the right editor to take this book through the last stages of labor. Which led me to Hachette's Grand Central—to Michael Pietsch and Ben Sevier, to Karen Kosztolnyik, Brian McLendon, to a team of talented Grand Central folks—and to Millicent Bennett, that right editor. The book's midwife and godmother, she has been relentless and gentle as she pushed and applauded the delivery, always calm in the face of my panic.

From the start my son Sam has been my sounding board and best friend, but I was afraid for my older sons, Peter and Eli, to read these pages. When they did I was overwhelmed by how lovingly each responded, sharing memories, giving astute notes, and allowing my words to open a new dialogue between us. As they have with Sam. How lucky I am to know these three men. Without them and each and every one of you, these pages would not be. Thank you.

Additional Copyright Acknowledgments

Holdings, S.A.R.L. controlled and administered by Spirit Two Music, Inc. All rights reserved used by permission. Reprinted by permission of Hal Leonard LLC.

All photos courtesy of the author unless otherwise noted. Page 10: courtesy of Paramount Pictures; page 49: courtesy of *TV Show* magazine; page 95: courtesy of 1964 Tomahawk yearbook; pages 114, 171: CPT Holdings, Inc., courtesy of Sony Pictures Television; page 116: courtesy of *TV Star Parade*; page 125: courtesy of *TV & Movie Screen*; pages 141, 146, 281, 284: courtesy of MGM Media Licensing; page 151: courtesy of Sai Saha, *TV Guide* magazine 2018; page 183: courtesy of *Movie Mirror* magazine; page 207: courtesy of *TV Radio Mirror*; pages 220, 223, 230, 240, 271: courtesy of Steven Craig; pages 314, 320: courstesy of Universal Licensing LLC; page 329: courtesy of Guy Webster; pages 348, 355: *Norma Rae* copyright © 1979 Twentieth Century Fox, all rights reserved; page 368: courtesy of Randy LaCaze; page 385: copyright © 2012 DreamWorks II Distribution Co., LLC, all rights reserved; page 401: upper left courtesy of Hourash Falati, upper right courtesy of Alex J. Berliner, bottom courtesy of Joy Marie Smallwood.